Democratic Government and Constitutional Jurisdiction

Democratic Government and Constitutional Jurisdiction

Clèmerson Merlin Clève
Bruno Lorenzetto

LEXINGTON BOOKS
Lanham • Boulder • New York • London

Published by Lexington Books
An imprint of The Rowman & Littlefield Publishing Group, Inc.
4501 Forbes Boulevard, Suite 200, Lanham, Maryland 20706
www.rowman.com

86-90 Paul Street, London EC2A 4NE, United Kingdom

British Library Cataloguing in Publication Information Available

Library of Congress Cataloging-in-Publication Data

Names: Clève, Clèmerson Merlin, author. | Lorenzetto, Bruno Meneses, author.
Title: Democratic government and constitutional jurisdiction / Clèmerson Merlin Clève, Bruno Lorenzetto.
Other titles: Governo democrático e jurisdição constitucional. English
Description: Lanham : Lexington Books, [2022] | Includes bibliographical references and index. | Summary: "With the focus on constructing a free, just, and compassionate society, this book provides a panoramic view of the most prominent discussions in constitutional law, democracy, and institutions of our time"—Provided by publisher.
Identifiers: LCCN 2021045363 (print) | LCCN 2021045364 (ebook) | ISBN 9781793648914 (cloth) | ISBN 9781793648921 (epub)
Subjects: LCSH: Constitutional law—Brazil. | Jurisdiction—Brazil. | Judicial power—Brazil. | Democratization—Brazil. | Human rights—Brazil.
Classification: LCC KHD2921 .C5713 2022 (print) | LCC KHD2921 (ebook) | DDC 342.81—dc23/eng/20211029
LC record available at https://lccn.loc.gov/2021045363
LC ebook record available at https://lccn.loc.gov/2021045364

Contents

Introduction

We are living in a time when boundaries still exist between the civil law and common law systems, although they are more tenuous than in the past. The changes occurring in the rational and practical substrate of the legal field are truly significant. Countless reasons can be given to explain the new structure of legal knowledge in Brazil: globalization, technological advances, greater access to and dialogue with other branches of knowledge, and the demystification of particular traditions. In certain areas, theoretical developments are being made at a rapid pace, while in others, much remains to be done. Consequently, just as appearances can be deceiving, not everything that seems to be "new" necessarily moves beyond the conditions that had previously been established or is able to prompt a profound change in the categories that are now being tested.

Although an assessment of our era indicates that there is not necessarily anything new in that which calls itself "neo," it is impossible to deny that a series of important structural readjustments have taken place in Brazil in recent decades. Despite missteps and considerable difficulties in certain situations, the institutional balance can still be seen as positive. As a result, discourses that were uncommitted to the rule of law and the democratic regime no longer have a place in the public arena.

Those are signs of a commendable institutional maturation, indicating the importance of changes occurring through the established democratic mechanisms (i.e., institutions opening up to contributions from the lifeworld), which occur through the appropriate procedures, without resulting in stagnation or purely maintaining the status quo. Perhaps it is time to say that we are (finally) learning from history, given the harsh lessons of a twentieth century shaped by various moments of exception, as well as a denial of democracy and fundamental rights. However, new challenges may arise in ways that we would have never imagined having to face again.

This book brings together a series of articles produced in recent years and contains elements that are intentionally addressed more than once, in some cases to construct an argument and in others to analyze the subject more accurately: constitutional jurisdiction, judicial activism, judicial deference, the relationship between law and politics and the relationship between constitutionalism and democracy, the legitimating conditions of judicial decisions, theories of interpretation, fundamental rights and institutional design, and tolerance, to name several of the most salient, are the topics considered; in our opinion, they can provide a panoramic view of the most prominent discussions in constitutional law in our time.

In short, we intend to scrutinize political issues within institutions or the institutionalization of political changes, guided by the precept that determines constitutionalism itself; namely, the *promise*—which may be more or less cogent in a particular society—that the intersubjective interactions that will occur in the political community shall be governed by a set of higher rules: by the Constitution, that is, a normative body that, defining how all the other rules will be produced, interpreted, and applied, not only occupies a privileged space in the normative hierarchy, but also constitutes the political community—constitutes us.

This occurs under the influence of a specific way of understanding the Constitution: not in a fragmented way or taking one part as primary to the detriment of others, but rather seeking to perceive the *structure* and *relationship* of the constitutional material,[1] that is, a way of reflecting on the structures in which social disputes are embedded and on how institutional responses to those conflicts are produced.[2] That choice inspires the proposal to continue the conversation between institutions, between institutions and people, and makes it possible to alter the construction of the very notion of jurisdiction, which comes to be seen as an attempt at justification, at presenting the reasons that will be (re)discussed in the public space and, in certain cases, revised or adopted as a foundation for the stabilization of social relations. The book is divided into five chapters, which cover the topics described below.

The first chapter is divided into two sections. The thread running through the first part of the article is *United States v. Carolene Products Co.* (1938) and its consequences on the activity of the U.S. Supreme Court. It observes how a procedural justification for constitutional judicial review was devised based on footnote 4 of the *Carolene Products* case. It presents the substantivist critiques that prove the limitations of the highly deferential stance derived from the case. In the second part, the study focuses on the Brazilian reality and emphasizes that our Federal Constitution has a substantive sense of justice. It discusses the phenomena of judicial activism and the judicialization of politics and points out the changes that have taken place within the Supreme Federal Court in recent years. In the propositional part, it juxtaposes the *Carolene Products* doctrine and the levels of scrutiny with Brazil's constitutional jurisdiction, distinguishing between cases of *strong* and *weak* constitutional review.

The second chapter is guided by an inquiry into which institution has better conditions for making decisions in controversial cases and which interpretative theory would be appropriate for steering the decision-making process. It thus recognizes that after the judiciary became a preferred forum for resolving conflicts, theories sought to, on the one hand, perfect the decision-making process through normative proposals for jurisdiction, and, on the other, to curb the role of courts by making them deferent to other branches of power. The article thus addresses the linguistic turn that has taken place in the law and the two normative interpretative theories that accompanied that process: Ronald Dworkin's law as integrity and William Eskridge's dynamic statutory interpretation. It presents the thesis of institutional capacities as an antagonist of the normative theories and outlines its central characteristics. Finally, it critiques the reception of that theory in Brazil and proposes an assessment of its central aspects, questioning the legitimacy of the decision.

The third chapter addresses the thesis of institutional dialogue as an alternative to the legitimacy of constitutional review. It presents a critical view of the dichotomy between law and politics and the proposal for a rigid separation of powers. It lays out the genesis of the theory of institutional dialogue in Canada and outlines the difference between the cases in which dialogue actually takes place and when it becomes a normative demand. It deals with the questions that arose regarding the theories of dialogue and presents its most promising theoretical version. It recounts the mechanisms for carrying out institutional dialogue in Brazil and reflects on the dichotomy between law and politics to suggest maintaining institutions in which disagreements can continue to occur.

The fourth chapter deals with the doctrine of effectiveness, presenting its main characteristics and the advances it has made in the Brazilian legal landscape. In parallel, it discusses the development of fundamental rights and the problems involved in realizing them. To this end, it debates the questions raised by the doctrine of effectiveness as well as the roles that the judiciary may play to achieve fundamental rights. It also addresses the concept of the Unconstitutional State of Affairs (*Estado de Coisas Inconstitucional*) and its structural aspects, indicating potential risks in its application.

The fifth chapter discusses the subject of tolerance. It begins by presenting its early religious and philosophical rationale, with contributions from Pierre Bayle and John Locke. It breaks new ground in recognizing the historical contingencies present in cases that demand tolerance and how important it is because it concerns the most complicated and persistent characteristics of human relationships. It also articulates the importance of tolerance for the construction of a democratic state of law, in terms of the formation of opinions and desires resulting from deliberative processes.

Given the challenges that Brazil must confront as part of the process of constructing a free, just, and compassionate society, this book is intended to be an additional tool for improving the country's institutions. In the inevitable presence of doubts and dreams, we seek to offer alternatives to ensure that this project continues.

We hope everyone enjoys reading this book.

Curitiba, June 2020
Clèmerson Merlin Clève
Bruno Lorenzetto

NOTES

1. Charles L. Black Jr., *Structure and Relationship in Constitutional Law*. Woodbridge: Ox Bow, 1985.

2. "We will have to deal with policy and not with grammar. I am not suggesting that grammar can be sidestepped, or that policy can legitimately be the whole of law. I am only saying that where a fairly available method of legal reasoning, by its very nature, leads directly to the discussion of practical rightness, that method should be used whenever possible. It is the best wisdom of every system of law to seek and to cleave unto such intellectual modes" (Charles L. Black Jr., *Structure and Relationship in Constitutional Law*, p. 23).

Chapter 1

Constitution, Democratic Government, and Levels of Scrutiny in Judicial Review

In modern times, the circular question between theory and praxis plays out against the backdrop of the functioning of a certain set of institutions. In the legal field, constitutional jurisdiction and the power relations embedded therein have a particular relevance. Constitutional jurisdiction has become a preferred locus of convergence between praxis and theory, demanding a critical analysis of its place and role in contemporary society.[1]

The role that *jurisdiction* has played in modern times is based on a redefinition of the concept of *politics*, which was distanced from its archaic Aristotelian character and took on a radically different position.[2] In his emblematic work "Leviathan,"[3] Hobbes scrutinized the modern sense of politics in the following way: 1) politics is responsible for establishing the appropriate conditions for the functioning of the state and society (with the aim of universalization); 2) in the move from theory to practice, application becomes a *technical* issue, with the provision of the general conditions organizing the state and society, requiring an accurate calculation of legislative output, intersubjective relations and the arrangement of institutions; and 3) the architects of the new social order should turn their efforts toward producing calculable behavior.[4]

Based on that, one might recall that major theoretical debates ultimately point back, on different occasions, to elementary questions about practical factors that pervade life in society, the foundation of the political community and the emergence of law as a way to prevent and resolve conflicts. In this context, it is worth asking: Who defines *what the law is,* and who must obey it? Who is allowed to *rule* on the law?

Those questions, which do not require definitive answers, elicit different arguments according to different lines of thought. However, Ronald Dworkin warns that any theory of law should endeavor to answer at least a portion of those problems. Formulations about legislation, adjudication and compliance with the law thus need to be developed.[5]

Those formulations have their respective recipients: those who produce laws; those who make decisions; and those who obey. While the concern of those who produce the set of rules is, in principle, related to the issue of legitimacy and to democracy, the theory of judicial decision-making must be relatively complex, encompassing 1) a "theory of controversy," establishing the standards for deciding *hard cases*; and 2) a "theory of jurisdiction," defining the reasons and moments when judges should make decisions based on the theory of controversy.[6]

At present, a theory of jurisdiction that sets out solely the arguments of justification used by judges is insufficient; it must dialogue with spheres that have a strong evaluative appeal, such as democracy and justice.

Given those appeals, the aim is to assess the role of constitutional jurisdiction in the contemporary world, governed by the idea of majority.

A BRIEF LOOK AT A U.S. DEBATE

Constitutional Jurisdiction and the Origins of Proceduralism

Each constitutional generation is organized according to events and texts that become the standards of a particular historical period. That set of legal data influences current practices while becoming material to challenge revitalized conceptions. This is the context in which footnote 4 of *United States v. Carolene Products Co.* (1938) becomes particularly important in U.S. constitutional law.

The footnote authorized the formulation of a complex decision-making theory in constitutional matters. The case that led to the decision containing the famous footnote involved the question of the constitutionality of a 1923 law (Filled Milk Act),[7] which had made it illegal to transport "modified milk" (Milnut) from one state to another.[8]

The historical context of the decision is relevant for understanding the paradigm shift it caused in U.S. constitutional law. The presumption of constitutionality, for normative acts of an economic nature, was contemporaneous with the government having a stronger presence in the economy through New Deal policies as well as the ongoing process of redefining the role of the branches of government.[9] It also marked a shift in the court's perspective, which had declared until the early 1930s that laws that regulated the economy and guaranteed rights for workers were unconstitutional; the case is thus positioned at the end of the Lochner era.[10] In that regard, the court, in exercising judicial review, would correct the defects in the democratic political process, allowing important decisions to be made by the branches that had been legitimized democratically through the electoral process.

The simplicity of questions that require complex theories to answer them has an important correlate in footnote 4, the most famous and fertile footnote in the history of the Supreme Court. Based upon it, there were different structural changes to the understanding of the court's "place" in the organization of the branches, particularly in terms of its supervisory role over the constitutionality of laws.

The doctrine that prevailed in the first three decades of the twentieth century was based on Supreme Court decisions that protected a vaguely defined set of substantive interests, which had been brought together under the title of "substantive due process."[11] The concern of those who initially opposed the decisions of the Lochner era (Holmes, Brandeis, and Stone) lay in the court's role in invalidating the outcome of a process that, in principle, was legitimate. However, it took an intervention by President Franklin Roosevelt to reconfigure the court, with the appointment of Justice Hugo Black, creating a majority that was critical of the old perspective of "substantive due process."[12]

It is prudent to examine the proposal contained in footnote 4.[13] It begins by asserting that there may be a more restricted scope for the presumption of constitutionality when legislation appears to be violating specific prohibitions of the Constitution. Next, it defines that legislation that restricts political processes ends up being subjected to more exacting judicial review, such as restrictions on the right to vote and the dissemination of information, interference in political organizations, and the prohibition of peaceful assembly. The same applies in the case of laws directed at religious, national, or racial minorities, as prejudice against *discrete* and *insular* minorities, implying an undue restriction on political processes, demands stricter judicial scrutiny.

What explains the importance achieved by that footnote? The protection against abuses in the political process, via the judiciary, and the defense of constitutional review. Constitutional jurisdiction should only be exercised when the legislation is preventing the participation of minorities, due to unacceptable reasons associated with belief, nationality, or race. In other circumstances, the court must base its work on the presumption of the constitutionality of the laws and be respectful of the legislative work.

As Robert Cover observed, footnote 4 combined a textual and functional justification for different levels of judicial review.[14] The importance and originality of the note lies in the fact that it seeks to set limits for the exercise of constitutional jurisdiction—although one might disagree with the role it establishes and the limitation of review to a proceduralist perspective. It is no exaggeration to say that footnote 4 was produced within a landscape of increasing abuse, a consequence of majoritarian politics and the decline in democratic constitutionalism, mainly on European soil, with the end of the Weimar Republic and the rise of totalitarian regimes.[15]

It is also important to understand the redefinition of the idea of a "minority." Based on the tradition present in The Federalist Papers, the judiciary's role in the protection of minorities would initially have an economic aspect, intending to protect private property from any impassioned majorities (factions) that could attack the "few" owners belonging to the emerging bourgeoisie.[16] Between 1787 and 1938, the semantics was radically diverse, including "discrete and insular" minorities that not only suffer temporary defeats in the political arena[17] but do not participate (they simply do not vote, and their members are not recognized as citizens) or do not have attributes that qualify them to participate in the discursive construction of the public sphere. The marginality of those minorities resulted in majoritarian political processes being placed under suspicion.[18]

There is no doubt that the judiciary's active role in the definition of national policies defies caution and may, in certain circumstances, contradict democratic demands. In *Carolene Products*, the intention was to both change the paradigm of the Court in relation to its previous activism and to present a set of "limits" that would guide the moments when it adopted a counter-majoritarian stance.[19]

It is therefore possible to draw out a theory of democracy from the *Carolene Products* decision. The democratic process is presented as a competition between groups, in which momentary defeats and victories must be accepted, for they are part of the "game."[20] However, it is not acceptable for competitors to be arbitrarily excluded or to never be able to participate in the "game." In analogous situations that assume the silencing of a portion of political actors, it might be justified to assign a consistent role to the judiciary, which would involve correcting the democratic process. At this point, the question that permeates the tension between constitutionalism and democracy is more than evident.[21]

In defending his theory of constitutional jurisdiction in "Democracy and Distrust,"[22] John Hart Ely sought to define the court's field of activity for resolving controversial cases: when and for which reasons should it interfere in the legislation enacted by Congress and declare its unconstitutionality, and when should it be silent, adopting a stance that is deferential to the production of the legislature? As is widely known, the perspective adopted by Ely was called "proceduralist."

Ely's work emerges in a different political context than footnote 4. Between *Carolene Products* (1938) and "Democracy and Distrust" (1980), there is a period of time filled by the Warren Court (1953 to 1969).[23] Ely's project was to defend Warren's legacy from conservative attacks by a new court.[24] He also intended to shift the accusation of "activism" aimed at that court's decisions or, at least, to revisit the democratic problem related to constitutional review.[25]

Ely distinguishes *interpretivist* and *noninterpretivist* approaches. While the former would be restricted to using explicit rules to construct the constitutional discourse, the latter are open to recognizing rules beyond the constitutional text. The distinction between the interpretivists and their opponents lies in the degree of interpretive clarity that can be drawn from the Constitution. For Ely, *Roe v. Wade* (1973) was a noninterpretivist decision.[26] His "distrust" arises as a result of this stance.

According to Ely, this variant of constitutional discourse is scarcely compatible with the democratic theory of the United States. Now, noninterpretivists would use fundamental rights to fill the gaps left by the legislature. This would be the central problem of constitutional review: "A body that is not elected or otherwise politically responsible in any significant way is telling the people's elected representatives that they cannot govern as they'd like. That may be desirable or not, depending on the principles on the basis of which it is done."[27]

For Ely, both the Lochner era and the Warren Court can be called "activist." However, the similarity between the interventionist courts ends with this initial characterization. Unlike the Lochner era, the Warren Court had a broad procedural concern, as it was the first to consider the link between political activity and the proper functioning of the democratic process.[28] Moreover, the *modus operandi* of the Warren Court was inspired by footnote 4, which stated that the Court's role would be to keep the democratic government machine running, ensuring open channels for political participation and communication.[29]

For this reason, during the Warren Court, the set of suspicious classifications was expanded beyond the central case of race. Suspicious classifications deal with laws that separate individuals according to a particular criterion because there is no doubt that as a result of the criterion—race, for example—the minority group experiences harm "One set of classifications we should treat as suspicious are those that disadvantage groups we know to be the object of widespread vilification, groups we know others (specifically those who control the legislative process) might wish to injure."[30]

Defending the Warren Court, Rebecca Zietlow emphasized that it promoted the expansion of "rights of belonging," that is, rights of inclusion, of integration into the country, and "equal membership" in the political community.[31] From the court's perspective, the rights of belonging recognized by the legislature would be less effective than those derived from judicial decisions. The argument for deference, in that regard, thus passed to the side of the conservatives.

However, Zietlow recalls that the Warren Court should also be observed in its moments of deference to the other branches. During the period when Warren was Chief Justice, the court declared that only twenty-three federal laws were unconstitutional.[32]

The Rehnquist Court replaced the activism adopted by the Warren Court with a conservative perspective. Rehnquist's type of activism focused on protecting state governments from demands for civil rights; state agents from federal regulatory requirements; private property owners from environmental protection laws; and whites from affirmative action.[33]

The Critique of Proceduralism

Ely was, as is only natural in an open society, the target of critiques. His theory of strengthening representation, presented as an appropriate justification for constitutional review, had its central arguments questioned.

For Paul Brest, constitutional jurisdiction, like any type of jurisdiction, always involves an interpretation. The dichotomy between interpretivists and noninterpretivists would therefore be false, as everyone would be interpreting the Constitution. If adjudication always substantiates a hermeneutic initiative, the most promising part of constitutionalism would thus lie in the investigation of the interpretive process.[34]

Brest also questioned Ely's "distrust" of jurisdictional action aimed at protecting substantive rights. The recognition that there are very significant substantive choices in constitutional texts opens the door to a step beyond the role that Ely sought to give constitutional jurisdiction.

There is a significant difference between a system in which representatives seek to present justifications for their decisions and a system determined solely by political power.[35]

For Ely, as stated above, constitutional review should pave the way for democratic procedures—without interfering with substantive causes. This is based on the idea that judges could not include their own values in their decisions. As Ackerman explains, the procedural perspective understands that although we cannot compel our legislators, we can insist that they treat our demands with respect, considering the moral and empirical arguments offered to them, rejecting them only by applying a scrutiny that assumes their inadequacy for the public interest. If a group does not receive this treatment, is not formally accepted to participate in the "debate," it is experiencing prejudice, which is different from analyses that address the possibility or impossibility of arguments, of their merits.[36]

The problem, Cass Sunstein observes, is that the Constitution specifies different substantive values.[37] In other words, the central idea of representative democracy requires the defense of *substantive values* because democracy itself is presented as a value. For that reason, even the procedural characteristics of democracy, such as the mechanisms that enable political participation and party plurality, are grounded in values, although they are always conveyed by rules contemplated by the constitutional order.

According to Laurence Tribe, one difficulty that arises for those who defend procedural theories is the substantive nature of the most important commitments set out in the Constitution, which defines the values that the political community adopts.[38] Religious freedom, the prohibition of slavery, and the protection of private property are examples of substantive values.

What Tribe finds puzzling is that some people argue that the Constitution should be concerned with *processes* rather than *substances*. However, even the most formal procedures cannot be understood in the absence of a theory requiring controversial substantive choices.

In a similar direction, for Sunstein, at least the basis of arguments should be supported by substantive reasons, and Ely does not present a defense of the substantive arguments that support his constitutional review.[39]

The problem with a strictly formalist perspective is that it is not concerned with the *communicative distortions* resulting from the use of interpretative principles, in the sense of attributing meaning to legal texts. Both the formalists and those who defend the status quo do not account for the substantive disputes that are fought when *attributing* normative *meaning* to texts, a characteristic that limits their epistemic scope.

Moreover, in regard to defining minorities, one might legitimately question whether a group has been marginalized from political processes by exogenous factors—outside its sphere of action—or by endogenous factors.[40] The court's decision will assess not only the minority group's degree of marginalization but also whether the group itself should participate in the political process.[41] The constitutional rhetoric that permeates the doctrine is that the court should not make substantive judgments, yet the decision about a group's marginal situation cannot be merely "technical"; it will necessarily be political and evaluative.

The critique of the doctrine derived from *Carolene Products* concerns the political role that jurisdiction must play when recognizing and protecting minorities, which, in principle, challenges the education of judges. Furthermore, the "lack of power" of certain minorities has also not been fully accepted, as the "insularity" (or marginality) of each social group has its own particular historical characteristics. It is thus essential to continuously ensure that the process of understanding groups considered to be excluded from the space for democratic deliberation is as up to date as possible.[42]

The Court, in this case, must authorize the substantive results that would be obtained in the political arena if minorities had not been historically or systematically excluded from the democratic processes of deliberation and bargaining. On this point, it is important to recognize that there are "anonymous and diffuse" groups (such as the poor) that end up at a perpetual disadvantage in a pluralist democracy.[43]

Ackerman criticizes the underinclusion that the minority concept produces as it relates to prejudice. Two examples illustrate the issue: the fact that homosexuals are a relatively anonymous minority does not reduce prejudice; similarly, sexism remains a problem for women, a "diffuse, if discrete" majority.[44]

For Ackerman, the emphasis on prejudice may open up another possibility for justifying constitutional review: in that hypothesis, the courts would not only be perfecters of the democratic process but also "pluralism's ultimate critics."[45] According to that prism, judges would begin to respond to a duty to protect minorities from prejudice, on substantive grounds derived from the set of principles contained in the Constitution.

The fertile construction around *Carolene Products* continues to be present in the background of different precedents and decisions by the Court.[46]

In *Bush v. Gore*, Balkin and Levinson note, the Supreme Court was able to "short circuit" the process of democratic representation.[47] Ruling on one of the country's most sensitive political processes, it decided to halt an electoral process that was still occurring (vote recount).

As a result of the decision, the Republicans came to have a majority and controlled the three branches of government for a certain period of time. The danger of the case lies in the use of constitutional jurisdiction to ensure one political group's dominance over the branches of government or that group remaining in power for an indefinite period of time, even without popular support. For Balkin and Levinson, this would be the "true counter-majoritarian difficulty"[48] rather than the interpretative changes that accompany the rise and fall of political parties, influencing the composition of the Supreme Court.

It is no accident that the theory derived from *Carolene Products* recommends using the highest level of scrutiny (strict scrutiny) for legislative measures that aim to strengthen the legislature's own powers. *Bush v. Gore* raised the alert for the possibility of an attack coming not only through the "traditional" route of the legislature but also by the judiciary.

The Court, Between Permanence and Change

The shifts that have occurred in the different configurations of the court at least partly explain the direction of its rulings. The repeated questioning of paradigmatic changes proposes considerations regarding the role that must be played by the judiciary in the organization of the branches and, as a consequence, how judicial review is exercised in this or that configuration.

Opponents of constitutional jurisdiction present arguments that range from a disrespect for precedents, such as the violation of the Constitution, to attacks on the interpretative modalities adopted. If the ideological stance is favorable, an activist position is defended by the court. If the court takes the opposite position, it argues in favor of self-restraint and deference, given the lack of democratic legitimacy of constitutional review.

Two of the most important objections to the contemporary role of the U.S. Supreme Court, such as the minimalism advocated for by Sunstein[49] and the proposal to place a high value on popular manifestations, defended by Mark Tushnet,[50] are part of that polarization, questioning the changes prompted by the Supreme Court in its most recent conservative configurations.[51]

According to Levinson and Balkin, the quality of a court will not be evaluated strictly based on its respect for precedents but also on the set of substantive principles it wields when it articulates new doctrines.[52] This applies to both the Warren Court and the Lochner era.[53]

It is therefore appropriate to analyze the constitutional principles that the court endorses either explicitly or implicitly in its decisions. It is essential to not only recognize that it has a prominent role in the institutional design of this or that political formation, but also that it has the ability to make decisions that decisively affect, for better or worse, the life of the community. For that reason, in the twenty-first century—more strikingly than in past historical scenarios—it is important to monitor the court's role when it is producing "high politics" as well as investigate how it gives "life" to the Constitution, by affirming or denying constitutional principles.[54]

Although the critiques of proceduralism are quite relevant and very often unanswerable, *Carolene Products* made it possible to identify a set of standards that the court would use in its decisions, adopting a stance that is more active—due to using more rigorous scrutiny—or deferential to the legislative production—given less demanding scrutiny.[55]

Footnote 4 offers a "direction" for the justification and functioning of constitutional jurisdiction, and thus, the *Carolene Products* decision can still guide contemporary debates on the subject, even in other countries.

Although it is imperative to recognize the difference in contexts and practices, the problems raised by the footnote are pertinent in any democratic rule of law.

That discussion is also relevant for those of us in the southern hemisphere, faced with the recent inquiries regarding the role of the Supreme Federal Court (Supremo Tribunal Federal—STF) in the Brazilian institutional framework. When, ultimately, should the STF be "activist" or "deferential"?

Although it is insufficient, particularly in the case of a substantively exuberant Constitution such as our own, to assert that the STF must protect political dissent (the right of political opposition), unblock the democratic process and protect marginalized minorities—in short, ensure that democracy remains open and inclusive and provide tools to combat potential adversities—is no small feat.[56]

Consequently, while procedural democracy and its justification for conducting judicial review cannot be embraced as a complete program for constitutional jurisdiction, they provide an important starting point for any discussion about the process and substance of democratic political organizations.

Influenced by that debate, we analyze the role of the STF following the redemocratization prompted by the 1988 Constitution.

FEDERAL CONSTITUTION, JUDICIAL REVIEW, AND LEVELS OF SCRUTINY

The New Role of the Supreme Federal Court

In the U.S. tradition, the difficulty of differentiating between processes and substances is due to the nature of the Constitution, as well as the use of an abstract language for fundamental rights.[57] Furthermore, there is a recurrent demand for the interpretation of implicit principles[58] and the pursuit of a "Living Constitution," in response to an old, incomplete constitutional text.[59]

In Brazil, those problems do not have the same power. Not only did the Constitution adopt a comprehensive list of fundamental rights,[60] but they are binding on all, producing vertical and horizontal effectiveness.[61] However, the existence of a detailed list of fundamental rights does not reduce the controversy surrounding the interpretation of the Constitution.[62] It merely indicates that the controversy over substantive rights in Brazil does not require, in most cases, appeals to extratextual rights.[63]

It is also important to recognize that the breadth of the rights that were established facilitates a reading and defense of often-opposed substantive positions.[64] This is due to the differences present in an extremely heterogeneous society like Brazil, segmented, fragmented, and characterized by the interaction of different ethos in a single political community. Every individual formulates their own ideological and religious conceptions of a dignified life, which ultimately increases the social complexity.[65]

The definition of the Brazilian state, in the 1988 Constitution, as a democratic rule of law is the result of a political decision that sought to demonstrate that democracy is not only a fundamental value but also a constitutive mark of the country's constitutional identity.[66]

Now, a democratic rule of law must be understood as a state of justice, not just any justice, subjectively and arbitrarily oriented or idealistically deduced from parameters residing outside or on the Constitution but, rather, a justice that is historically determined and legally formed by the Constitution itself. The legal order of a democratic rule of law must be understood not only as something formally designed by the action of legislative bodies. Rather, it is a matter of understanding it as a normative organizational block resulting from the action of those bodies but endowed with a determined substantive meaning.

The content of the normative emanations of the Brazilian state is oriented toward producing a just legal order. According to the preamble of the 1988 Constitution, the constituent assembly met "to institute a democratic state for the purpose of ensuring the exercise of social and individual rights, liberty, security, well-being, development, equality and justice as supreme values of a fraternal, pluralist and unprejudiced society, founded on social harmony and committed, in the domestic and international orders."

Based on a careful reading of the Constitution, a set of principles and objectives are deduced that indicate the content of the dynamics in that legislative process. That content is expressed through rules or principles embodied in the Constitution (democracy, republic, legality, security, social justice, and equality, among others) that, grouped around fundamental rights, produce the substantive nucleus of the Brazilian legal order.

Now, the reserve of justice concentrated in the Constitution binds all the constitutional bodies.[67] Although it authorizes different readings (communitarian, republican, and egalitarian liberal) and rejects others (libertarian, anarchic, perfectionist, or communist), that reserve concentrates a substantive nucleus shared by the most important theories of justice. Furthermore, different *conceptions of justice*, plural and substantive, imply singular worldviews regarding what is just to—supplying the formal *concept* with content—provide scrutiny criteria to classify or justify situations (normative or factual) as just or unjust. Now, in an open and democratic society, "insofar as we know where the disagreements are, the more likely we are to overcome them."[68]

In any case, there is a hard nucleus in the Constitution's reserve of justice that points to equality—simultaneously a right, a principle, and an objective—as a criterion for scrutinizing social positions. The connection between justice and equality must therefore be present not only when the law is applied but also in the former, identified with its normative and institutional construction. Equality, in that hypothesis, is "an ideal to be achieved and is implicit in any plausible conception of political justice."[69] In this case, society is fair because it considers citizens equal. Now, "this requires institutions and rules that foster factual equality, i.e., social policies for equality or parity."[70]

There is, however, a set of obstacles in the transposition or translation of social manifestations produced in the "lifeworld" and their compatibility with substantive values from democratic political institutions.[71] One concerns the disconnect between the representatives and the represented.[72]

At the same time that the legislature saw its (albeit contingent) capacity to produce consensus diminished, it began to support replacing its activity with a strategic or "statistical" action. The ideal of representative democracy remains a fundamental pillar of the democratic rule of law, but it becomes insufficient for dealing with the plurality and complexity arising from the different social identities of the groups that make up the country.

Responsibility for producing those consensuses also began being exercised, in special cases, by the judiciary. In that branch of government, interests, in their ordinary language, are received and transformed into "reasons," finding a technical language that can accommodate them, which remains open to receiving that data from the "lifeworld." Furthermore, there is a procedural guarantee of the contradictory and of an institutional response, formulated a priori according to the set of rules that regulates social life.

It is also understood that the new role played by the judiciary in its relationship with the legislature is the result of the following reconfigurations: The courts began to regulate parliamentary activity by imposing substantive limits on the legislative process, through judicial review; substantive policies started to be derived from jurisdiction; and the judiciary began interfering in political activity itself, imposing restrictions on the behavior of interest groups, political parties, and political agents.[73]

John Ferejohn presents two theses to explain the judicialization of politics.[74] The first concerns the *fragmentation* of power within the branches: in situations where the branch's capacity for political action is constrained, people seek to resolve their conflicts in institutions that can provide an answer, which leads to the judiciary replacing the legislature on certain occasions. The second thesis is the *rights hypothesis*, in which the courts are seen as protecting important substantive values from potential political abuse; in other words, they perform the *countermajoritarian* role to protect minorities—in the terms of the theory derived from *Carolene Products*.

In the sphere of constitutional jurisdiction, those theses take on more salient dimensions. In situations where the legislature refuses to decide on a matter due to its potential political cost, the discussion is transposed to the judiciary, which does not have to worry about the electoral consequences of its decisions.[75]

Transferring the legislature's authority to other spheres of decision-making also occurs in its relationship with the executive, who can issue Provisional Measures (*Medidas Provisórias*). The constituent assembly sought to empower the executive to—without requiring prior authorization from Congress and in particularly relevant and urgent situations—issue a regulatory order endowed with the force of law,[76] which can thus operate as a provisional "test" of the final legislation to be approved by Congress.[77]

The judicialization of politics in our reality must therefore be treated as a historical phenomenon, derived from the institutional structure designed by the constituent assembly, which in turn made it possible to channel demands repressed in society during the dictatorship to the constitutional text.[78] As a result, there is a great profusion of rules in the Brazilian constitutional text, while the principles largely reside in Titles I and II, in the part concerning the "reserve of justice," which deals with fundamental rights.[79]

There will be no changes to the current state of the judicialization of politics phenomenon in Brazil unless a deep constitutional reform were to redefine the country's constitutional identity.[80]

Until the advent of the 1988 Federal Constitution, the most common form of Brazilian judicial review was diffuse; from that moment on, abstract review gained prominence. This is a consequence of the provision of new actions that trigger a review in theory, an increase in the list of legitimate assets, and the provision of mechanisms that enhance abstract review.

The significant number of Direct Unconstitutionality Actions before the STF reflects not only the rise of abstract review but also Brazilian constitutional jurisdiction itself.[81] With the 1988 Constitution, the theory of the normative force of constitutional provisions was applied, which resulted in constitutional jurisdiction playing a larger role.

It is important to emphasize that the Brazilian judiciary does not have a corresponding model at the international level, as the 1988 Constitution, unlike any other, gave it a unique role. The constituent assembly, absent any prior experience in drafting Constitutions, sought to provide the judiciary with a standard for action that was able to powerfully assist with the process of making the Constitution effective.

However, while the initial focus of Brazilian constitutionalism was on the effectiveness of the constitutional rules, once that lesson had been learned, it became time to emphasize the tensions inherent in the growth of judicial activity with democratic postulates. It is not a question of defending an ever-deferential stance for constitutional jurisdiction but of considering that its use can be problematic in an environment characterized by a democratic commitment.[82]

Constitutional jurisdiction in Brazil must therefore seek a difficult balance between the separation of powers and the STF's need to uphold the Constitution.[83] As noted above, the Constitution has an expansive nature, which implies a broader scope for the STF's activity as a "constitutional guardian."[84]

It is true that many STF decisions involve hard cases.[85] However, they are not the majority. In addition, the *modus* used by the Court to resolve controversial issues does not always entail the adoption of an activist orientation.

Activism, present in expansive decisions, often appears in situations where the other branches have not acted, particularly to protect minority or vulnerable groups.[86] However, on different occasions, the STF ruled a different way, choosing *deference* to the other branches, in situations involving hard cases.[87]

The judiciary transitioned from an almost silent past to a paradigm of necessary interaction with the other branches, at times in the sense of cooperation, at times as a brake, or even as the protagonist of a productive tension.[88]

In Brazil, there has been a gradual bringing together of the U.S. model, which prefers diffuse judicial review,[89] and the European model,[90] which emphasizes concentrated review operated by a constitutional court. The STF, contemporaneously, despite favorable declarations in this direction, has not yet taken on the role of a true body restricted to "guarding the Constitution," or a constitutional court.[91]

There is thus a convergence between the diffuse-incidental and concentrated-primary forms of review. Ultimately, both are oriented toward the protection of substantive rights referenced in the fundamental rights established in the Constitution. It can therefore be argued that abstract review is not limited to defending the objective constitutional order.[92]

There are thus no doubts about the gradual strengthening of the judiciary and, particularly, the STF, following the democratic stabilization of Brazil. That observation does not attempt to divert attention to the eminently agonistic, adversarial aspect that characterizes democracy.[93] In contrast, the stabilization and constancy of a certain set of elementary processes guaranteeing democracy during the last two decades resulted in a deepening of political discussions and the inclusion of new problems for deliberation in the public arena. However, despite the constitutional commitment to representative democracy and the role of the legislature, the inertia of the latter on certain occasions ends up leaving power vacuums that are filled by the judiciary, to such an extent that some justifications for judicial activism are woven around the omissions of the other branches.[94]

While it is true that the STF's activism should not be confused with that of the entire judiciary, the reasons presented in support of a less deferential stance by the court are, in general, as follows: 1) the Constitution is a fundamental order "guarding" substantive principles rather than merely a "framework law"[95]; 2) the defense of fundamental rights and the fundamental principles that underlie our political community is the task of the judiciary[96]; 3) that task often demands the use of new decision-making techniques, to be able to confront the country's social complexity and advance senses of constitutional justice; and 4) the Court's activism is subsidiary, appearing only in circumstances when the other branches demonstrate inertia.

The strengthening of the STF can also be explained by other factors. The binding effect of its decisions,[97] the general repercussion in the extraordinary appeal (*recurso extraordinário*)[98] and the possibility of issuing binding precedents[99] are mechanisms that have been accompanied by new decision-making techniques, such as conforming interpretation, the declaration of unconstitutionality without a reduction in text,[100] and the appeal to the legislator,[101] as well as greater attention on the institute of the complaint,[102] adherence to *ratio decidendi*, and transcendence of determining motives in decisions.[103] All this resulted in a revision of the STF's own role in constitutional jurisdiction, involving a reinterpretation and enhancement of the procedural institutes originally provided by the constituent assembly.

What, then, would be the STF's role within the institutional design established by the constituent assembly? Would the Court be a revisional deliberative space? Would its function be to present strong or weak remedies in the event of possible violations of the fundamental law?[104] The STF must not only constantly question itself about its role—which motivations justify constitutional review—but also about the intensity of that review.

The STF has neither adopted an activist behavior nor a stance that solely embraces deference as a position. The insufficiency of those models, as well as the political pendulum that may exist within the court's ideological configuration, has been observed in the different arrangements of the U.S. Supreme Court.

In a certain historical context, activism can be a fundamental element for promoting civil rights, but the same discourse can also be used to dismantle hard-won achievements. The argument for weakening the Court's role appears to be a radical measure from a context that is foreign to us. That position, in the present, is a consequence of the lengthy tenure of a conservative court in the United States, which has been shaping key aspects of the U.S. political community through its decisions.

That reality, which has recently seen progressives defending other spaces for legal production beyond the court, implies the return of the unending problem of judicial review. Given the counter-majoritarian difficulty,[105] is it more productive to defend only one of the different forms of democracy and abandon constitutionalism or, alternatively, to confront the tension between them, defending the need for a commitment?

A sophisticated version of the argument in defense of judicial review should point out that the ideal prerequisites of the democratic process have *epistemic value*.[106] Carlos Santiago Nino's epistemic theory of democracy questions the use of judicial review but presents three exceptions. In this line of thought, reviewing the constitutionality of parliamentary decisions would be justified at certain moments, to ensure that they are reliable or effective.

The first exception involves the review of democratic procedure. Democratic procedure is the result of a (previous) set of rules that should be guided by the *epistemic maximization* of the political process.[107] The fundamental problem lies in giving democracy the responsibility of determining what democracy is. The proposal of procedural democracy is therefore relevant, as it considers the importance of the conditions of democratic discussions and decisions.

The second exception concerns the protection of personal autonomy. Judicial review makes sense for policies that aim to impose perfectionist ideals on individuals or personal ideals on the entire political community. For Nino, the rationale for not following the commands of a perfectionist legislation would be that its real foundation is based on an ideal of human excellence.[108] In those situations, it is thus understood that judges can interfere in the legislation and remove rules that seek to impose excellent behavior on all individuals and, as a consequence, restrict their field of ethical choices.

The third exception suggested by Nino considers the effectiveness and preservation of social practices based on the Constitution. Judicial review is justified in cases where the objective is to protect the constitutional convention that guarantees the effectiveness of democratic decisions.[109] The aim is to preserve the *real possibility* of implementing the ideal dimensions of a certain Constitution. Even in the case of a law that meets the necessary requirements for parliamentary deliberation, that device can radiate out to impede other democratic practices. In those situations, judicial review could be justified; however, there is no "formula" that can accurately establish what those cases are.[110]

In our reality, it is not possible—given the role assigned to the STF by the Constitution—nor would it be desirable for the judiciary to be purely deferential to the other branches. Even Nino's doctrine would have difficulty passing through the filter of the Brazilian constitutional experience.

Judicial Review and Levels of Intensity

In certain situations, the functionality of judicial review is related to ensuring the legality of democratic processes, even justifying an additional round of deliberations on any matter under discussion, which implies that judicial review is classified as majoritarian debate. Even among ourselves, however, it would not be compatible with a model of activist justification, which proposes that—in all cases—a group of unelected judges can make decisions, solipsistically, about the lives of the entire population.

The principle of the *presumption of constitutionality* therefore becomes a vital guide for the actions of the courts. Derived from the separation of powers, this principle operates as a limit to activist outbursts, as Barroso explains: "Judges and courts shall not, as a rule, declare the unconstitutionality of a law or normative act when: 1) the unconstitutionality is not evident and unequivocal, there being a reasonable legal thesis for preserving the rule; 2) it is possible to rule on the matter using other grounds, without invalidating an act by another branch; and 3) there is an alternative interpretation, making it possible to confirm the rule's compatibility with the Constitution."[111]

In the United States, in the exercise of constitutional jurisdiction, the "three-tier test" has been adopted to assess the degree of legitimacy of the contested legislative text. The ruling as to which type of scrutiny will be used for the legal provision is usually supported by the precedents of the Court. In circumstances involving the violation of a fundamental right, the control will be more rigorous (i.e., the more important the right, the more active the Court will be).

The most basic test is rational basis review or minimum scrutiny. Any law that is subjected to judicial review undergoes this test, regardless of its content. It is a rather elementary judgment in which the argumentative demand to justify the constitutionality of the law is low. The test is passed by simply demonstrating that the law is a rational and reasonable means for the pursuit of a certain legitimate aim. It is thus characterized as a type of scrutiny that prioritizes the Court's deference to the legislation produced by Congress. The most recurrent examples involve cases dealing with economic matters.[112]

The second level is intermediate scrutiny. It requires the government to prove that the law in question deals with an important interest and, moreover, that there is a *substantive* relationship between that interest and the legal prescription.[113] Based on the "equal protection" clause (Fourteenth Amendment to the U.S. Constitution), a test is used to examine the constitutionality of laws involving gender discrimination and cases of restrictions to freedom of expression.[114] Testing for "quasi-suspect" classifications is undertaken using this type of scrutiny.

At its final level, judicial review applies strict scrutiny, the highest degree used by the Court in very specific situations, particularly when the legislation adopts suspect classifications—such as restrictions on voting rights and nondiscrimination rights[115]—and also when it adopts classifications that encumber fundamental rights, as in the guarantees provided for in the Fourth Amendment to the U.S. Constitution[116] or in access to the courts.[117]

Strict scrutiny requires the authority to demonstrate that the classification adopted by the contested act satisfies three requirements for its legitimacy to be recognized by the Court:[118] 1) it must reflect a *compelling* interest; 2) it must be *narrowly tailored* to achieving the interest; and 3) and it must be the *least restrictive means* necessary to achieve that end.[119]

Although the Court has not defined the concept of a *compelling* government interest with great precision, it is understood to refer to something necessary and crucial, rather than something that can be chosen at the discretion of political actors.

If the policy developed by the government is not *tailored* to achieving its objective, thus overstepping the bounds of the public interest, the rule cannot be considered appropriate.[120]

Furthermore, the law or policy should adopt the least restrictive means in pursuing the interest. Although that assessment may be carried out in conjunction with the above, the Supreme Court ultimately conducts a separate analysis of each aspect related to the constitutionality of the law.

The demand for more exacting judicial scrutiny was derived from footnote 4 of *Carolene Products*, in addition to its rationale for judicial review in the sense of developing a high standard for oversight, which would complement rational basis review, in cases of rights that demand special attention.

Strict scrutiny was not created as a mechanism to repudiate the constitutionality of any law but as an instrument that sought to combine doctrinal elements from different eras to review laws defending rights.[121] The term was expressly used in a later case: *Skinner v. Oklahoma* (1942).[122]

The U.S. Supreme Court, however, did not always know how to handle this set of instruments in an appropriate way. *Korematsu v. United States* (1944) is an example of the fact that even applying rigid scrutiny,[123] the Court may fail, mistakenly adopting a deferential stance and confirming the constitutionality of an Executive Order that mandated the detention of Japanese Americans in internment camps during World War II, regardless of whether or not they were U.S. citizens.[124]

Nevertheless, despite the risk of a bad ruling, standards can be used to guide constitutional oversight, which does not preclude—but on the contrary, demands—a simultaneous assessment of other data that emerge from the political situation, the diagnosis of the historical moment and the intensity of deliberations on the matter, as well as considering the precedents and the consistency of the chain novel.[125]

Following upon the idea of different levels of scrutiny, standards are useful for discussing the parameters for judicial review in Brazil. They are therefore not intended to preclude other comparable formulations that might refine the considerations presented. Some might think that an emancipatory constitutional dogma implies a practice that contradicts democratic demands, as it instrumentalizes supposed judicial activism. Nothing could be more false. It is true that this dogma is concerned with implementing constitutional commands, in particular those addressing fundamental rights. And in doing so, it recognizes the important role to be played by the Brazilian judiciary, specifically in the exercise of constitutional jurisdiction. It neither proposes a role for the judge that goes beyond what was designed by the architect of the structure of powers in the Constitution nor implies an undue constriction of the legislature's sphere of legitimate choices through an open process of deliberation with repercussions in the public arena.[126]

A judiciary that is occupied with constitutional promises will be neither activist nor deferent to the legislature's choices. It will operate according to the case but always on rational grounds, supported by the Fundamental Law, sometimes with a stronger review and sometimes with a weaker review of the contested act (omissive or commissive). It will move between self-restraint, deferring to the legislature's choice, and stronger review (activism) for protection in this or that situation,[127] using the postulate of proportionality in an appropriate manner.[128]

In any case, however, the judiciary will have to adopt a vigilant stance towards the postulates of democracy (implying self-government and the definition of choices primarily through the public deliberation process). There are moments that demand strong judicial review, such as those involving protecting minorities from discrimination, protecting freedom of expression and opinion, and protecting the existential minimum, true conditions for the exercise of democracy.

There are others, however, that—prima facie—challenge a position of self-restraint and deference to the legislature's decision. In those cases, very robust arguments are needed to justify different action by the judiciary, for example, the difficult questions involved in interpreting (open) constitutional clauses authorizing different and reasonable conceptions in an environment of moral pluralism.

In those cases, as a rule, the legislature's choice, which is the result of a public deliberation process, should not be replaced by that of the judge. If it were replaced, it might prove to be in contrast with the democratic experience.

The judge must therefore not act against democracy but, rather, in favor of democracy. We want a society of free and equal citizens, not an inappropriately paternalistic society where the judge acts as a kind of caring father. That said, it is important to reiterate that, given a broad, analytical Constitution such as our own, many issues that once remained in the exclusive field of politics are now brought before the judiciary, based on the choice made by the constituent assembly. However, here again, we must remember that judicialization does not necessarily imply activism.

In short, we argue that strong judicial review, or stricter scrutiny, makes sense in the following circumstances: A) to protect the conditions for the exercise of democracy in matters involving 1) the freedom of expression (right to protest[129] and freedom of speech)[130]; 2) the protection of the democratic process (legality of the legislative process and review of political or economic power in the electoral process)[131]; 3) the protection of minorities (legislation suspected or deemed to be unconstitutional)[132]; 4) other basic rights in terms of what is necessary (though not sufficient) for the protection of human dignity[133]; and 5) social rights,[134] particularly those granted by the state, in cases of an inherent effectiveness or when protecting the existential minimum[135] (not to be confused with the bare minimum), true material conditions for democracy; and B) to protect against perfectionist laws, from the left (everyone should be supportive, generous, good, and virtuous) or the right (undue criminalization of behavior—homo-affective relations, *verbi gratia*).[136]

Constitutional jurisdiction preserves the substantive values necessary for legitimate public deliberation. This, however, is not sufficient; those substantive values must be interpreted by everyone who will be affected by the decision, hence the importance of preserving deliberative spaces and institutions that transform the plural expressions emanating from society into rights.

The spaces in which those manifestations may occur are present in both the classic representative sphere as well as through other less traditional forms. Public hearings and *amicus curiae*, for example, are important for determining the reasons for the exercise of constitutional jurisdiction.

In addition to cases that require, as a rule, the court to take an active stance, other occasions demand a soft review, self-restraint, or deference to the legislature's decisions: A) in the case of public policies that instrumentalize social rights in terms of derived effectiveness or that overstep the bounds of the existential minimum; B) in eminently political matters, always considering, however, that those matters are not an immunizing clause. There is a need to respect the political dimension of life as well as legislative latitude for what is not constitutionally binding; and C) in election results, referendums, citizen initiative laws, constitutional drafting,[137] and even new laws resulting from a legal and open process of deliberation, which, in principle, must defer to the results and the reasons of the legislature.

This is not a question of admitting a proceduralist stance. It is a question—in the argumentative and deliberative process carried out by the judiciary—of giving appropriate weight to the reasons of the legislature. In those cases, there is a strong presumption of the constitutionality of the laws, which can nevertheless be dismissed for other—even unpopular—overriding reasons. It is good to remember that the constitutional judge is a guardian of the permanent principles of the constitutionalized political community.

Finally, there are a number of difficult issues, which—when they are judicialized—will only be resolved smoothly on rare occasions. Topics involving the right to life, euthanasia, or abortion, for example, as *contentious issues*, test the foundations of any theories that seek to offer a solution to the tension between judicial review and majority rule. This includes problems that suggest the impossibility of formulating a consensus, as they involve the presentation of reasons that can be used to defend different points of view with identical constitutional support.

Although those cases cause some consternation, they cannot always "wait for" intense deliberations by the legislature or even the judiciary. In those circumstances, the decision is made—because there is no other way—that, as a rule, the *reasonable and current* solutions offered by the legislature should be preferred.

CONCLUSION

In a limited examination of the period, the role of the STF appears to have changed. That new feature, however, is still being constructed, and not all of the bolts and screws have been tightened. It is now time to discuss that new role, with humility, openness, and critical reasoning. We should warn, however, that the STF is still part of the political game. As in any democratic environment,[138] judicial decisions—whether they are correct or not—must be enforced. That does not mean that they cannot be questioned in the public arena, with all due respect and compelling arguments. After all, in an open society, yesterday's losing vote may be tomorrow's winning vote.[139]

NOTES

1. In the case of Brazil, the Supreme Federal Court is not solely a constitutional court, and a significant portion of its decisions thus have a scope restricted to the parties involved in the proceedings. One example of significant structural changes in society as a whole was provided by Ronald Dworkin, with regard to *Brown v. Board of Education* (1954): "When the Court decided in 1954 that no state had the right to segregate public schools by race, it took the nation into a social revolution more profound than any other political institution has, or could have, begun." Ronald Dworkin, *Law's Empire* (Cambridge, MA: Harvard University Press, 1986), 2.

2. Politics was understood as the continuation of ethics, and for that reason, the ethical character of (political) action was not separated from law and customs. *Polis* was the space to pursue a "good life." *Praxis* was distinct from *techne*, which was related to the production of artifacts and the skillful mastery of certain activities. Given the ontological inconsistency of abstract concepts such as justice, the aim is thus to use (modern) politics to ensure knowledge about the essential nature of justice, now identified with the world of laws and contracts. See: Aristotle, *Politics* (London: William Heinemann, 1932); Thomas Hobbes, *Leviatã* (São Paulo: Ícone, 2000).

3. "Though nothing can be immortal which mortals make, yet if men had the use of reason they pretend to, their commonwealths might be secured at least from perishing by internal diseases. For by the nature of their institution they are designed to live as long as mankind, or as the laws of nature, or as justice itself, which gives them life. Therefore, when they come to be dissolved, not by external violence, but intestine

disorder, the fault is not in men as they are the *matter*, but as they are the *makers* and orderers of them." Hobbes, *Leviatã*, 230.

4. For Habermas, the separation between politics and morality replaced the directive that guided the production of a "good" and "just" life with the possibility of achieving a life of well-being within a correctly instituted order. Jürgen Habermas, *Theory and Practice* (Boston: Beacon Press, 1973), 43.

5. Ronald Dworkin, *Taking Rights Seriously* (Cambridge, MA: Harvard University Press, 1978), vii.

6. Dworkin, *Taking Rights Seriously*, viii. Dworkin, in turn, presented theoretical proposals for resolving hard cases and a theory of jurisdiction. Those formulations identified problems related to the traditions of utilitarianism, realism, and legal positivism. In particular, the legal positivist tradition was criticized for its inability to understand the importance of standards that are not rules; positivism would thus be a model of and for a system of rules. Another aspect that was lacking in the legal positivist repertoire is the absence of a "theory of jurisdiction." Faced with a case in which there is no rule that can be subsumed to resolve the conflict, the judge should use his or her judicial discretion to decide the unprecedented case, "creating" a new law. As a way to confront those problems, Dworkin proposed his own version of a theory of controversy and a theory of jurisdiction, which aim to include a protocol for resolving hard cases as well as ways of presenting reasons in decisions. Dworkin, *Taking Rights Seriously*, 30–31; Ronald Dworkin, *Law's Empire*.

7. "'Filled milk' was condensed milk in which the fat normally found in milk was replaced with vegetable oil. Filled milk was cheaper than regular condensed milk, and today we would regard it as healthier. Apparently it did not taste any different. . . . It is not difficult to see the Act as a piece of interest group legislation that favored the condensed milk industry by effectively driving a competitor out of business." (David A Strauss, "Is Carolene Products Obsolete?" *University of Illinois Law Review* 4 (2010): 1252.

8. The precedent for the case was *Nebbia v. New York* (1934), in which the state of New York created a board with the power to regulate the price of milk. Nebbia, who owned a grocery store, was convicted of selling milk outside of the established prices and defended his right to do so before the Supreme Court, based on the Fourteenth Amendment to the U.S. Constitution, according to which the government could not violate his right to enter into contracts without the guarantee of due process. By a majority, the Supreme Court ruled that neither property rights nor contract rights were absolute. It also took a deferential stance, ruling that states were free to adopt policies to promote public welfare and that courts had neither the authority to enact policies nor to overrule them when they were produced by the legislature. Price control would only be unconstitutional if it were arbitrary.

9. "During the 1930s, the nation struggled with the constitutional implications of the Great Depression; during the 1940s, with those of the Second World War. In both cases, the basic thrust was the same—away from laissez-faire and toward activist government first at home and then abroad." Bruce Ackerman, *We the People: Transformations* (Cambridge, MA: Harvard University Press, 1998), 280.

10. *West Coast Hotel Co. v. Parrish* (1937) is considered crucial to the Court's shift in perspective. While *Lochner* is an example of the Court's activism in overruling the regulation of bakers' working hours and thus defending a more extreme model of contractual freedom, *West Coast Hotel* addresses a Washington State law that demanded the payment of a minimum wage for women and minors. Unlike what happened in *Lochner*, the Court upheld the legislation and ensured Parrish's right to receive the difference in wages between her salary and the minimum required by law. Chief Justice Hughes presented the majority vote, stating that the Constitution did not recognize absolute and uncontrollable freedom; he also noted that the minimum wage in Washington State had been established after it was the subject of public debate and discussions by employees and employers.

11. Robert Cover, "The Origins of Judicial Activism in the Protection of Minorities," *Yale Law Journal* 91, no. 7 (1982): 1287. Laurence Tribe notes that several critics of the old perspective on the "substantive due process" theory had indicated the inconsistency between the clause in the Constitution protecting due process and the doctrine derived from it and that, regardless of our current perspective on due process, the majority would agree with the fact that in 1787, the constituent assembly had adopted a federal system, to, among other things, protect private property. Laurence H. Tribe, *Constitutional Choices* (Cambridge, MA: Harvard University Press, 1985), 10–11.

12. As Eduardo Enterría explains: "This crisis has been positively beneficial, as it is now possible to refine the limits of judicial review and channel it predominantly toward the protection of fundamental rights, abandoning the arbitrary terrain of economic conceptions." Eduardo García de Enterría, *La Constitución como norma y el Tribunal Constitucional*, 4th ed. (Madrid: Civitas, 2006), 180.

13. "There may be narrower scope for operation of the presumption of constitutionality when legislation appears on its face to be within a specific prohibition of the Constitution, such as those of the first ten amendments, which are deemed equally specific when held to be embraced within the Fourteenth. See *Stromberg v. California*, 283 U.S. 359, 283 U.S. 369–370; *Lovell v. Griffin*, 303 U.S. 444, 303 U.S. 452. It is unnecessary to consider now whether legislation which restricts those political processes which can ordinarily be expected to bring about repeal of undesirable legislation is to be subjected to more exacting judicial scrutiny under the general prohibitions of the Fourteenth Amendment than are most other types of legislation. On restrictions upon the right to vote, see *Nixon v. Herndon*, 273 U.S. 536; *Nixon v. Condon*, 286 U.S. 73; on restraints upon the dissemination of information, see *Near v. Minnesota ex rel. Olson*, 283 U.S. 697, 283 U.S. 713–714, 283 U.S. 718–720, 283 U.S. 722; *Grosjean v. American Press Co.*, 297 U.S. 233; *Lovell v. Griffin*, supra; on interferences with political organizations, see *Stromberg v. California*, supra, 283 U.S. 369; *Fiske v. Kansas*, 274 U.S. 380; *Whitney v. California*, 274 U.S. 357, 274 U.S. 373–378; *Herndon v. Lowry*, 301 U.S. 242, and see Holmes, J., in *Gitlow v. New York*, 268 U.S. 652, 268 U.S. 673; as to prohibition of peaceable assembly, see *De Jonge v. Oregon*, 299 U.S. 353, 299 U.S. 365. Nor need we enquire whether similar considerations enter into the review of statutes directed at particular religious, *Pierce v. Society of Sisters*, 268 U.S. 510, or national, *Meyer v. Nebraska*, 262 U.S. 390; *Bartels v. Iowa*, 262 U.S. 404; *Farrington v. Tokushige*, 273 U.S. 284, or racial

minorities, *Nixon v. Herndon*, supra; *Nixon v. Condon*, supra: whether prejudice against discrete and insular minorities may be a special condition, which tends seriously to curtail the operation of those political processes ordinarily to be relied upon to protect minorities, and which may call for a correspondingly more searching judicial inquiry. Compare *17 U.S.* Maryland, 4 Wheat. 316, 17 U.S. 428; *South Carolina v. Barnwell Bros.*, 303 U.S. 177, 303 U.S. 184, n 2, and cases cited."

14. Cover, "The Origins of Judicial Activism," 1291.

15. See: Hannah Arendt, *The Origins of Totalitarianism* (San Diego, CA: Harcourt Brace, 1976).

16. Alexander Hamilton, James Madison, and John Jay, *The Federalist Papers* (Washington, DC: Library of Congress, 1787).

17. Strauss explains that: "They are 'discrete' in the sense that they are separate in some way, identifiable as distinct from the rest of society. They are 'insular' in the sense that other groups will not form coalitions with them—and, critically, not because of a lack of common interests but because of 'prejudice.'" Strauss, "Is Carolene Products Obsolete?" 1257.

18. Cover recalls that the meaning of "minority" adopted in footnote 4 had already been used internationally in the 1930s: "Furthermore, the premise for this international protection was that the nation-state, ordinarily dominated by a single racial, religious, or ethnic group, might fail to afford the benefits of its political processes to the racial, religious, or ethnic minorities within the state." Cover, "The Origins of Judicial Activism," 1298. For critiques of the concept of the nation-state, see: Bruno Meneses Lorenzetto, *Direito e desconstrução: as aporias do tempo, do direito e da violência* (Belo Horizonte: Arraes Editores, 2013).

19. "*Carolene* promises relief from the problem of legitimacy raised whenever nine elderly lawyers invalidate decisions of a majority of our elected representatives. The *Carolene* solution is to seize the high ground of democratic theory and establish that the challenged legislation was produced by a profoundly defective process." Bruce Ackerman, "Beyond Carolene Products," *Harvard Law Review* 98, no. 4 (1985): 715.

20. For Ackerman, the case provides a New Deal theory of democracy as an organizational structure: "While judges should defer to the legislature in ordinary economic disputes, 'a more exacting judicial scrutiny' might be required when the democratic process malfunctioned—either when the majority denied opponents crucial political rights or when legislation was motivated by prejudice against 'discrete and insular minorities.'" Ackerman, *We the People: Transformations*, 369.

21. Robert Post and Reva B. Siegel, *Constitucionalismo democrático: Por una reconciliación entre Constitución y pueblo* (Buenos Aires: Siglo Veintiuno Editores, 2013). "The starting point that 'haunts' the tension between democracy and constitutionalism lies in constitutional review. The idea, presented in the foreground, is uncomfortable: how can the government explain or justify an apparently undemocratic practice by the judiciary, in which popular and democratic productions (laws) are subjected to a 'test' of legality by a higher law (constitution)? The quest to harmonize those two sides is the reason for the haunting and involves poles that end up being radically compromised: the defense of the ideal of a government limited by norms (constitutionalism) and the ideal of a government exercised by the people

(democracy)." Bruno Meneses Lorenzetto, "Os Caminhos do Constitucionalismo para a Democracia" (Phd diss., Universidade Federal do Paraná, 2014), 104–105.

22. John Hart Ely, *Democracy and Distrust: A Theory of Judicial Review* (Cambridge, MA: Harvard University Press, 1980).

23. Warren was Chief Justice between 1953 and 1969, but according to Owen Fiss: "The Warren Court refers to that extraordinary phase of Supreme Court history that began in the mid-1950s, with *Brown v. Board of Education* and the appointments of Earl Warren (1954) and William J. Brennan Jr. (1956), and which reached its apogee in the early 1960s, when Justice Frankfurter retired and the liberal wing of the Court achieved a solid majority. Aside from Warren and Brennan, that majority included Hugo Black, William O. Douglas, and Frankfurter's replacement, Arthur J. Goldberg, who served from 1962 until 1965 and then was replaced by Abe Fortas. In 1967, the group of five was strengthened when Thurgood Marshall replaced Tom Clark. Now and then, they picked up the vote of Potter Stewart or Byron White or even that of their most forceful critic, John Harlan, a conservative who often found himself encumbered by his commitment to stare decisis. Earl Warren retired from the chief justiceship in 1969, but the phase of Supreme Court history that bears his name continued into the early 1970s, probably until 1974." Owen Fiss, "A Life Lived Twice," *Yale Law Journal* 100 (1991): 1117.

24. "In 1968, Richard Nixon ran against the Warren Court, and in so doing, attacked Justice Brennan as much as anyone, perhaps more so, given the commanding role that Brennan played on that Court." Fiss, "A Life Lived Twice," 1121. "Ely's position is not intended to be his own imaginative construction, but rather is presented primarily as an explanation or interpretation of Warren jurisprudence." Enterría, *La Constitución como norma y el Tribunal Constitucional*, 227.

25. Ely explains that the Warren Court's reputation as an "activist" is appropriate, but that perspective must be refined: "These were certainly interventionist decisions, but the interventionism was fueled not by a desire on the part of the Court to vindicate particular substantive values it had determined were important or fundamental, but rather by a desire to ensure that the political process—which is where such values *are* properly identified, weighed, and accommodated—was open to those of all viewpoints on something approaching an equal basis." John Hart Ely, *Democracy and Distrust: A Theory of Judicial Review* (Cambridge, MA: Harvard University Press, 1980), 80.

26. John Hart Ely, *Democracy and Distrust: A Theory of Judicial Review*, 4–5. In *Roe v. Wade* (1973), although the U.S. Constitution does not expressly mention the right to privacy, the Supreme Court has recognized that this right or the guarantee of certain zones of privacy exists under the Constitution. Furthermore, he concluded that the personal right to privacy included the decision regarding abortion. In his concurring opinion, Justice Stewart explained that: "The Constitution nowhere mentions a specific right of personal choice in matters of marriage and family life, but the 'liberty' protected by the Due Process Clause of the Fourteenth Amendment covers more than those freedoms explicitly named in the Bill of Rights."

27. John Hart Ely, *Democracy and Distrust: A Theory of Judicial Review*, 4–5.

28. "These were certainly interventionist decisions, but the interventionism was fueled not by a desire on the part of the Court to vindicate particular substantive values it had determined were important or fundamental, but rather by a desire to ensure that the political process—which is where such values are properly identified, weighed, and accommodated—was open to those of all viewpoints on something approaching an equal basis." John Hart Ely, *Democracy and Distrust: A Theory of Judicial Review*, 80.

29. John Hart Ely, *Democracy and Distrust: A Theory of Judicial Review*, 101. "Unblocking stoppages in the democratic process is what judicial review ought pre-eminently to be about, and denial of the vote seems the quintessential stoppage." John Hart Ely, *Democracy and Distrust: A Theory of Judicial Review*, 117.

30. John Hart Ely, *Democracy and Distrust: A Theory of Judicial Review*, 153.

31. Rebecca E. Zietlow, "The Judicial Restraint of the Warren Court (and Why It Matters)," *Ohio State Law Journal* 69 (2008): 257.

32. Zietlow, "The Judicial Restraint," 274.

33. Jack M. Balkin and Sanford Levinson, "Understanding the Constitutional Revolution," *Virginia Law Review* 87, no. 6 (2001): 1089.

34. Paul Brest, "The Fundamental Rights Controversy: The Essential Contradictions of Normative Constitutional Scholarship," *Yale Law Journal* 90, no. 5 (1981): 1063–1109.

35. Cass Sunstein argues that the idea of forcing governments to present reasons can be seen as very abstract. He thus lists three paradigmatic cases that help to illustrate the importance of this practice: *Plessy v. Ferguson* (1896), in which the Supreme Court ruled that race-based segregation did not violate the Constitution; *Lochner v. New York* (1905), in which the Supreme Court invalidated a law that established a maximum number of working hours for bakers; and *Muller v. Oregon* (1908), in which the Supreme Court upheld a law that established a maximum number of working hours for women. The main problem with the decisions, for Sunstein, was the following: "In all three cases, the Court took existing practice as the baseline for deciding issues of neutrality and partisanship. It did so by assuming that existing practice was prepolitical and natural." Cass Sunstein, *The Partial Constitution* (Cambridge, MA: Harvard University Press, 1993), 41.

36. The courts should thus seek to remedy those procedures in an appropriate manner, without judges facing the "suspicious" task of prescribing substantive values: "If *Carolene* somehow hoped to find a shortcut around this substantive inquiry into constitutional values, its journey was fated to fail from the outset. The difference between the things we call 'prejudice' and the things we call 'principle' is in the end a substantive moral difference. And if the courts are authorized to protect the victims of certain 'prejudices,' it can only be because the Constitution has placed certain normative judgments beyond the pale of legitimacy." Ackerman, "Beyond Carolene Products," 740.

37. Sunstein, *The Partial Constitution*, 104.

38. Laurence Tribe, "The Puzzling Persistence of Process-Based Constitutional Theories," *Yale Law Journal* 89, no. 6 (1980): 1063.

39. Sunstein, *The Partial Constitution*, 106.

40. As an extreme example, a group of criminals is not a minority group with legitimate political appeals; they were excluded for committing a crime (i.e., for due reasons). That scenario is completely different from minorities who are unable to access appropriate social positions or do not have the right to vote, or people who are persecuted for belonging to a minority religious group, which are cases of undue exclusion from the democratic process.

41. "Do gays and lesbians, for example, constitute a discrete and insular minority within the meaning of the *Carolene Products* footnote, so that courts should develop special rules to protect them against laws that disadvantage them?" Strauss, "Is Carolene Products Obsolete?" 1266. Kenji argues that: "The gay tipping point might suggest that Justice Stone was correct in his original assessment that 'discrete and insular minorities' were more likely to be politically powerless. Opponents of gay rights have long argued that gays are an extremely politically powerful minority, and therefore should not receive the protection of the courts. The temptation here might be to argue that political powerlessness should not be necessary to a finding of heightened scrutiny. But we should not jettison the concept of political powerlessness as a precondition of heightened scrutiny. Instead, we should refine it." Kenji Yoshino, "The Gay Tipping Point," *UCLA Law Review* 57 (2010): 1542.

42. The *Carolene Products* decision was uncomfortably close to the Nuremberg Laws that deprived German Jewish people of their civil rights. This served to remind Americans of the deprivation of black people's civil rights. The consequences of majoritarian political decisions were stark. The marginality of those minorities allowed Jewish and black people to be targets for exclusion from the political body.

43. Ackerman, "Beyond Carolene Products," 724.

44. Ackerman, "Beyond Carolene Products," 731.

45. Ackerman, "Beyond Carolene Products," 741.

46. Justice Ginsburg's dissent in *Fisher v. University of Texas* (2013) is an example of this. For Ruth Ginsburg, affirmative action is a way for members of the majority to provide an advantage for those in the minority, rather than treating them unfairly. The legacy of *Carolene Products* warns that in the case of rights affecting minorities, the Court must use "strict scrutiny," the most rigid form of constitutional review. However, Ginsburg understood that it would not be appropriate to use that measure because affirmative action, rather than victimizing a minority, seeks to modestly raise their social condition. In her dissent, she noted that: "Texas' percentage plan was adopted with racially segregated neighborhoods and schools front and center stage. . . . It is race consciousness, not blindness to race, that drives such plans." Another relationship that can be traced is John Hart Ely's influence on Justice Stephen Breyer, as noted by Cass Sunstein: "Like Ely, Breyer does not rule out the view that courts should take an aggressive role in some areas, above all to protect democratic governance." Cass Sunstein, "Justice Breyer's Democratic Pragmatism," *Yale Law Journal* 115, no. 7 (2006): 1722. See: Stephen Breyer. *Active Liberty* (New York: Vintage, 2006).

47. Balkin and Levinson, "Understanding the Constitutional Revolution," 1081.

48. Balkin and Levinson, "Understanding the Constitutional Revolution," 1083. On the counter-majoritarian difficulty, see: Alexander Bickel, *The Least Dangerous*

Branch: The Supreme Court at the Bar of Politics (New Haven, CT: Yale University Press, 1986).

49. Cass Sunstein, *One Case at a Time: Judicial Minimalism on the Supreme Court* (Cambridge, MA: Harvard University Press, 1999).

50. Mark Tushnet, *Taking the Constitution Away from the Courts* (Princeton, NJ: Princeton University Press, 1999).

51. Balkin and Levinson, "Understanding the Constitutional Revolution," 1084. Under Chief Justice Roberts, the Supreme Court is expected to follow a more conservative agenda, allowing greater interference by religion in the public sphere, greater participation by corporations in electoral processes, and a broadening of the spectrum that guarantees the right to bear arms, provided for in the Second Amendment. In turn, rights linked to affirmative action, abortion, and the defense of criminal defendants would tend to be reduced.

52. Balkin and Levinson, "Understanding the Constitutional Revolution," 1084.

53. "Chief Justice Roger Taney's poor reputation is not based on his embrace or rejection of minimalism, but on his support for slavery. Justice William Brennan's towering reputation rests not on his treatment of precedents or his embrace of judicial restraint but on the fact that he was on the politically progressive side of most controversies concerning civil liberties and civil equality. Stated more correctly, he was on the right side as judged by subsequent history (at least so far), whereas Taney was not." Balkin and Levinson, "Understanding the Constitutional Revolution," 1084.

54. Those principles are largely protected in both the formal and material sense of the Constitution.

55. Attacks on a certain type of judicial activism seem to desire for things to return to a place that never existed. More relevant than accusing another branch of exceeding the bounds of its authority would be to realize that there is a (contingent) fluctuating change between legitimate spaces for decision-making and that, in future terms, there is no way to rigidly control who will rule on which matters. Preserving the tension between constitutionalism and democracy requires institutional mechanisms, to ensure that one does not colonize the other entirely.

56. For discussions on the important proposal of deliberative democracy, see: Jürgen Habermas, *Between Facts and Norms* (Cambridge, MA: MIT Press, 1998); Carlos Santiago Nino, *La constitución de la democracia deliberative* (Barcelona: Gedisa, 1997); Ian Shapiro, *The State of Democratic Theory* (Princeton, NJ: Princeton University Press, 2003).

57. Even with the abolition of slavery and the ratification of the Fourteenth and Fifteenth Constitutional Amendments, the nefarious policy of "separate but equal" continued to be practiced in the United States. The doctrine was derived from *Plessy v. Ferguson* (1896), treating a law from the state of Louisiana, which mandated different train cars for white and black people, as constitutional.

58. The Ninth Amendment to the U.S. Constitution refers to constitutional protections not necessarily provided for in the Constitution's text. Tribe indicates the production of extratextual substantive norms: "The idea that the invisible Constitution in fact embodies certain *substantive* principles central to defining both the structure of government and the rights of persons—and that those norms are parts of the

Constitution *actually in force* rather than of some merely *possible* Constitution—is likely to be among the most controversial of the propositions put forth in this book." Laurence Tribe, *The Invisible Constitution* (New York: Oxford University Press, 2008), 79.

59. David A Strauss, *The Living Constitution* (Oxford, UK: Oxford University Press, 2010).

60. Clèmerson Merlin Clève and Alexandre Freire, *Direitos fundamentais e jurisdição constitucional* (São Paulo: Editora RT, 2014).

61. Daniel Sarmento, *Direitos fundamentais e relações privadas* (Rio de Janeiro: Lumen Juris, 2003), 374–375; Virgílio Afonso da Silva, *Direitos Fundamentais: conteúdo essencial, restrições e eficácia*, 2nd ed. (São Paulo: Malheiros, 2010).

62. "We thus understand today that general and abstract laws do not eliminate the problem of law; in fact, contrary to what Enlightenment thinkers might also believe, with their excessive confidence in reason, they lead to the problem of modern law, which is precisely that of applying general and abstract rules to necessarily specific, determined and concrete situations." Menelick de Carvalho Netto and Guilherme Scotti, *Os direitos fundamentais e a (in)certeza do direito: a produtividade das tensões principiológicas e a superação do sistema de regras* (Belo Horizonte: Fórum, 2011), 134.

63. It should also be emphasized that this possibility is not impeded in Brazil; in addition to the fundamental rights that have been established, others arising from the regime and the principles adopted by the Constitution can be incorporated. Art. 5§2º—Federal Constitution (*Constituição Federal – CF*).

64. "Moreover, it is easy to see how tenuous the transition is from the acceptance of 'grotesque rights' to the acceptance of actions over which there is no consensus in terms of the protection of a fundamental right. To use a simple example: are outdoor parties, in a place open to the public, protected by the rule that guarantees the right of assembly (art. 5, XVI)? For the external theory and a broad model of factual support, the answer is more than obvious: *prima facie* yes, although it may be restricted later, due to an eventual collision with other fundamental rights or collective interests. For those who support restricted factual support and an internal theory, the answer may be *no*, but it may be *yes*. The problem is that once it is rejected—based on a restricted and internal conception—that outdoor parties are an exercise of the right of assembly, that decision—since it is final—has to be valid, even in cases where parties do not disturb anyone or have any public interest." Afonso da Silva, *Direitos Fundamentais*, 154–155.

65. "The problem of modern law, now clearly visible thanks to accumulated experience, is precisely the consistent challenge of appropriately applying general and abstract rules to life situations that are always individualized and concrete, to what is called the application situation, which is always unique and unrepeatable, by definition. Modern law, as a set of general and abstract rules, makes society more rather than less complex." Carvalho Netto and Scotti, *Os direitos fundamentais e a (in)certeza do direito*, 127.

66. According to Article 1, *caput*, of the 1998 Federal Constitution. The German Constitution, approved in May 1949, provides in Art. 20.1: "The Federal Republic of

Germany is a democratic and social federal state." In the 1978 Spanish Constitution, Art. 1, the constituent assembly established that "Spain is hereby established as a social and democratic State." With regard to the 1976 Portuguese Constitution, Art. 2 provides that "The Portuguese Republic is a democratic state based on the rule of law."

67. "Following Rawls's critique of utilitarianism and Habermas's critique of legal and sociological positivism, which reduced the normativity or legitimacy of the right to one's own strength, it is no longer possible to think about the Constitution, yet alone intangible constitutional clauses, without considering their content, their intrinsic qualities. For certain constitutional clauses to be accepted as limiting the power of each generation to alter its own constitutions, their content must be able to be justified and accepted rationally. The fact that they were established by a previous constituent power is not enough to ensure their legitimacy." Oscar Vilhena Vieira, "A Constituição como Reserva de Justiça," *Lua Nova* 42 (1997): 78. Clèmerson Merlin Clève, *Atividade Legislativa do Poder Executivo* (São Paulo: Revista dos Tribunais, 2011), 138–139.

68. Marina Velasco, *O que é justiça: o justo e o injusto na pesquisa filosófica* (Rio de Janeiro: Vieira & Lent, 2009), 55.

69. Velasco, *O que é justiça*, 91.

70. Velasco, *O que é justiça*, 91.

71. "Normatively substantive messages can circulate *throughout society* only in the language of law. Without their translation into the complex legal code that is equally open to lifeworld and system, these messages would fall on deaf ears in media-steered spheres of action. Law thus functions as the 'transformer' that first guarantees that the socially integrating network of communication stretched across society as a whole holds together." Habermas, *Between Facts and Norms*, 56.

72. For Paul Hirst, the best way to analyze representation is to ask how well a politician represents a group of desires, interests, or individuals; for him, the question has no answer: "In fact the critique of 'representation' proves one thing, that there is no 'true' form of representation of the interests of the represented. All schemes of representation involve some element of substitution, and all such schemes have distinct political effects." Paul Hirst, *Representative Democracy and its Limits* (Cambridge, UK: Polity Press, 1990), 12.

73. John Ferejohn, "Judicializing Politics, Politicizing Law," *Law and Contemporary Problems* 65, no. 3 (2002): 41.

74. Ferejohn, "Judicializing Politics," 55.

75. In a traditional approach, one of the main functions of constitutional review is to limit majoritarian political decisions contrary to the Constitution and aid in their removal from the legal system, even in situations where the law is defended by the majority of the population. From that perspective, it would be inconsistent with the role of an independent judiciary for the courts to consider the public effects of the decision, in terms of causing a public outrage or counter-demonstrations. Sunstein suggests two strategies—the consequentialist and the epistemic—that characterize the discussion about the public impacts of court decisions, see: Cass Sunstein, "If People

Would be Outraged by Their Rulings, Should Judges Care?" *Stanford Law Review* 60, no. 1 (2007).

76. Clèmerson Merlin Clève, *Medidas provisórias*, 3rd ed. (São Paulo: Revista dos Tribunais, 2010), 44.

77. "The understanding of Art. 62 of the Constitution cannot be a prisoner of the literal interpretation. Only a systematic interpretation is able to reveal the meaning of the constitutional provision. For this reason, once adopted, the provisional measure (law or legislative act) must be immediately submitted to the National Congress, to be converted into a formal law. This thus involves the conversion of a provisional law into a permanent law, as a result of the public process inherent to the drafting of a formal law. Nothing more than that: one type of law (the provisional measure: provisional act) is converted into another type of law (the formal law, in this case, an ordinary law: a permanent act)." Clève, *Medidas provisórias*, 76–77.

78. "The first major cause of judicialization was the country's *redemocratization*, which culminated in the enactment of the 1988 Constitution. In the last few decades, with the restoration of judicial guarantees, the judiciary has ceased to be a specialized technical department and has become a true political power, capable of enforcing the Constitution and the laws, even when it involves confronting the other branches. . . . The second cause was *comprehensive constitutionalization*, which included countless matters in the Constitution that had previously been left up to the majoritarian political process and to ordinary legislation. . . . The third and final cause of the judicialization, which will be examined here, is the *Brazilian system of constitutional review*, one of the most comprehensive in the world." Luís Roberto Barroso, "Judicialização, Ativismo Judicial e Legitimidade Democrática," *Revista de direito do estado* 13 (January/March 2009): 73–74.

79. One example of this lies in the possible dichotomy that can be drawn from the constitutional text, both in the sense of heteronomous philosophical perspectives as well as in others that seek to guarantee the greatest autonomy for individuals. Those philosophical perspectives collide in situations involving hard cases (or tragic decisions).

80. Luís Roberto Barroso, *O novo direito constitucional brasileiro: Contribuições para a construção teórica e prática da jurisdição constitucional no Brasil* (Belo Horizonte: Fórum, 2012), 244.

81. Not only has there been an increase in abstract review, but there has also been an "abstraction" of concrete review. In this sense, the STF has already applied the modulation of effects technique (inherent to abstract review) in incidental review (RE-AgR n. 516,296, Justice Rapporteur Joaquim Barbosa, j. 04.10.2007) and conferred general effects on the decision issued in Writ of injunction (*Mandado de injunção – MI*) n. 670 (MI n. 670, Justice Rapporteur Gilmar Mendes, j. 10.25.2007, *Informativo STF* 485), an instrument that triggers an incidental constitutional review.

82. Clèmerson Merlin Clève, *Temas de Direito Constitucional*, 2nd ed. (Belo Horizonte: Fórum, 2014), 395–396.

83. For Conrado Mendes: "In the separation of powers, interaction is inevitable. Deliberative interaction is a gain; purely adversarial interaction—if it is not a loss—wastes its epistemic potential. . . . Judicial review does not need to be seen as solely

a dike or a containment barrier but also as a driving mechanism for better deliberations. It not only serves to (try to) protect us from politics when it succumbs to panic or irrationality but to challenge it to excel in quality." Conrado Hübner Mendes, *Direitos fundamentais, separação de poderes e deliberação* (São Paulo: Saraiva, 2011), 211–212.

84. The normative critique of the STF's role as a "guardian" does not change its structural function, but it is relevant because it points to other forms of institutional interaction, seeking to move beyond the tricky question of the "final word": "The deliberative type of interaction is the ideal that permeates, hence that exercise. It provides a conditioned justification for the STF's role while simultaneously taking it down from its pedestal as a 'guardian.' . . . But it also does not reject the STF's legitimacy to practice strong activism in certain circumstances. This is in line with the concept of the separation of powers outlined in the previous chapter, according to which there are no (and never will be) abstract and preset recipes that exhaust the definition of functions." Mendes, *Direitos fundamentais, separação de poderes e deliberação*, 214.

85. Dworkin explains that: "even when no settled rule disposes of the case, one party may nevertheless have a right to win. It remains the judge's duty, even in hard cases, to discover what the rights of the parties are, not to invent new rights retrospectively. I should say at once, however, that it is no part of this theory that any mechanical procedure exists for demonstrating what the rights of parties are in hard cases." Dworkin, *Taking rights seriously*, 81.

86. For Barroso, "The idea of *judicial activism* is associated with a broader and more intense participation by the judiciary in the implementation of constitutional values and aims, with greater interference in the space of action of the other two branches. The activist stance appears in different behaviors, which include (i) directly applying the Constitution to situations not expressly set out in its text, regardless of the activities of the ordinary legislator; (ii) declaring the unconstitutionality of normative acts emanating from the legislator, based on less rigid criteria than those of a patent and ostensible violation of the Constitution; and (iii) imposing behaviors or abstentions upon the government, notably in matters of public policies." Barroso, "Judicialização, Ativismo Judicial e Legitimidade Democrática," 75. The author claimed to have ceased using the term "judicial activism," due to its strictly negative association, as it had become a derogatory rhetorical device. Luís Roberto Barroso, "Não tenho nenhum orgulho do volume de processos que o Supremo julga," *Os Constitucionalistas*, February 23, 2015, http://www.osconstitucionalistas.com.br/entrevista-luis-roberto-barroso-nao-tenho-nenhum-orgulho-do-volume-de-processos-que-o-supremo-julga. While the concept ends up being subjected to a low semantic rigor on certain occasions, it has not lost its descriptive explanatory potential. Carlos Campos notes that: "Although it is indisputable from a descriptive point of view, judicial activism is not unanimous from a normative perspective. The political rise of judges and courts has always received much critique. The practice is accused of defying the democratic principle and the value of popular self-government. There is talk of a mutation in the 'parliamentary legislative state in a jurisdictional state governed by the Constitutional Court' and that 'the Court becomes, in a peculiar sense, sovereign

over the constitution' in a clear violation of the principle of the separation of powers." Carlos Alexandre de Azevedo CAMPOS, *Dimensões do ativismo judicial do Supremo Tribunal Federal* (Rio de Janeiro: Forense, 2014), 35.

87. Three emblematic cases can be cited to illustrate the argument. 1) In the case of the demarcation of indigenous lands, known as Raposa Serra do Sol (PET 3388—RR, Justice Carlos Brito, j. 03.19.2009, *DJE* 09.25.2009), the Constitution has defined the rule regarding domain over those areas by indigenous populations and traditional populations, such as quilombolas. The rule was already being used by the executive terms of its implementation, with the President of the Republic having the authority to define the demarcation of the area—it would be possible to transfer that authority to the legislature if the rule was enacted as a law. At the time of the STF's decision on the issue, the Court was generally not an activist—except for the provisions stipulated by Justice Menezes Direito, which once again had to be taken before the STF. In the ruling on the Motions for Clarification (*Embargos de Declaração – ED*) for the case in 2013 (PET 3388 ED—RR, Justice Rapporteur Roberto Barroso, j. 10.23.2013, *DJE* 02.04.2014), the rapporteur, Justice Roberto Barroso, removed the binding nature of the conditions and explained that the guidelines cannot be questioned in other proceedings. The Court thus deferred to the executive, who has better technical resources for understanding the matter, such as, for example, carrying out anthropological studies. 2) The Biosafety Law (11,105/2005) followed a legislative process filled with broad discussions promoted by the legislature itself, close to what is desirable for any matter that will be submitted to the legislature. The STF's decision (ADI 3510, Justice Rapporteur Carlos Britto, j. 05.29.2008, *DJE* 05.28.2010), also aided by popular participation through public hearings, deferred to the legislative process by recognizing the constitutionality of the law. 3) In the case of same-sex unions (ADPF 132, Justice Rapporteur Carlos Britto, j. 050.05.2011, *DJE* 10.14.2011), the STF took a more activist stance by using the technique of constitution-conforming interpretation; this was done, however, within the logic of protecting minority groups, one of the reasons that justify constitutional jurisdiction.

88. "An institutional design involves allocating powers to enact and powers to veto in different agents. Between vetoes and enactments, a decision-making process is designed, powers are distributed, institutional incentives are shaped, healthy channels of dialogue are created. In a series of tests, a collective decision is ultimately made. . . . Constitutional review would be an additional veto in the intricate network of the powers of veto and enactment that make up the engineering of the separation of powers." Conrado Hübner Mendes, *Controle de constitucionalidade e democracia* (Rio de Janeiro: Elsevier, 2008), 132.

89. *Marbury v. Madison* (1803).

90. Hans Kelsen, *Jurisdição constitucional*, trans. Maria Ermantina de Almeida Prado Galvão (São Paulo: Martins Fontes, 2007).

91. Clèmerson Merlin Clève, *A Fiscalização Abstrata de Constitucionalidade no Direito Brasileiro*, 2nd ed. (São Paulo: RT, 2000), 413.

92. "The three dimensions analyzed above—legality, constitutionality, fundamental rights—indicate that the principle of the rule of law is informed by two ordering ideas: (1) the idea of subjective ordering, guaranteeing a legal status to individuals that is

essentially anchored in fundamental rights; and (2) the idea of objective ordering, based on the principle of constitutionality, which in turn embraces the principle of the separation of powers as an objectively structuring principle. These two dimensions are not divorced from one another, but the stress accent will now fall on the objective functional ordering of the rule of law." J. J. Gomes Canotilho, *Direito Constitucional e Teoria da Constituição*, 7th ed. (Coimbra: Almedina, 2003), 250.

93. Chantal Mouffe recalls that democracy is fragile and must constantly be defended: Chantal Mouffe, *El retorno de lo politico* (Barcelona: Paidós, 1999).

94. With regard to activism, Carlos Campos notes its multi-dimensionality: "Those decisions have different dimensions, rather than solely a single form of expression, which means that judicial activism involves decision-making practices, generally multifaceted, and therefore cannot be reduced to unique identification criteria. There are multiple indicators of judicial activism, such as the expansive interpretation of constitutional texts, the lack of institutional deference to the other branches of the government, the judicial creation of general and abstract rules, etc." Campos, *Dimensões do ativismo judicial do Supremo Tribunal Federal*, 163.

95. A law whose general provisions guide the application of the rules of a given legal system. See: Canotilho, *Direito Constitucional e Teoria da Constituição*, 785–786.

96. In this sense, Dworkin emphasizes the importance of arguments of principle over political arguments, when exercising constitutional jurisdiction: "If we want judicial review at all—if we do not want to repeal *Marbury v. Madison*—then we must accept that the Supreme Court must make important political decisions. The issue is rather what reasons are, in its hands, good reasons. My own view is that the Court should make decisions of principle rather than policy—decisions about what rights people have under our constitutional system rather than decisions about how the general welfare is best promoted—and that it should make these decisions by elaborating and applying the substantive theory of representation taken from the root principle that government must treat people as equals." Ronald Dworkin, *A Matter of Principle* (Cambridge, MA: Harvard University Press, 1985), 69.

97. RCL 2189 MS, Justice Rapporteur Gilmar Mendes, j. 02.03.2003, *DJU* 02.07.2003. Gustavo Binenbojm, *A nova jurisdição constitucional*, 2nd ed. (Rio de Janeiro: Renovar, 2004), 195.

98. Art. 102, CF: § 3 "In an extraordinary appeal, the appealing party must demonstrate the general repercussion of the constitutional issues discussed in the case, under the terms of the law, so that the Court may examine the possibility of accepting the appeal, and it may only reject it through the opinion of two thirds of its members." The general repercussion was regulated by Law 11,418 of 12.19.2006. The STF, in turn, issued Amendment of the Rules (*Emenda Regimental—ER*) n. 21, of 04.30.2007.

99. "It is evident, however, that binding precedent, as its name implies, will have the power to directly bind the judicial bodies and the bodies of the public administration, opening up the possibility that any interested party can enforce the STF's guidance, not through a simple appeal but by filing a complaint for non-compliance with a court decision (CF, art. 103-A)" (Gilmar Ferreira Mendes and Paulo Gustavo Gonet Branco, *Curso de direito constitucional*, 7th ed. (São Paulo: Saraiva, 2012), 1040.

100. "As an interpretation technique, the principle requires judges and courts to interpret ordinary legislation to implement the constitutional values and aims in the most appropriate manner. That is to say, among the possible interpretations, it is necessary to choose the one that has the greatest affinity with the Constitution. . . . As a mechanism of constitutional review, constitution-conforming interpretation allows the interpreter—in particular, the constitutional court—to preserve the validity of a law that, in its most obvious reading, would be unconstitutional. In that hypothesis, the court simultaneously *invalidates* one of the possible interpretations, declaring it unconstitutional, and *affirms* another, which makes the rule compatible with the Constitution. This is a 'corrective' activity, which is important in a declaration of unconstitutionality without reduction of text." Luís Roberto Barroso, *Curso de direito constitucional contemporâneo: os conceitos fundamentais e a construção do novo modelo* (São Paulo: Saraiva, 2009), 301.

101. "The 1988 constituent assembly created two instruments to deal with unconstitutional omissions: the writ of injunction and the direct action of unconstitutionality by omission. It thus responded to a generalized complaint from society and the doctrine, seeking greater effectiveness for the constitutional rules and confronting one of the main historical dysfunctions of Brazilian constitutionalism." Luís Roberto Barroso, *O controle de constitucionalidade no direito brasileiro: exposição sistemática da doutrina e análise crítica da jurisprudência* (São Paulo: Saraiva, 2011), 153–154.

102. "The jurisprudence of the STF, as regards the use of the institute of the complaint in a concentrated review of rules, showed signs of a great evolution in the ruling on the point of order in an interlocutory appeal in Complaint 1,880, on 05–23–2002, when the Court confirmed that the complaint is appropriate for all those who prove harm resulting from decisions contrary to the STF's theses, recognizing the binding effect *erga omnes* of decisions on the merits in concentrated review Mendes, and Branco, *Curso de direito constitucional*, 1456.

103. "In successive decisions, the STF extended the objective and subjective limits of the decisions in abstract constitutional review, based on a construction that has been called *transcendence of determining motives*. In this line of understanding, a binding effect is recognized not only for the ruling but also for the very grounds that supported the decision. In other words, judges and courts must respect not only the conclusion of the ruling but also the reasons for the decision." Barroso, *O controle de constitucionalidade no direito brasileiro*, 230.

104. "In a conversationalist theory of judicial review, for example, the role of courts is simply to deliberate, not to decide, so that weak remedies, because they entail less sacrifice of judicial efficacy, will almost always be preferred over weak rights. On the other hand, in a democratic minimalist understanding, a key part of the court's role is to resolve concrete controversies without resort to the kind of broad or deep judicial reasoning that can destabilize constitutional order, so that weak rights will almost always be preferred to weak remedies. Similarly, in a departmentalism understanding, the courts' role is simply to decide the particular concrete controversy; judicial opinions are not afforded any presumptive respect in the broader political process and, thus, nothing is lost when courts adopt a weak rights, as opposed to weak

remedies, approach." Rosalind Dixon, "Creating Dialogue about Socioeconomic Rights: Strong-Form versus Weak-Form Judicial Review Revisited," *International Journal of Constitutional Law* 5, no. 3 (2007): 411.

105. Bickel, *The Least Dangerous Branch*, 16.

106. "An alternative theory for establishing an appropriate connection between the value of democracy and constitutional judicial review would be to argue that the former requires certain preconditions. When judges interpret the Constitution and it prevails over ordinary legislation, they are actually protecting those preconditions." Nino, *La constitución de la democracia deliberativa*, 272.

107. Nino, *La constitución de la democracia deliberativa*, 273.

108. Nino, *La constitución de la democracia deliberativa*, 279.

109. Nino, *La constitución de la democracia deliberativa*, 281.

110. "Ultimately, it is a matter of judgment as to whether it is justified to limit the functioning of democracy, not to directly promote democracy as in the first case of constitutional judicial review but to preserve a practice that gives efficacy to democratic decisions." Nino, *La constitución de la democracia deliberativa*, 282.

111. Barroso, *Curso de direito constitucional contemporâneo*, 300. Along the same lines, see: Cláudio Pereira de Souza Neto and Daniel Sarmento, *Direito constitucional: teoria, história e métodos de trabalho* (Belo Horizonte: Fórum, 2012), 458.

112. One of the most radical defenses of the judiciary's deference is attributed to James Thayer: James Bradley Thayer, *The Origin and Scope of the American Doctrine of Constitutional Law* (Boston: Little, Brown and Company, 1893). On the relationship between Thayer and minimum scrutiny, see: Richard H Fallon Jr., "Strict Judicial Scrutiny," *University of California Law Review* 54 (2007). Another relevant historical example is Holmes' dissent in *Lochner v. New York* (1905): "[A] Constitution is not intended to embody a particular economic theory, whether of paternalism and the organic relation of the citizen to the state or of *laissez faire*. It is made for people of fundamentally differing views . . . I think that the word 'liberty,' in the 14th Amendment, is perverted when it is held to prevent the natural outcome of a dominant opinion, unless it can be said that a rational and fair man necessarily would admit that the statute proposed would infringe fundamental principles." On the relationship between Holmes and Thayer, see: Richard Posner, "The Rise and Fall of Judicial Self-Restraint," *California Law Review* 100 (2012): 526.

113. In *Craig v. Boren* (1976), Justice Brennan asserted: "To withstand constitutional challenge, previous cases establish that classifications by gender must serve important governmental objectives and must be substantially related to achievement of those objectives." The second level of scrutiny was created as a result of that case.

114. In *Clark v. Jeter* (1988), Justice O'Connor established that: "Between [the] extremes of rational basis review and strict scrutiny lies a level of intermediate scrutiny, which generally has been applied to discriminatory classifications based on sex or illegitimacy. To withstand intermediate scrutiny, a statutory classification must be substantially related to an important governmental objective." The Pennsylvania law requiring that an "illegitimate child" must prove paternity before seeking support from their father and that the statute of limitations was six years was declared unconstitutional by the Supreme Court.

115. In *Grutter v. Bollinger*, Justice O'Connor observed: "We have held that all racial classifications imposed by government 'must be analyzed by a reviewing court under strict scrutiny.' . . . We have never held that the only governmental use of race that can survive strict scrutiny is remedying past discrimination. Nor, since *Bakke*, have we directly addressed the use of race in the context of public higher education. Today, we hold that the Law School has a compelling interest in attaining a diverse student body. . . . We [also] find that the Law School's admissions program bears the hallmarks of a narrowly tailored plan." *Grutter v. Bollinger* (2003).

116. It protects individuals from unsubstantiated searches of their property and documents and demands probable cause for searches and seizures.

117. Sergio Fernando Moro, *Legislação suspeita? Afastamento da presunção de constitucionalidade da lei*, 2nd ed. (Curitiba: Juruá Editora, 2003).

118. ". . . extremely rigorous, in which there is practically a reversal in the presumption of constitutionality of the normative act." Souza Neto and Sarmento, *Direito constitucional*, 459.

119. A comparison between the levels of scrutiny and proportionality was made as follows: "The first stage of PA mandates inquiry into the 'suitability' of the measure under review. The government must demonstrate that the relationship between the *means chosen* and the *ends pursued* is rational and appropriate, given a stated policy purpose. This mode of scrutiny is broadly akin to what Americans call 'rational basis' review, although under PA, the appraisal of government motives and choice of means is more searching. In most systems, few laws are struck down at this stage. The second step—'necessity'—embodies what Americans know as a 'narrow tailoring' requirement. At the core of necessity analysis is a least restrictive-means (LRM) test, through which the judge ensures that the measure at issue does not curtail the right more than is necessary for the government to achieve its goals. . . . The third step—balancing *stricto sensu*—is also known as 'proportionality in the narrow sense.' In the balancing phase, the judge weighs, in light of the facts, the benefits of the act (already found to have been narrowly tailored) against the costs incurred by infringement of the right, to decide which side shall prevail." Jud Mathews and Alec Stone Sweet, "All Things in Proportion? American Rights Doctrine and the Problem of Balancing," *Emory Law Journal* 60 (2011): 106–107.

120. See *Adarand Constructors, Inc. v. Peña* (1995): "The decision here makes explicit that federal racial classifications, like those of a State, must serve a compelling governmental interest, and must be narrowly tailored to further that interest. Thus, to the extent that Fullilove held federal racial classifications to be subject to a less rigorous standard, it is no longer controlling. Requiring strict scrutiny is the best way to ensure that courts will consistently give racial classifications a detailed examination, as to both ends and means. It is not true that strict scrutiny is strict in theory, but fatal in fact."

121. Mathews and Sweet, "All Things in Proportion?" 130–131. *Carolene Products* was less an introduction of a more rigorous level of scrutiny and more a shift in focus—towards deference—in judicial review. Adam Winkler, "Fatal in Theory and Strict in Fact: An Empirical Analysis of Strict Scrutiny in the Federal Courts," *Vanderbilt Law Review* v. 59 (2006): 799. For Tribe, in *Carolene Products*,

the Supreme Court stated that it would maintain regulations in the socioeconomic sphere if any set of known facts, or facts that could be inferred, supported the political decision. Such limited review turned out to be nearly a complete judicial abdication. The Court began to use hypothetical facts and reasons to maintain laws on economics and health or, in certain cases, had no substantive reasons. Laurence Tribe, *American Constitutional Law*, 3rd ed. (New York: Foundation Press, 2000), 1362.

122. The Supreme Court ruled that the Oklahoma law providing for the potential sterilization of criminals following their third conviction was an infringement of an important fundamental right: the right to reproduction. Furthermore, the failure to provide for sterilization following white-collar crimes violated the Fourteenth Amendment's Equal Protection Clause: "He is forever deprived of a basic liberty. We mention these matters not to reexamine the scope of the police power of the States. We advert to them merely in emphasis of our view that strict scrutiny of the classification which a State makes in a sterilization law is essential, lest unwillingly or otherwise invidious discriminations are made against groups or types of individuals in violation of the constitutional guaranty of just and equal laws."

123. "It should be noted, to begin with, that all legal restrictions which curtail the civil rights of a single racial group are immediately suspect. That is not to say that all such restrictions are unconstitutional. It is to say that courts must subject them to the most rigid scrutiny. Pressing public necessity may sometimes justify the existence of such restrictions; racial antagonism never can."

124. "The story of Japanese Americans and strict scrutiny begins with *Hirabayashi v. United States* and *Korematsu v. United States*. In these cases, the Court justified its upholding of race-based restrictions on American citizens of Japanese ancestry on the grounds of the exceptional demands of wartime military necessity." Greg Robinson and Toni Robinson, "*Korematsu* and beyond: Japanese Americans and the origins of strict scrutiny," *Law and Contemporary Problems* 68 (Spring 2005): 30.

125. Dworkin, *Law's Empire*. The following criteria may also be used: "(1) The first aspect is the normative act's *degree* of democratic *legitimacy*. . . . (2) Democracy should also calibrate judicial self-restraint, in the other direction. . . . (3) An equally important criterion is related to the protection of stigmatized minorities. . . . (4) Another criterion concerns the material relevance of the fundamental right at stake. . . . (5) Another important element is the comparison between the institutional capacities of the judiciary and the body that issued the normative act under discussion. . . . (6) Finally, another element is the era when the normative act was issued." Souza Neto and Sarmento, *Direito constitucional*, 460–463.

126. Clèmerson Merlin Clève, *Para uma dogmática constitucional emancipatória* (Belo Horizonte: Fórum, 2012).

127. Clèmerson Merlin Clève, *Jurisdição constitucional, ativismo e democracia*, Opening lecture at the IX Latin American Law Convention (*Convenção Latino-americana de Direito – Colad*), Curitiba, Paraná (October 27, 2011).

128. In Brazil, we have the postulate of proportionality, which is widely used as an instrument to review governmental acts: "It is only applicable in situations where there is a causal relationship between two empirically discernible elements—a means and an end—such that three fundamental tests can be carried out: adequacy (does the

means promote the end?); necessity (among the means available and equally adequate for promoting the end, is there a less restrictive means for the fundamental right(s) affected?); and proportionality in the strict sense (do the advantages offered by promoting the end correspond to the disadvantages caused by adopting the means?)." Humberto Ávila, *Teoria dos Princípios: da definição à aplicação dos princípios jurídicos* (São Paulo: Malheiros, 2004), 112–113. See also: Afonso Silva, *Direitos Fundamentais*, 167–182.

129. See: Roberto Gargarella, *El Derecho a la Protesta: el primer derecho* (Buenos Aires: Ad-Hoc, 2005). For those for whom the right to protest is the "first right," it makes it possible to demand the restoration of other rights.

130. Fiss seeks to redefine the state's role as it concerns freedom of expression. Rather than simply thinking about that right in terms antagonistic to the state, it would be possible to see freedom of expression as a public right, an instrument of collective self-determination, and the state as a "friend of freedom" of expression. Owen Fiss, *Libertad de Expresión y Estructura Social* (México, D.F.: Fontamara, 1997), 13–14.

131. ". . . thereby reflecting a strengthening constitutional commitment to the proposition that all qualified citizens are to play a role in making public decisions." John Hart Ely, *Democracy and Distrust: A Theory of Judicial Review*, 123.

132. According to the type of discrimination and how it affects a minority. In cases of "suspect classifications," the Court's level of scrutiny must be high to protect minorities. Some laws may "pass the test," but most should eventually be declared unconstitutional, given the government's difficulty justifying the discriminatory measure. Furthermore, in the case of "quasi-suspect" classifications, the intermediate level of scrutiny is recommended. However, even the very definition of "suspect classifications" is not placid. Some courts may emphasize the minority being "discrete and insular," while others may focus on the immutability of the group's characteristics, as well as the history of discrimination related to the minority group. Per Marcy Strauss: "Thus, although described in different ways, the basic factors for determining suspect class status were in place by the early 1980s: (1) prejudice against a discrete and insular minority; (2) history of discrimination against the group; (3) the ability of the group to seek political redress (i.e., political powerlessness); (4) the immutability of the group's defining trait; and (5) the relevancy of that trait. Using some combination of these factors, the Court has deemed various groups suspect, others quasi-suspect, and still others nonsuspect since the 1970s. Facial classifications based on race, national origin, and religion are considered suspect and receive strict scrutiny. Gender and illegitimacy are considered quasi-suspect and receive intermediate scrutiny. Age, socioeconomic status, and mental disability are subject to rational basis review. All other classifications (such as sexual orientation) either have not been decided or are reviewed under the default rational basis standard." Marcy Strauss, "Reevaluating Suspect Classifications," *Seattle University Law Review* v. 35 (2011): 146.

133. According to Barroso: "an open, elastic and plural notion of human dignity must be accepted. Roughly speaking, this is my minimalist conception: human dignity identifies 1. the intrinsic value of all human beings as well as 2. the autonomy of each individual and is 3. limited by certain legitimate restrictions imposed upon it in the name of social values or state interests (community value)." Luís Roberto

Barroso, *A dignidade da pessoa humana no direito constitucional contemporâneo: a construção de um conceito jurídico à luz da jurisprudência mundial* (Belo Horizonte: Fórum, 2012), 72.

134. ". . . they are, in a material sense, rights to factual positive actions, which, if the individual was financially able and found sufficient supply in the market, could be obtained from other individuals; however, in the absence of these conditions and considering the importance of these social rights, the granting or non-granting of which cannot remain in the hands of the simple parliamentary majority, they can be directed against the state through a constitutional provision." Paulo Gilberto Cogo Leivas, *Teoria dos direitos fundamentais sociais* (Porto Alegre: Livraria do Advogado, 2006), 89.

135. "The existential minimum, as a fundamental right, has—just as the latter does—different facets: it is both a subjective law and an objective rule. As a *subjective law*, it gives the citizen the ability to invoke procedural and institutional guarantees to defend their minimum rights. From an *objective* point of view, the existential minimum appears as a rule declaring fundamental rights, which should encompass the broader field of claims to citizenship. But, as it is pre-constitutional, the fact that it is implicit in the constitutional discourse does not impair its effectiveness." Ricardo Lobo Torres, *O direito ao mínimo existencial* (Rio de Janeiro: Renovar, 2009), 38–39.

136. Perfectionist legislation can be presented in different ways and thus involves discussions about the control of drug use, drinking while driving, cigarettes in public spaces, and the right to health. Perfectionism is characterized by the understanding that what is good for an individual or satisfies their interests is independent of their own desires or the choice of their way of life and the state is thus responsible for choosing which values and life plans are objectively best for individuals. Carlos Santiago Nino, *Ética y derechos humanos: un ensayo de fundamentación* (Buenos Aires: Astrea, 1989).

137. Bruce Ackerman, *We the People: Foundations* (Cambridge, MA: Harvard University Press, 1993).

138. "I maintain that democracy should not be understood as simple majoritarianism—let the political branches have their say—but rather as a deep and broad-based deliberative process in which we—all of us—give content to the values that define us as a nation. Constitutional pronouncements do not prevent or even stifle such deliberations, but rather, by fully revealing the threat that is posed to our basic commitments, give such deliberations a certain vitality." Owen Fiss, "The Perils of Minimalism," *Theoretical Inquires in Law* 9, no. 2 (2008): 647–648.

139. See: Mark Tushnet, *I Dissent: Great Opposing Opinions in Landmark Supreme Court Cases* (Boston: Beacon Press, 2008). "Undoubtedly, the intertemporal scrutiny of the Supreme Court's decisions, which is never confused with contempt, authorizes us to assert that a dissenting vote was the best, which should serve as an inspiration for a change of opinion, along with encouragement for civil rights movements, new environmental attitudes and civilizing moral approaches. It is not unusual for the Court's majority to understand cases according to epochal tendencies and to take interpretative paths that conflict with the wishes of future generations. Conversely, some dissenting votes showed that they had a long-term vision,

backed by a perspective that was lacking in the majority" (Gabriel Wedy and Juarez. Freitas, "O legado dos votos vencidos na Suprema Corte dos Estados Unidos," *Revista Consultor Jurídico*, March 26, 2015, http://www.conjur.com.br/2015-mar-26/legado-votos-vencidos-suprema-corte-estados-unidos.

Chapter 2

Interpretive Theories, Institutional Capacities, and Criticism

The question of who or, alternatively, which institution has the best conditions to make decisions in controversial cases is not a new theoretical concept. Nonetheless, different normative responses have been offered within the modern paradigm as regards the appropriate institutional arrangement between the branches and, as a consequence, who would have the best conditions to carry out constitutional interpretations.

The aim is to establish the most appropriate way to read, understand, and apply the texts of a constitution. One reason why that activity has been recognized as fundamental to the tensions between the branches of government is the expansion of the functions granted to the judiciary in recent decades in democratic countries.[1]

In Brazil, those discussions are relevant to the consolidation and untangling of the different theoretical perspectives that are used to justify the practice of constitutional jurisdiction.

In that context, the theory of institutional capacities has gained attention both internationally and nationally as an alternative to activist actions by the judiciary. Theories of deference were reestablished in opposition to constructions that sought normative paths for explaining the "best response" to be presented by magistrates.

In light of the theoretical struggle described, the chapter presents considerations on language games and connects two normative interpretive theories: one that proposes the reading of law as integrity, by Ronald Dworkin, and the dynamic interpretive theory, by William N. Eskridge.

An overview is then provided of the thesis of institutional capacities by Cass Sunstein and Adrian Vermeule, and the main characteristics are described: the attempted rereading of formalism, the defense of consequentialism and textualism, their grounding in an empirical vision, and the revival of the judiciary's deference. The theory of institutional capacities has several distinctive features: the institutional concern, the advancement of the theory of incompletely theorized agreements, the choice of second-order decisions, and the elevation of agencies as the most appropriate decision-making bodies for resolving controversial cases. These categories are discussed and critiqued in the final part of the chapter.

The critiques seek to point out the limits of the theory of institutional capacities, the insufficiency of textualism and consequentialism, the impossibility of the judiciary simply deferring to the executive branch and the inapplicability of political and normative factors to the decision.

LANGUAGE GAMES

Having overcome the notion that the meaning of texts emanates only from a specific place or that there is a necessary relationship between the designated objects and their respective "proper names," this section will reflect on how normative texts that configure legal systems are dependent on the production of meaning by their interpreters. The different ways in which it is possible to carry out the semantic construction is thus underpinned, in the legal sphere, by the guidelines stipulating the grounds for sentences, the presentation of reasons by their interpreters, to communicate their decisions in such a way that they can be understood by their subjects.[2] That idea is important for substantiating the dialogical legal constructions and the understanding that the law is an ongoing conversation.

No rule is detached from the hermeneutic operation. The production of rules and their meanings are activities that demand interpretation, that is, for them to have normative force, *the force of law*, they require someone with authority to say what the law is for the situation being disputed. It therefore follows that the provisions that will be interpreted will, in principle, result in a rule.

However, there is not necessarily a correlation between a rule and its provisions.[3] That analysis makes it possible to eliminate the false image establishing a simultaneous relationship between text and rule, as a rule is not always derived from a "text."[4]

Accordingly, the construction of meanings through interpretation does not correspond to the *nonexistence* of meanings established before the hermeneutical process. This is inferred from the distinction between the different *uses* of language and the limits on the appropriate use of means of communication.

Wittgenstein, when addressing language games, sought to break with the understanding that each word would correspond to a specific object. He therefore proposed to differentiate between the "bearer of the name" and the "meaning of a name," as the meaning would not depend on the existence of its bearer.[5] He also emphasized the importance of use, of the pragmatic aspect of language,[6] which occurs when a correction is made, given a set of minimum rules for the appropriate use of linguistic expressions.[7]

Formulating *language games*,[8] Wittgenstein argues that intentional acts that give meaning are not essential to understanding language. The search should therefore be focused on the variety of circumstances in which linguistic signs are constructed.[9] The fact that they are part of a guided activity does not necessarily result in a system of rules being defined for each specific language game but points out the conventional nature of this human activity.

Rather than proposing a general form of communicative propositions and for language itself or identifying something common to everything that can be called language, Wittgenstein emphasized that those phenomena are related in disparate ways and that there is no definition of the "essence" of the game.[10]

What can be analyzed is the result of a complex web of overlapping and intersecting similarities in certain cases, whether these similarities are generic or refer to details.[11] Although *family similarities* reaffirm the lack of boundaries for language, they also require the creation of certain boundaries.[12] Grammatical rules therefore do not only conform to instructions for the correct use of language but also express the rules of a language that produces meaning, of a meaningful language.

Grammar, for Wittgenstein, is not situated on an abstract plane but, rather, underpins a normal human activity in which language games are interwoven, which emphasizes the fact that language is an activity, part of a *life-form*.[13] In this sense, the hermeneutic task is not a unilateral production of meanings but, rather, reaffirms a semantics that is already ongoing in a discursive community, presenting itself as the product of social conventions.[14]

The set of reformulations engendered by the "linguistic turn" has reverberated on the legal plane.[15] It led to the understanding that theories of interpretation are a crucial component of constitutional production.[16] Having rejected the old idealized visions of textual interpreters as unwilling agents—who could only apply the series of decisions made in the political sphere, in which they were not active participants—different ways of articulating appropriate methods for formulating decisions have been devised.[17]

CONSTITUTIONAL INTERPRETATION

In those circumstances, constitutional interpretation became more prominent, given a plethora of political and historical factors that established the constitution as the supreme law. The charter's elevation to the status of a roof and foundation for the legal system was accompanied by increased attention on the activities of those who had the duty to "guard" or "protect" the constitution.[18]

Considering the importance ascribed to that activity, the specificity of the constitution's present role—understood as a normative source in its entirety—is related to the existence of a set of rules that are not self-evident or self-enforcing and cannot be subjected to a simple subsumption. As Wojciech Sadurski analyzes, it was the example of the US Constitution that convinced Europeans that the constitution could not be applied only in the political sphere, as it required the creation of legal instruments to confirm its supremacy, in terms of implementation. The idea that a legal institution should have the authority to guarantee constitutional supremacy had long been anathema on the European continent.[19]

In Brazil, after the 1988 Constitution, the doctrine of effectiveness sought to affirm constitutional normativity in opposition to readings that considered the Constitution to be a political text lacking normative force. The proposal of the "dogma of effectiveness" focused on filling a theoretical gap in the country and maximizing the effects that could be derived from the charter, wagering, at that time, on a certain leadership by the judiciary.[20]

Moreover, written constitutions do not present—in a complete way, within their text—a set of guidelines on how they should be interpreted.[21] What can be said, however, is that constitutions are laden, from their origins, with a dense narrative that cannot define itself without exogenous factors; it is a narrative that passes through different historical moments, demanding that successive generations produce meaning from it, whether based on the constitutional history, structure, or text.[22]

As a result, constitutional courts were also given a privileged position in the debate and the understandings that seek to strengthen or mitigate the function of constitutional jurisdiction began to challenge the theoretical scenario. This can be seen, for example, in the clash between "interpretivist" and "noninterpretivist" lines of thought in the United States.[23]

The "interpretivist" perspective emphasizes the interpretative limits present in the semantic texture and in the supposed will of the legislature, which would be justified by the democratic principle, that is, judges may not want to occupy the role of politicians in defining the rules that organize the state of law.[24] Judicial review would therefore only be admissible in situations where a clear "rule" for the "judgement on constitutionality" is identified, while the constitution would fulfill an institutional and procedural function—defining the powers of public bodies and not establishing substantive content to guide society.[25]

The "noninterpretivist" perspective, however, emphasizes that judges are responsible for identifying and applying substantive values to preserve the constitution. In that context, it is not democracy only that should be regarded as a value that deserves protection by the judiciary. Justice, equality, and freedom must also be considered when judges are carrying out hermeneutic activity.[26]

The dichotomy was underlined in the detection of "hard cases," cases in which there is no previously established rule that determines—with a certain confidence—a specific direction for the decision.[27] As it is not supported by a rule, it can be based on principles or policies, and for Dworkin, they would ideally be grounded in legal principles,[28] as, in those cases, judges make decisions that are able to justify other decisions, which can also be incorporated into a comprehensive theory of principles.[29]

INTERPRETATION AND INTEGRITY

Dworkin was one of the most important proponents of "noninterpretivism,"[30] and his reflections include the famous "Olympian" theory about how hermeneutics should be adjusted,[31] as well as questions about the very concept of law.[32]

Dworkin's theory focuses on interpretive activity while seeking to articulate assessment criteria, establishing the parameters of fit and justification as principles related to the legal system and its practices. He is guided by integrity, the pursuit of the best interpretation possible in the legal system, seeking "to show what is interpreted in the best light possible."[33] He makes several criticisms of what he calls the "semantic theory" of law. He thus questions Herbert Hart's positivism, as the author supposedly turned the use of state power into a "mere game of words."[34] He also identifies a moral judgment in the propositions capable of affirming *what is the* appropriate *law* in a certain case.

The configuration of the so-called hard cases is discussed by the academy, especially after the Hart's work.[35] These are cases that cannot be resolved through an answer that, according to the law, is given; its solution requires a certain discritionarity on the part of the judge. It is well known how Dworkin contests this thought. Is there, after all, a right answer that is offered by law and it is up to the judge to find it?[36] The best solution, the adequate solution, requires an adjusted hermeneutical effort, but it can and must be found.[37]

In his holistic hermeneutics, legal statements must be drawn from a set of principles that can even arrive at the "right answer"[38] given the entire established legal system.[39] His theoretical proposal is a general theory of interpretation based on principles, grounded in the idea that there are objective truths. According to Dworkin, some institutions are effectively unfair, and some acts are truly wrong, no matter how many people understand it differently.[40]

The example of courtesy aids in understanding that proposal. For the author, the practice of courtesy cannot only be observed in factual terms; it has a value in and of itself, is in accordance with some interest or reinforces some principle that is independent of the description of the rules that make up the practice.[41] Once an interpretative stance towards courtesy has been adopted, it is no longer a mechanical activity but, rather, a practice to which people try to attribute certain meaning and potentially restructure it in light of that meaning,[42] thusly: "Interpretation folds back into the practice, altering its shape, and the new shape encourages further reinterpretation, so the practice changes dramatically, though each step in the progress is interpretive of what the last achieved."[43]

His "constructive interpretation" stipulates different levels of consensus at each of the three stages of interpretation: a) first, in a "preinterpretative" moment, standards that provide the tentative content for the practice are identified; b) in the next stage, he proposes the creation of a general justification for the main elements of the previous practice; in that case, the justification must be sufficient to ensure that the interpreter is able to see himself or herself as someone performing a hermeneutic activity, rather than creating a new practice; and c) finally, there is a postinterpretive or reforming stage, in which the appropriate practice and justification are adjusted.[44]

Dworkin's interpretive theory is part of the broader perspective of "law as integrity," in which all of law and its artifacts, rules, and decisions experience an ongoing process of interpretation. Integrity also guides the production of the legislature, such that it must seek to make the State's set of rules morally consistent.

Dworkin's formulations indicate that there is no going back to a period in time where constitutional interpretation ceases to be a constructive practice performed by its interpreters. However, and not excluding the author's important contributions, it is not necessary to agree with the entire theoretical apparatus that has been presented to reach similar conclusions.[45]

Moreover, the dispute over interpretative activity—whether it should be concentrated to a greater or lesser extent in the judiciary or in the legislature[46] or be carried out by the "people" themselves[47]—does not alter the divergent nature of the theories that dispute the definition of *who* has the capacity to produce the best answers: the judge, the legislature, the members of the executive branch, or the people themselves?[48]

DYNAMIC INTERPRETATION

William Eskridge seeks to answer that question through a dynamic theory of interpretation. The dynamic interpretation of constitutional cases is part of a deliberative process that demands that the voice of the people be heard when there is tension between the laws and factual changes in society.[49]

The proposal would correspond to the provisions established in the Constitution itself concerning the dynamic creation of policies, in which the preferences of the majority are shaped by the deliberations of their representatives. Dynamic interpretation would therefore be a valuable instrument for legitimating the government, and in cases involving significant factual changes in circumstances, the problems presented by the counter-majoritarian difficulty[50] would not preclude dynamic interpretations by the courts.

One recurrent way of interpreting legal provisions focuses on the text and the system of precedents. Eskridge also suggests a cautious dynamic interpretive theory, through which he seeks to scrutinize subsequent interpretative stances, developments in constitutional matters and social facts that are current in their context.[51]

The insufficiency of static interpretive theory challenges the proposal of dynamic theory. Static theory expects judges to reproduce the meanings of old rules without considering the context in which they will be applied, often ruling out the possibility of dialectic hermeneutics[52] by transforming this activity into a mere "discovery," a locating of past meanings, as if the interpreter could (re)create a connection with the legislators or judges of the past and faithfully reproduce the meanings established in those moments, without interference from contemporary contingencies.

For Eskridge, rather than being limited to the conventional perspective, dynamic theory should observe and reconcile three dimensions: 1) the text, the formal part of interpretation, which places a limit on the number of hermeneutic possibilities; 2) the legislators' original expectations and the compromises they reached; 3) and the subsequent evolution of the rules and their present context, particularly in cases where changes have taken place in the legal and social realm.[53]

To illustrate his theory, Eskridge refers to *United Steelworkers v. Weber* (1979). In his view, although the Supreme Court's response was adequate, the justices found it difficult to justify the decision based on traditional interpretative theories. The case discusses the Civil Rights Act of 1964, which had prohibited any form of discrimination based on race, color, religion, gender, or nationality.

Brian Weber, a white employee, questioned the constitutionality of a collective labor agreement that guaranteed quotas for black workers, centered on Title VII of the Civil Rights Act, which prohibited discrimination in employment relationships. It therefore questioned the constitutionality of affirmative actions adopted in labor practices, given the presence of legislation that did not adequately address the questions raised by Weber regarding discrimination.[54]

The Supreme Court ruled by a majority that the alleged discrimination against whites made no sense and that the company's affirmative actions should be maintained. Justice Brennan presented the Court's ruling, using legislative history, the intent of Congress and the normative text itself as arguments. It ruled that Title VII of the Civil Rights Act did not condemn private, voluntary, and race-conscious affirmative action plans.[55]

In Eskridge's view, if dynamic interpretation were used, it would recognize that there had been a change in the concept of discrimination between the year the act was signed into law (1964) and the year of the ruling on the case (1979), as well as in the legal and social contexts. Those transformations could be observed in subsequent decisions, where the meaning of the ruling was expanded to guide affirmative actions related to women and racial minorities.[56]

Dynamic theory suggests an ongoing relationship between textual, historical, and contextual aspects. In different situations, the normative text will suggest responses to cases, particularly when the law is recent and the legislative production involved major deliberations—under those conditions, the text is paramount. However, in some cases, neither the text nor legislative history indicate an answer, and there have been significant social and legal changes—under those conditions, the context prevails. The following structure can aid in the interpretative activity: 1) the more detailed the normative text, the greater the textual considerations should be; 2) the more recent the law and the more evident the legislative intentions, the greater the consideration for historical aspects should be; and 3) the more remarkable the changes in the circumstances, the more attention should be given to the evolutionary aspect.[57]

Given such a proposal, it is possible to advocate for a reading of the normative texts carried out over a sustained period of time.[58] However, the theory of dynamic interpretation poses questions about the very "nature" of the interpretative activity. Hans-Georg Gadamer, in particular, understands that the method adopted for interpretation does not restrict or even guide the interpreter in a specific way, as the legal literature often seems to assume; interpretation is a search for a common understanding of the truth of the text by the interpreter, through a historical tradition.[59]

There is thus no single method that is able to respond to all the vicissitudes that the hermeneutic activity must confront. Eskridge argues that the text, the legislature's expectations and the current political arrangements can be used to improve hermeneutics. Interpretation should therefore be understood as a *conversation* between the interpreter's contemporary perspective and the trio of elements that help construct the normative meaning.[60]

BETWEEN DYNAMIC AND INTEGRITY

As for the question of who would be the authority with the best conditions to make constitutional interpretations, a brief comparison can be made between Eskridge and Dworkin. Both formulate normative proposals that seek to expand the range of possible instruments for carrying out constitutional hermeneutics. Furthermore, they both place their wagers on the judiciary as the branch of power equipped to make hard decisions.

In their own way, each of the two theories questions "static" interpretations. For Eskridge, the alternative lies in a cautious dynamic perspective and in the view of judges as "diplomats,"[61] whose authority is limited by their "superiors" but who nonetheless have the power to bring their orders up to date, given new circumstances. Dworkin defends the interpretative updating that occurs in accordance with law as integrity (i.e., the interpretative activity itself is able to impart another perspective on the rules through a cogent and Olympian [Herculean] reading of the law).

For Dworkin, integrity must be sought not only in decisions but must also be a guide for legislative production, making it imperative for legislators to construct a morally cogent legal order. Under the mantle of law as integrity, legal propositions are true if they are in harmony with principles of justice, equality, and legal due process, which can construct the best legal interpretation. To produce a constructive interpretation, it is necessary to perceive the interpretative activity as the construction of a novel—a chain novel—an ongoing story, in which the understanding changes with the development of the narrated story itself (which is narrated by law).[62]

Dworkin's proposal is not dissimilar to the confluence of horizons presented by Gadamer, that is, the ways in which tradition can connect past and present,[63] and a way of performing that activity in the legal realm—in particular, in common law—occurs through a reading of the precedents. The sequence of precedents, practices, and customs form a chain of meanings for Dworkin, which accurately connect court decisions with present decisions. The interpreter is responsible for considering not only the origins of the rules but also their *life* and their transformations.

As a result of those characteristics, Dworkin's view was treated as "romantic"[64] or a "dream."[65] One of the problems arising from Dworkin's theory is the difficulty of maintaining the coherence of the legislative production, as new rules may not only have internal inconsistencies but may also conflict with earlier provisions that expressed different political views. The challenge lies in the complex articulation of the coherence between the different fields protected by law as well as finding a balance between old rules and precedents and new legal and social configurations.

Eskridge's dynamic theory seems to offer answers that are more attuned to that question. The dynamic model suggests that when judges are interpreting texts, they act as "diplomats." Diplomats are required to follow ambiguous orders in unusual situations. They are, ultimately, agents in the service of the state, and their freedom of interpretation is restricted by previous orders, which are not always consistent and coherent over time.[66]

Eskridge acknowledges that in certain cases, judges may approach the Olympian thesis. Justice Earl Warren and his colleagues came close in *Brown v. Board of Education* (1954), but most magistrates end up having an activity similar to that of diplomats.[67] This is not all bad, as in certain circumstances, when certain judges believe they are judging like Hercules, their decisions end up being reversed. As a result, for Eskridge, the public agent who applies—with decency and fairness—the rules of a system plagued by incoherence performs a noble activity, a nobility that is constructed every day, and thus does not dwell in the book of fables of Utopia.

Another problem concerns how Dworkin deals with policies. The importance of the author's distinction between principles and policy cannot be denied.[68] However, the proposal of the political ideal of integrity, which would transform a political community into a community of principles,[69] encounters resistance. Eskridge acknowledges that the community of principles transcends the proposal of a political organization based on compromises and thus seems to be more valuable.[70] Dworkin, however, ends up simplifying the role of policy, placing his wager on law as a transformational agent of the political community in a community of principles. However, his theory does not seem to be able to dispel the common political rationality, which is based on rules and political compromises.

Nonetheless, Eskridge and Dworkin agree on the hermeneutical foundations and on topics related to coherence. Eskridge supports Dworkin's proposal regarding the pursuit of coherence as it concerns public values, which should be protected by the courts from potential legislative usurpations. Moreover, when the courts bring old laws closer to modern policies, they end up making the normative order more coherent.

Dynamic theory and the notion of law as integrity depart from less complex hermeneutic discourses, presenting sophisticated developments[71] defining the relationship between the text and the interpreter.[72] In this instance, the images suggested by Dworkin and Eskridge—of Hercules or the diplomat, respectively—are fertile and, moreover, truly useful for deepening the debates around constitutional interpretation.

INSTITUTIONAL CAPACITIES: THE INSTITUTIONAL TURN

The two theories presented sought to provide normative answers to questions concerning legal interpretation. When a judge is confronted by a case, how should he or she formulate an appropriate answer and interpret the available set of rules to produce their decision?

This type of approach is not endorsed by all hermeneutical perspectives. Different interpretative (normative) proposals have been criticized for not focusing on a salient aspect of hermeneutic practice, namely the definition of who would have the best institutional conditions to provide answers for controversial cases. The critique attempted to demonstrate that normative hermeneutic theories end up focusing their attention on an idealized image of the judiciary as well as a very negative view of the legislature.

Furthermore, the institutionalist perspective stressed that an earlier problem needed to be (re)included on the agenda, to ascertain who has the appropriate instruments to respond to the controversial questions posed to public institutions. A shift in this perspective was suggested by a "non-normative" view of the production of judicial decisions. Rather than asking "what *should* the interpretation *be*?" attention would be shifted to assessing what institutional conditions *are* effectively available for judges to produce the interpretation of laws.

Adrian Vermeule and Cass Sunstein sought to emphasize the influences of institutional aspects in the formulation of decisions by actual judges. This occurred based on the understanding that normative interpretative theories generally gave little attention to *institutional capacities* and ended up engaging in abstract discussions about substantive values, such as democracy, legitimacy, and authority.[73] For Vermeule and Sunstein, these types of formulations are difficult to translate to the courts and are therefore less likely to be instrumentalized as indicators when determining responses in disputes between appropriate methods of interpretation.[74]

They thus proposed to differentiate between theories based on a decision scenario involving optimal conditions—"first-best" conditions—for resolving conflicts and those where levels of perfection cannot be achieved, identifying "second-best" responses.[75] The idea of the second-best decision would be to provide a more realistic overview of the conditions under which a judge makes his or her decisions.

Disconnected from institutional considerations, normative theories would operate under ideal first-best conditions, but this would make it impossible to reach adequate conclusions on forms of interpretation.[76] Admitting that judges may not achieve the perfection outlined in the normative theories opens up the possibility of institutional arguments, as according to the authors, it is impossible to derive interpretative rules directly from first-best considerations.[77]

They also believe that a second-best assessment may not only be necessary but sufficient for resolving conflicts over interpretative theories, thus enabling people with different perspectives to agree on what the appropriate practices are. This is supported by Sunstein's theory of "incompletely theorized agreements."[78]

For Sunstein and Vermeule, modern interpretative theories have neglected institutional analysis and its centrality when choosing interpretative techniques. Based on that finding, the authors proposed a formalist perspective as the most appropriate for resolving questions around the choice of *who* has the best conditions for decision-making. It is essential, however, to heed the specificity of the way the term was used.

By admitting that formalism can encompass different meanings,[79] Vermeule sought to define his perspective as a decision-making strategy that could be adopted by the courts, in which second-best decisions would be formulated, with an emphasis on the legal certainty that could be derived from interpretation.[80] To this end, judges should follow the "clear" and "specific" meaning of legal texts and adopt a deferential stance towards the interpretations presented by the legislature and government agencies.[81] Vermeule's formalism attempts to define a decision-making strategy limited by rules and emphasize the consequentialist grounds of a decision[82] (i.e., following formalism will result in better outcomes for the entire legal system).[83]

According to that perspective, judges who make decisions under conditions of profound uncertainty and with limited rationality should restrict both the amount of information and the complexity of their behavioral repertoire and thus follow simple rules and limit the potential harm their decisions may cause. A generalist court that has limited information and time would perform better if it ignored or overlooked certain interpretative sources. In turn, a court specializing in a particular matter may have an activity that is detached from formalism and adopt bolder interpretative techniques.[84] The formalistic perspective is thus defended as more attractive given certain specific empirical situations in which systemic effects must be assessed.

For Vermeule and Sunstein, the "institutional turn" was not followed by hermeneutic theories and has not been fully achieved in constitutionalism. For the authors, topics such as judicial review have an extensive history of institutional blindness.[85] Since its creation with *Marbury v. Madison* (1803), judicial review has devoted little attention to institutional issues, ignoring the risks of errors made by the judiciary, as well as their consequences.[86] The conclusion that it is the judiciary's duty and responsibility to say *what the law is*—pursuant to the Supremacy Clause—is supported, in the United States, by weak textual and structural inferences, and any assessment of those arguments depends on institutional considerations.

The question, therefore, is whether one institution can oversee the actions of another and the scrutiny with which this should occur. Vermeule and Sunstein's proposal is that constitutional interpretation should observe the limits set by the institutions themselves,[87] which leads to a struggle against the romanticized perspective of the branches of government (primarily the judiciary) and the selection of second-best choices and incompletely theorized agreements. To this end, the type of formalism supported by the authors is advocated as the "best path" for reducing complexities and guiding the decisions of generalist judges, who have few institutional instruments for resolving political issues.

However, they are placing a wager on the role played by administrative agencies; given the agencies' closer proximity to reality and, therefore, better institutional position for assessing specific situations, they should be allowed greater flexibility in interpretations. For Vermeule and Sunstein, the agencies' privileged position would allow them to recognize whether a particular outcome is appropriate or whether departing from the text will destabilize the regulatory structure.[88]

When the normative text is "clear and specific," notes Vermeule, judges should adhere to its literal meaning and discard collateral sources that could expand its meaning, as is the case for legislative history. Otherwise, in situations where the legal text is ambiguous or vague, judges should defer to interpretations established by administrative agencies or agents of the executive branch. Furthermore, the doctrine of precedents should have the authority to guide judicial decisions, but the case law itself must be subjected to the interpretative updating carried out by the public administration.[89] Given those assumptions, Vermeule's skeptical position regarding the possibility of judicial review becomes apparent, befitting his version of "Thayerism."[90]

Sunstein, in turn, heightens the questions around the fallibility of judges by criticizing theories that support "first-order perfectionism," such as Dworkin's theory of law as integrity. "Second-order perfectionism" seeks to make constitutional jurisdiction alert to the fact that judges may err.[91]

For Sunstein, outside of "Olympus," there are no guarantees that real-world judges will enforce the normative projects contained in constitutional interpretative theories. It is necessary to consider the costs of decisions and their potential errors, factors that first-order perfectionist theories do not consider. Furthermore, the limitations of judges should be admitted, particularly those relating to moral and political discourses.[92]

For the perspective of institutional capacities, the first-best concept is incapable of producing conclusions on the design of the interpretative procedures leading to a decision; it is an incomplete theorization that does not adequately assess the true capacities of the judging agents. This produces the "nirvana fallacy," which compares the best-case scenario of one institution (judiciary) with the worst-case scenario of other institutions (legislature).[93] As a result, rather than seeking the perfect interpretation, what would need to be assessed would be how certain institutions, with their abilities and limitations, should interpret certain texts.[94]

When considering flesh-and-blood judges, it is impossible to rule out the possibility of the judiciary formulating responses, but assessing the limitations of the branch—compared to the range of mechanisms available in other institutions—leads to the understanding that the judiciary does not have the best position for resolving the questions brought before it.

That questioning is not, in and of itself, new. A recurrent topic in the critique of the judicialization of politics ultimately adopts a similar argumentative line, asserting that a certain matter should not have been decided by the judiciary and that the appropriate space for political decisions is the parliament rather than the court. Those argumentative lines tend to be invoked by lawsuits, in the sense of a restrained stance by the courts.[95]

For Diego Arguelhes and Fernando Leal, the idea of an institutional capacity is accompanied by a concept of the separation of powers and institutional design. They seek to distribute functions and ensure that they are exercised within the institutional framework according to their corresponding specialty. In those terms, the constitution is compared to a blueprint for the institutional architecture that seeks to streamline and maximize the achievement of its objectives.[96] Furthermore, as regards the difference between the ideal conditions and the actual plan for the practice of jurisdiction, the theory of institutional capacities advocates for separating theory and reality, as normative theories would not have suitable mechanisms for addressing the errors committed by institutional actors with limited access to information.[97]

Vermeule, in line with his statements on the appropriate roles to be played according to the institutional design, criticizes the stance of constitutionalism in common law, which mistakenly transposes the idea that a few heads in the judiciary are better than one (an image that is related to the importance of precedents) to the idea that a few heads in the judiciary are better than all heads in the legislature.[98]

The theory of institutional capacities is not focused only on solving the specific cases presented to the judiciary. It gives preference to a more comprehensive scope and seeks to reflect on the structure and relationships among the branches of government. It can therefore encompass decision-making methods that are intended to be valid for different situations. Jeff King advocates for an institutional approach to judicial self-restraint.[99] This is because judges often rule on conflicts that raise questions about the level of rigor they should use when scrutinizing acts originating in the legislature and the public administration.[100]

According to King, formalism can be criticized for its attachment to abstract categories such as "law" and "politics" without considering the context in which they are used. Rigid divisions between law and politics therefore do not have the subtlety to advocate for a proper role for the judiciary.[101] In turn, "non-doctrinal" perspectives place too much trust in the judiciary, assuming that each case is unique, underestimating the possibility of unpredictable errors coming from the judiciary and undermining the idea of limited government in a state of law.[102]

A CRITIQUE OF INSTITUTIONAL CAPACITIES

The theory of institutional capacities has come to be viewed rather cautiously due to what it sought to promote: an "institutional turn." There is, however, an appealing aspect to the theory, which is the consideration of which institutional sphere is best suited for making decisions. During times when there has been an intense judicialization of different subjects and a potential inertia or lack of effectiveness in the other branches, the judiciary came to be seen as a key forum for resolving different types of social conflicts, including issues that were seen as preferably belonging to the political sphere, such as the eligibility of politicians and the possibility of forming party coalitions. That phenomenon was countered by different arguments, including the theory of institutional capacities, which advocates for deference by the judiciary, among other proposals.

The theory of institutional capacities has thus far been received unilaterally in Brazil. Rather than questioning the adaptability of those theoretical apparatuses for solving problems related to the Brazilian reality, there has been an attempt to make its use more rigorous, which has rendered its sterile vision of the judiciary's role even more difficult to justify.[103]

Beyond the most obvious conflict with the type of formalism proposed by Brazilian theory and legal culture, the lack of questions regarding *who* would decide which matters are more appropriate for one of the branches or another is a significant gap in the theory. While there is an idealization of the role of the judiciary to be critiqued in the normative theories, the argument that the low operational effectiveness of the judiciary will diminish the possibility of it committing errors is a discourse that can be extended, in the same manner, to the other branches.

Although Dworkin and Eskridge commit the "nirvana fallacy," Vermeule and Sunstein's theory of institutional capacities ultimately encounters similar difficulties to those they are denouncing, producing an idealized image of agencies and the legislature as well as not offering an adequate answer regarding which public agent would be capable of reducing errors within the "second-best" logic.

Furthermore, by following the line of thought that appears to be attempting to erode the judiciary's powers and restore a "Thayerist" perspective, the theory of institutional capacities demands that a set of "procedures" are followed. For those authors, the flesh-and-blood judge must be guided by the understanding that their institutional capacities are limited. They should therefore choose, whenever possible, to be deferential and rule in such a way that it does not cause major shake-ups in the structure of the political community. However, institutional design is not considered, in the sense that once the deferential stance has been taken, people begin to demand a response from another government body. There can thus be no guarantee that the response from another body will be protected by the set of principles that guide jurisdiction, such as legality or legal due process.

Moreover, it seems that the partial acceptance of the theory cannot be reconciled with the characteristics of Brazilian legal practices. It is unlikely that Vermeule and Sunstein's perspective will be adopted in regard to the normative aspects implicitly and indirectly assumed in the "institutional turn." The formalism presented would, according to Vermeule, demand empirical and institutional objections, not arguments about the nature of language.[104] The problem is that there is no effective reduction in errors in that institutional design, only the transposition of agents who will commit errors in other institutional spheres. Additionally, the question of who would make the "prior" decision—the decision about which institution would be the most appropriate for deciding the problem and the appropriate criteria for assessing that decision—is left unanswered.

Vermeule's consequentialism also proposes the fragile idea that it would be best for judges to cling to the superficial meaning of texts, rather than making other types of considerations, such as referring to legislative history or public values. Those formulations are accompanied by the indication that highly abstract topics should be placed beyond the reach of the judiciary.[105] Both proposals do not seem sustainable.

First, there is an initial or "superficial" meaning that a term may have, but it is impossible to prevent—even at the level of the use of common language—other meanings from arising or being extracted from a term. The explanation of language games—maintaining a central meaning of a sign, which is accompanied by successive changes in the use of language according to different contexts and practices—seems to be enough to highlight the difficulty of performing a "superficial" reading. There are cases in which the judicial questioning itself is based on the possibility of more than one interpretation of the normative texts. Opting for a superficial reading to guarantee formalism does not ensure a reduction in errors or even any type of appropriate response, in either normative or systemic terms.

Second, the reduced degree of abstraction, or institutional analyses of a lesser degree, cannot be considered as an alternative to restructuring the practice of the judiciary. The problem, in this case, lies in situations where what is brought before the judiciary is precisely the meaning of highly complex and abstract topics. Not infrequently, constitutional courts use arguments regarding the protection of democracy, the violation of the separation of powers, and even the meaning of certain fundamental rights.

Not only is this a recurrent factor in the argumentative construction of the courts, but it is also possible to observe that controversial issues are raised in different cases, and given the silence of the other branches, it is the task of the judiciary to settle (even if momentarily) disputes around the conflict. The problem lies not only in the impracticality of the theory that is proposed as making the institutional turn but also in the inevitability of dealing with abstract topics as well as topics on which no consensus can be reached—neither political nor legal.

Another critique of the theory of institutional capacities concerns its "novelty." To treat their theory as unique and innovative, the authors disregard other contributions that had previously been made by Henry Hart and Albert Sacks' theory of the legal process[106] as well as by those who furthered it. John Hart Ely, for example, advocated for a theory in which the judiciary's active role was focused on correcting dysfunctions in the legislature, and judicial review would therefore be justified—on certain occasions—to correct those errors. [107]

Vermeule's proposal thus furthers this procedural aspect, without assuming its legacy and with a more radical perspective regarding the role of the courts. It is therefore similar to the arguments of Antonin Scalia, for whom judges—when interpreting—should set aside legislative history as well as the evolution of the legal order, as those artifices would increase the discretionary power of magistrates.[108] For Vermeule, judges should not have access to materials about the context and should limit their action to applying the superficial meaning of normative texts. Thus, while Eskridge accuses certain authors of suffering from the nirvana fallacy, he claims that the theory of institutional capacities suffers from "agency nirvana."[109]

For Vermeule, the constitutional debate does not signal the adoption of any specific interpretative theory; that is, based on the constitution, it would not be possible to derive any interpretative procedure of how to read the constitutional text.[110] The problem is that Vermeule is reviving a type of barren theory that emphasizes instrumental aspects of the decision-making process and disregards—due to the absence of normative aspects—the fact that decisions have a political dimension, not merely a technical one. This is reflected, for example, in the problem of the legitimacy of decisions.

The barrenness of the theory conflicts with the constitutive characteristics of the law,[111] with the fact that the law reflects a number of historical, political, moral, and technical factors. It would therefore be imperative to deny that moral concerns and concerns about legitimacy constitute the law; they are also adopted at the moment of the decision.

Take, for example, a law regulating the entry of vehicles into a park. By prohibiting the entry of vehicles, it can be deduced that motorcycles are also not allowed entry, but the simple prohibition does not make it possible to state with any certainty whether it should also be extended to bicycles, tricycles, and skateboards. The stipulation that a "vehicle" includes any means of transport that carries a person from one place to another does not offer any assistance because, for example, would wheelchairs be included in that description? Would the park come to not allow entry to wheelchair users? If a child is on a tricycle, would the prohibition also apply?

For these types of problems, Eskridge suggests that the interpretation should be made using 1) the clear meaning of the text; 2) the legislative structure and the content of other relevant laws; 3) the legislative history of the rule, its compromises and proposals; 4) previous interpretations by the courts and agencies (precedents); 5) the observation of legislative developments, including new practices and standards; and 6) substantive canons of legislative interpretation (normative sources).[112]

As simple as it may seem, a judge's decision regarding the possibility of vehicles entering the park also reflects a series of moral values and is part of the deliberations that take place in different spheres of power. It is thus understood that the courts' decisions are components of a people's moral constitution. Moreover, they are part of the public sphere, which is the stage for social, moral, and normative tensions and disputes. Those disputes cannot be resolved in a trivial manner by limiting judges' interpretative resources, particularly in matters involving highly political aspects.

A child who is prohibited from entering the park with their tricycle is not only questioning the literal nature of the law, but also the case raises concerns related to the democracy of rules, legal due process, the right to equality, and the state's legitimacy to impose prohibitions—the reasons that the state authority must present to justify the prohibition of certain behaviors. Vermeule's textualism, which values the costs and benefits of decisions, does not seem to consider the costs related to the loss of a law's legitimacy.[113]

When ruling out a theory of state legitimacy, it is not possible to determine whether interpretations are good or bad. Furthermore, for this to be assessed, it is necessary to determine which institution is the most competent to make decisions—the earlier question regarding who should decide which is the best decision-making institution. Determining the most capable institution also requires normative and empirical assessments.

For some time now, the question has no longer been restricted to defining "how judges should decide" but also defines how the decision can be justified as legitimate to the political community. The most widely held answer to the question of legitimacy refers to the need for judges to present justifications, an element that does not seem to be supported by the theory of institutional capacities.[114]

In that sense, it is timely to recall that "*it is impossible to divide the act of application into two parts: decision and grounds. One is part of the other, a question that has been clearly explained by the ontological-fundamental theorem of the hermeneutic circle.*"[115] The concern with legitimacy is in line with the new paradigm established by the democratic rule of law, in which the law is tasked with not only stabilizing social relations but also transforming them.[116] The constitution becomes a legitimizing source of intersubjective relations and guides the process of "re-founding" society: "*The constitution is ultimately the result of its interpretation, as a thing only exists (something, a thing) to the extent that it is interpreted (because it is understood 'as' something).*"[117]

This is a demand for "*conditions enabling intersubjectively valid judgements about the world,*"[118] given the impossibility of expressing the world outside of language and the understanding that it is only through language—which is perceived as a condition of possibility—that it is possible to have access to the world. To deny access to deep relationships with the meaning of the text or to try to limit the role of the interpreter to that of reproducing the "superficiality" of the text is thus to demand the renunciation of entry into the "world" constructed in the legal narratives that are presented to the courts and is an instrumental vision of language as a simple object mediating the subject-object relationship.[119]

The pursuit of simplification, for Vermeule's simplified (simplifying) interpreter, disregards the fact that our way of being (human) is interpretative: "*The horizon of meaning is given to us by our understanding of something. The human being is understanding. We are only made through understanding. We only exist through understanding.*"[120]

Such considerations are far removed from what Vermeule proposed; for him, much of the canon of interpretative forms is dismissed as a collection of abstractions or "high-level" issues that should be separated from how they are imagined by a judge with limited capacities, which would lead to a decision guided by cost-benefit and the possibility of harm reduction at the empirical level. The result is one of the most "austere" theories on the interpretive role of the judiciary ever presented.[121]

Additionally, the theory does not provide guarantees for one of its most forceful proposals: adopting a deferential stance towards the executive or legislative branches (in the case of ambiguous texts) would reduce the costs linked to adopting interpretative methods other than the surface reading of texts, hence why there is little in the theory of institutional capacities that may be used to refine Brazilian jurisdictional practice.

FINAL CONSIDERATIONS

Theories that address the deference of the judiciary are important, at the very least, as a reminder that constitutional oversight cannot be carried out in a manner that would destabilize democratic institutions or allow the judiciary to supplant the legislature. Theories that advocate for self-restraint are also relevant for emphasizing the institutional particularities of each of the branches and exploring the question about which branch can provide better answers for the hard cases that are brought before the state.

The hermeneutic normative theories sought to pave the way for discussions on the best response that could be produced by the judiciary. In response, the theory of institutional capacities sought to delineate the empirical limits of transposing those theories to the factual world. Ultimately, however, the image envisioned by (new) formalism turns out to be the revival of past proposals to wrest controversial issues from the judiciary, alleging that its decisions have a high cost and that this branch would not be in an appropriate institutional position to perform those activities.[122]

Old theoretical skeletons continue to be exhumed from their graves and have their coffins replaced. The uncertainty that plagues the judiciary is not reduced—nor are the costs of decisions diminished—when other bodies replace the judiciary as a result of its self-restraint. Although the courts do have limitations and can make incorrect decisions, the judiciary has institutional advantages compared to other decision-making spaces.[123] Romanticized wagers on any of the branches of government (or even on the "people") run the risk of forgetting the problems that can afflict any of the institutions in question.[124]

It is inevitable that powers will eventually be abused. There is nothing new about the fact that constitutional oversight could become an instrument for usurping rules with democratic support that have been produced in a technically appropriate manner.

The answer to the (old) question of who has the best conditions to respond to hard cases is that the construction of legal knowledge must be an ongoing conversation between all those involved in its production and revision. Finally, if there is a genuine concern about increasing the legitimacy of the decisions made by the branches, the choice to reduce complexity seems to run counter to the choice that proposes intrainstitutional and interinstitutional dialogue in the creation of a true democratic rule of law.

NOTES

1. Ran Hirschl explains the different ways of understanding how the judiciary has become an important power through constitutionalization in different parts of the world, a phenomenon that he treats as "global." "The hegemonic preservation thesis may help us understand judicial empowerment through constitutionalization as part of a broader trend whereby crucial policy-making functions are increasingly insulated from majoritarian control. As we have seen, the world seems to have been seized by a craze for constitutionalization and judicial review. The transformation of judicial institutions into major political actors has not been limited to the national level." Ran Hirschl, "The Political Origins of the New Constitutionalism," *Indiana Journal of Global Legal Studies* 11, no. 1 (2004): 105.

2. Ludwig Wittgenstein, *Philosophical Investigations* (Oxford: Basil Blackwell, 1986). "Those meanings, by virtue of the duty to state the grounds, must be understood by those who manipulate them, even as a condition for them to be understood by their subjects." Humberto Ávila, *Teoria dos Princípios: da definição à aplicação dos princípios jurídicos*, 3rd ed. (São Paulo: Malheiros, 2004), 16.

3. Ávila, *Teoria dos Princípios*, 22.

4. "In some cases, there is a rule but no provision. What are the provisions that provide for the principles of legal certainty and certainty of law? None. There are thus rules, even without specific provisions that lend them physical support. In other cases, there is a provision but no rule. What rule can be constructed from the constitutional statement that provides for the *protection of God*? None. There are thus provisions from which no rule is constructed" (Ávila, *Teoria dos Princípios*, 22). In similar terms, the same question can be observed in the following assertion by Laurence Tribe: "Like *McCulloch v. Maryland*, and in a manner reminiscent even of the Gettysburg Address, our hypothetical case would undoubtedly be governed by a defining principle drawn from the invisible Constitution: the principle that ours is a 'government of the people, by the people, for the people.' . . . Why? Where does the constitutional status of that simple idea come from? There are a few textual points reflecting it, but examining them merely confirms that the broad principle at issue here cannot be extracted from the text alone but must instead be interpolated from features of the Constitution that remain invisible." Laurence Tribe, *The Invisible Constitution* (Oxford, UK: Oxford University Press, 2008), 87–88.

5. Wittgenstein, *Philosophical Investigations.* In legal terms, the question can be clarified as follows: "When the individual ruler dies his legislative work lives on; for it rests upon the foundation of a general rule which successive generations of the society continue to respect regarding each legislator whenever he lived." Herbert L. A Hart, *The Concept of Law* (Oxford, UK: Oxford University Press, 1961), 63.

6. "But if we had to name anything which is the life of the sign, we should have to say that it was its *use*." Ludwig Wittgenstein, *O Livro Azul* (Lisboa: Edições 70, 1992), 30.

7. See the difference between surface and depth grammar presented by Wittgenstein. Wittgenstein, *Philosophical Investigations*, 168.

8. "I will call these game 'language-games' and will sometimes speak of a primitive language as a language-game. And the processes of naming the stones and of repeating words after someone might also be called language-games. Think of much of the use of words in games like ring-a-ring-a-roses. I shall also call the whole, consisting of language and the actions into which it is woven, the 'language-game.'" Wittgenstein, *Philosophical Investigations*, 5. "The employment of the expression 'language game' is not accidental. The point of view from which Wittgenstein considers language leads almost necessarily to the comparison with a complicated game, such as chess. The analogy turns out to be fruitful in many respects. For Wittgenstein, what stands especially in the foreground is the *operative aspect* common to games and language. To realize a game is to *operate with playing pieces* in a particular way, and to actualize a language as a language game is to *operate with words and sentences*." Wolfgang Stegmüller, *A filosofia contemporânea: introdução crítica*, 2nd ed. (Rio de Janeiro: Forense Universitária, 2012), 418.

9. "Think of the tools in a tool-box: there is a hammer, pliers, a saw, a screw-driver, a rule, a glue-pot, glue, nails and screws. The functions of words are as diverse as the functions of these objects." Wittgenstein, *Philosophical Investigations*, 6.

10. "For if you look at them you will not see something that is common to *all*, but similarities, relationships, and a whole series of them at that." Wittgenstein, *Philosophical Investigations*, 31.

11. Wittgenstein, *Philosophical Investigations*, 32.

12. "What still counts as a game and what no longer does? Can you give the boundary? No. You can *draw* one; for none has so far been drawn. (But that never troubled you before when you used the word 'game')." Wittgenstein, *Philosophical Investigations*, 33. Along the same lines, Herbert Hart asserts: "Very often the ordinary, or even the technical, usage of a term is quite 'open' in that it does not *forbid* the extension of the term to cases where only some of the normally concomitant characteristics are present." Hart, *The Concept of Law*, 15.

13. Wittgenstein, *Philosophical Investigations*, 11.

14. In line with that understanding, Hart states: "Courts regard legal rules not as predictions, but as standards to be followed in decision, determinate enough, in spite of their open texture, to limit, though not to exclude, their discretion." Hart, *The Concept of Law*, 147.

15. Herbert L. A. Hart, *The Concept of Law* (Oxford, UK: Claredon Press, 1994), 15 and 125. Richard Rorty, *The Linguistic Turn: Essays in Philosophical Method* (Chicago: University of Chicago Press, 1992). See also: Lenio Luiz Streck, *O que é isto: decido conforme a minha consciência?* (Porto Alegre: Livraria do Advogado, 2010).

16. Herbert L. A Hart, *Essays in Jurisprudence and Philosophy* (Oxford, UK: Clarendon Press, 1983).

17. "We no longer interpret in order to understand, but understand in order to interpret, thus breaking with epistemological perspectives that place(d) method as a supreme moment of subjectivity and a guarantee of the (positivist) certainty of interpretation. The consequence, I repeat, will be the need for a decision theory." Lenio Luiz Streck, "Superando os diversos tipos de positivismo: porque hermenêutica é *applicatio*?" *Nomos: Revista do Programa de Pós-Graduação em Direito da UFC* 34, no. 2 (2014): 278.

18. Hans Kelsen, *Jurisdição constitucional*, trans. Maria Ermantina de Almeida Prado Galvão (São Paulo: Martins Fontes, 2007).

19. Wojciech Sadurski, "Constitutional Review in Europe and in the United States: Influences, Paradoxes and Convergence," *Sydney Law School Research Paper* no. 11/15 (2011). Along the same lines: "Until the mid-twentieth century, in the hegemonic model in continental Europe and in other countries linked to the Roman-Germanic legal system, the regulation of social life gravitated around laws issued by parliaments, with an emphasis on codes. The political assumption underlying this conception was that the legislative branch, which embodied the will of the nation, had the legitimacy to create the law, but the judiciary did not, as it was only responsible for applying the rules previously established by parliaments to specific cases." Cláudio Pereira de Souza Neto and Daniel Sarmento, *Direito constitucional: teoria, história e métodos de trabalho* (Belo Horizonte: Fórum, 2012), 84.

20. "Just as the doctor-surgeon intervenes in the patient's body to fulfill their mission, using surgical instruments, the lawyer is responsible for intervening in the legal world using their own instrument: dogma." Clèmerson Merlin Clève, *Para uma dogmática constitucional emancipatória* (Belo Horizonte: Fórum, 2012), 36. See also: Luís Roberto Barroso, *O direito constitucional e a efetividade de suas normas: Limites e possibilidades da Constituição brasileira*, 8th. ed (Rio de Janeiro: Renovar, 2006).

21. Tribe, *The Invisible Constitution*, 78.

22. Tribe, *The Invisible Constitution*, 69.

23. "A long-standing dispute in constitutional theory has gone under different names at different times, but today's terminology seems as helpful as any. Today we are likely to call the contending sides 'interpretivism' and 'noninterpretivism'—the former indicating that judges deciding constitutional issues should confine themselves to enforcing norms that are state or clearly implicit in the written Constitution, the latter the contrary view that courts should go beyond that set of references and enforce norms that cannot be discovered within the four corners of the document." John Hart Ely, *Democracy and Distrust: A Theory of Judicial Review* (Cambridge, MA: Harvard University Press, 1980), 1.

24. J. J. Gomes Canotilho, *Direito Constitucional e Teoria da Constituição*, 7th ed. (Coimbra: Almedina, 2003), 1195.

25. Canotilho, *Direito Constitucional e Teoria da Constituição*, 1196. Ronald Dworkin critiques that perspective with the following argument: "Judges cannot decide what the pertinent intention of the Framers was, or which political process is really fair or democratic, unless they make substantive political decisions of just the sort the proponents of intention or process think judges should not make. Intention

and process are mischievous ideas because they cover up these substantive decisions with procedural piety and pretend they have not been made." Ronald Dworkin, *A Matter of Principle* (Cambridge, MA: Harvard University Press, 1985), 34.

26. "The *law* is not only the 'content' of concrete legal rules, it is also comprised of *open legal principles* such as justice, impartiality, equality, freedom. Judicial mediation that puts these principles into practice is an undeniable task of judges." Canotilho, *Direito Constitucional e Teoria da Constituição*, 1197. "Noninterpretive theories are said to suppose, on the contrary, that the Court is at least sometimes justified in holding legislative decisions to standards taken from some source other than the text, like popular morality, or sound theories of justice, or some conception of genuine democracy." Ronald Dworkin, *A Matter of Principle*, 34–35.

27. "Even when no settled rule disposes of the case, one party may nevertheless have a right to win. It remains the judge's duty, even in hard cases, to discover what the rights of the parties are, not to invent new rights retrospectively." Ronald Dworkin, *A Matter of Principle* (Cambridge, MA: Harvard University Press, 1985), 81. As an illustration, see the low number of actions that typically involved constitutional jurisdiction in the STF's history: ADC, 32 (0.002%); ADI, 5.040 (0.331%); ADO, 24 (0.002%); ADPF, 300 (0.020%). Joaquim Falcão, Ivar A. Hartmann, and Vitor P. Chaves, *III Relatório Supremo em Números: o Supremo e o tempo* (Rio de Janeiro: Escola de Direito do Rio de Janeiro da Fundação Getulio Vargas, 2014), 143–144. According to the Court's annual report, there were 75,137 cases judged in 2020 by the Supreme Federal Court, in which only 503 correspond to constitutional jurisdiction (among ADC, ADI, ADO, ADPF). Brazil. Supremo Tribunal Federal (STF). Relatório de atividades 2020. Brasília: Supreme Federal Court, Secretariat for High Studies, Research and Data Management, 2021, 35. Without ruling out the possibility of judicial review in other actions, as well as the fact that the "hard cases" are not limited to the four modalities mentioned above, it is clear that, proportionally, the STF has a lower number of "hard cases."

28. "I propose, nevertheless, the thesis that judicial decisions in civil cases, even in hard cases like *Spartan Steel*, characteristically are and should be generated by principle not policy." Dworkin, *Taking Rights Seriously*, 84. "My own view is that the Court should make decisions of principle rather than policy—decisions about what rights people have under our constitutional system rather than decisions about how the general welfare is best promoted—and that it should make these decisions by elaborating and applying the substantive theory of representation taken from the root principle that government must treat people as equals." Ronald Dworkin, *A Matter of Principle*, 69.

29. Dworkin, *Taking Rights Seriously*, 87. "There are many situations where there is no preestablished solution in law. The solution will have to be constructed argumentatively, considering the elements of the specific case, the parameters set out in the rule and elements outside the law. These are hard cases. There are three main situations that produce hard cases: a) *Ambiguity of language*. . . . b) *Reasonable moral disagreements*. . . . c) *Conflicting constitutional rules or fundamental rights*." Luís Roberto Barroso, *O novo direito constitucional brasileiro: Contribuições para a*

construção teórica e prática da jurisdição constitucional no Brasil (Belo Horizonte: Fórum, 2012), 37–38.

30. To a certain extent, the dichotomy between interpretivists and noninterpretivists has been surmounted by recognizing the impossibility of excluding interpretive activity by judges. For Dworkin, any theory of judicial review is interpretive: "in the sense that it aims to provide an interpretation of the Constitution as an original, foundational legal document, and also aims to integrate the Constitution into our constitutional and legal practice as a whole." Ronald Dworkin, *A Matter of Principle,* 35. In Kingwell's terms: "judges—like readers—are interpreting all the time, whether they like it or not. From this point of view, interpretivism is really just a rather strict and old-fashioned school of interpretation, one that is further impaired by insufficient self-awareness." Mark Kingwell, "Let's Ask Again: Is Law Like Literature?" *Yale Journal of Law and the Humanities* 6, (1994): 323. See also: Owen Fiss, "Objectivity and Interpretation," *Stanford Law Review* 34, no. 4 (April 1982), https://doi.org/10.2307/1228384.

31. "I must try to exhibit that complex structure of legal interpretation, and I shall use for that purpose an imaginary judge of superhuman intellectual power and patience who accepts law as integrity." Ronald Dworkin, *Law's Empire* (Cambridge, MA: Harvard University Press, 1986), 239. "Dworkin concedes that no actual human judge as distinct from his mythical ideal judge 'Hercules' could accomplish the feat of constructing an interpretation of all his country's law at once." Hart, *The Concept of Law*, 264.

32. "When two sides disagree, as often happens, about a proposition 'of law,' what are they disagreeing about, and how shall we decide which side is right? Why do we call what 'the law' says a matter of legal 'obligation'? Is 'obligation' here just a term of art, meaning only what the law says? Or does legal obligation have something to do with moral obligation? Can we say that we have, in principle at least, the same reasons for meeting our legal obligations that we have for meeting our moral obligations?" Dworkin, *Taking Rights Seriously*, 14

33. Dworkin, *Law's Empire*, 243. "Judges who accept the interpretive ideal of integrity decide hard cases by trying to find, in some cogent set of principles about people's rights and duties, the best constructive interpretation of the political structure and legal doctrine of their community." Dworkin, *Law's Empire*, 255.

34. Dworkin, *Law's Empire*, 41. "Semantic theories like positivism crimp our language by denying us the opportunity to use 'law' in this flexible way, depending on context or point. They insist that we must choose, once and for all, between a 'wide' or preinterpretive and a 'narrow' or interpretive sense. But this buys linguistic tidiness at much too high a price." Dworkin, *Law's Empire*, 104.

35. "The open texture of law means that there are, indeed, areas of conduct where much must be left to be developed by courts or officials striking a balance, in the light of circumstances, between competing interests which vary in weight from case to case" (Herbert Lionel Adolphus Hart, *The Concept of Law* (Oxford, UK: Oxford University Press, 1994), 135. The Postscript: "The sharpest direct conflict between the legal theory of this book and Dworkin's theory arises from my contention that in any legal system there will always be certain legally unregulated cases in which on some point no decision either way is dictated by the law and the law is accordingly

partly indeterminate or incomplete." Herbert Lionel Adolphus Hart, *The Concept of Law*, 272.

36. Ronald Dworkin, *Justice in Robes*. Cambridge, MA: Harvard University Press, 2006.

37. Scott J. Shapiro, "The Hart–Dworkin Debate: A Short Guide for the Perplexed." *Public Law and Legal Theory Working Paper Series*, no. 77. Available at SSRN 968657, 2007.

38. "The very idea of a right answer (in accordance with the Constitution) is thus a (new) perspective for thinking about the problem of the relationship between law and morality: the judge's duty—which arises from the correlated fundamental right—instituted a (new) moral beginning for the law. In other words, the right answer must be understood in a dual perspective: 1) as a possibility, demonstrating how right answers are possible in law; 2) as a duty, within which a theory is produced for how judges must determine the reasons for their ruling, rather than only how they can (choose to) rule." Lenio Luiz Streck, "O direito como um conceito interpretativo," *Pensar* 15, no. 2 (2010): 511.

39. "If there are such moral facts, then a proposition of law might rationally be supposed to be true even if lawyers continue to disagree about the proposition after all hard facts are known or stipulated." Ronald Dworkin, *A Matter of Principle*, 138. Per Ronaldo Porto Macedo Junior: "The thesis of the right answer, as will be demonstrated, is based on an interpretative conception of truth and objectivity, according to which affirming the objectivity of a proposition means recognizing that it is justified by the best possible arguments . . . legal objectivity, or even 'possible objectivity'—because other conceptions would be contradictory—is governed by law's language game." Ronaldo Porto Macedo Junior, *Do Xadrez à Cortesia: Dworkin e a teoria do direito contemporânea* (São Paulo: Saraiva, 2013), 48.

40. Ronald Dworkin, *Justice for Hedgehogs* (Cambridge, MA: Harvard University Press, 2011), 7–8. Dworkin continued his arguments: "*That* there are truths about value is an obvious, inescapable fact. When people have decisions to make, the question of what decision they should make is inescapable, and it can be answered only by noticing reasons for acting one way or another; it can be answered only in that way because that is what the question, just as a matter of what it means, inescapably calls for. No doubt the best answer on some occasions is that *nothing* is any better to do than anything else. Some unfortunate people find a more dramatic answer unavoidable: they think nothing is *ever* the best or right thing to do." Dworkin, *Justice for Hedgehogs*, 24.

41. Dworkin, *Law's Empire*, 47.

42. Dworkin, *Law's Empire*, 48.

43. Dworkin, *Law's Empire*, 48.

44. Dworkin, *Law's Empire*, 65–66.

45. See, for example, Frank Michelman's critiques of Dworkin's theory: Frank I. Michelman, *Brennan and Democracy* (Princeton, NJ: Princeton University Press, 1999).

46. "What I want to do is apply the cannon of symmetry in the other direction. I want to ask: What would it be like to develop a rosy picture of legislatures and

their structures and processes that matched, in its normativity and perhaps in its naïvety, the picture of courts—'forum of principle' etc.—that we present in the more elevated moments of our constitutional jurisprudence?" Jeremy Waldron, *Law and Disagreement* (Oxford, UK: Oxford University Press, 2004), 32.

47. "America's Founding generation, in daring contrast, embraced a political ideology that celebrated the central role of 'the people' in supplying government with its energy and direction, an ideal that remained at all times in the forefront of their thinking—Federalist and Anti-Federalist alike. Preserving liberty demanded a constitution whose internal architecture was carefully arranged to check power, just as it demanded leaders of sufficient 'character' and 'virtue.' But structural innovations and virtuous leadership were 'auxiliary devices' to channel and control popular politics, not to isolate or eliminate it. The people themselves remained responsible for making things work." Larry D. Kramer, *The People Themselves: Popular Constitutionalism and Judicial Review* (Oxford, UK: Oxford University Press, 2004), 6.

48. Madison sought to mitigate popular participation through representative democracy, in which the people's representatives would be responsible for speaking on behalf of those they represented: "Under such a regulation, it may well happen that the public voice pronounced by the representatives of the people, will be more consonant to the public good, than if pronounced by the people themselves convened for the purpose." Alexander Hamilton, James Madison, and John Jay, *The Federalist Papers* (Washington, DC: Library of Congress, 1787). The deliberative modes imagined by the founding fathers would be mediated by representatives and they would place themselves beyond the private preferences of the citizens.

49. William N. Eskridge Jr., "Dynamic Statutory Interpretation," *University of Pennsylvania Law Review* 135, no. 6 (1987): 1529, https://doi.org/10.2307/3312014

50. However, even Alexander Bickel admits that commitment to the majoritarian ideal cannot be absolute. Alexander Bickel, *The Least Dangerous Branch: The Supreme Court at the Bar of Politics* (New Haven, CT: Yale University Press, 1986), 51. One problem with the objections raised by the counter-majoritarian difficulty is that it expects judges to limit themselves to implementing the wishes or guidelines of legislators, but Eskridge notes that hermeneutics demonstrates the inevitability of judicial creation when the normative text is interpreted over time. William N. Eskridge Jr., "Gadamer/Statutory Interpretation," *Columbia Law Review* 90, no. 3 (1990): 613.

51. "Statutes, however, should—like the Constitution and the common law—be interpreted 'dynamically,' that is, in light of their present societal, political, and legal context." William N. Eskridge Jr., "Dynamic Statutory Interpretation," 1479.

52. William N. Eskridge Jr., "Dynamic Statutory Interpretation," 1482–1483.

53. William N. Eskridge Jr., "Dynamic Statutory Interpretation," 1483.

54. "The statutory text does not decisively answer the interpretive issue, contrary to labored readings by both the majority and dissenting opinions. . . . The operative word is 'discriminate,' which is not defined in the Act. Weber interpreted the antidiscrimination rule of section 703(d) to prevent any and every differential treatment of employees on racial grounds." William N. Eskridge Jr., "Dynamic Statutory Interpretation," 1489.

55. Justice Burger's dissent is based on his reading of the "explicit language of the law": "Often we have difficulty interpreting statutes either because of imprecise drafting or because legislative compromises have produced genuine ambiguities. But here there is no lack of clarity, no ambiguity. The quota embodied in the collective bargaining agreement between Kaiser and the Steelworkers unquestionably discriminates on the basis of race against individual employees seeking admission to on-the-job training programs. And, under the plain language of § 703(d), that is 'an unlawful employment practice.'" *United Steelworkers v. Weber* (1979).

56. "*Weber* suggests a lesson: When societal conditions change in ways not anticipated by Congress and, especially, when the legal and constitutional context of the statute decisively shifts as well, this current perspective should, and will, affect the statute's interpretation, notwithstanding contrary inferences from the historical evidence." William N. Eskridge Jr., "Dynamic Statutory Interpretation," 1494.

57. William N. Eskridge Jr., "Dynamic Statutory Interpretation," 1496.

58. For Hans-Georg Gadamer, textual interpretation occurs in a fusion of horizons, in which the reader grasps the past perspective while understanding the present context of the text; it is an ongoing process. Hermeneutics is a dialogue between the interpreter and the text and the tradition that surrounds the writing. "Ernst Forsthoff has shown in a valuable study that for purely legal reasons it was necessary for an awareness of historical change to develop, which involved distinguishing between the original meaning of a law and that applied in current legal practice. It is true that the jurist is always concerned with the law itself, but he determines its normative content in regard to the given case to which it is to be applied. In order to determine this content exactly, it is necessary to have historical knowledge of the original meaning, and only for this reason does the judge concern himself with the historical value that the law has through the act of legislation. But he cannot let himself be bound by what, say, an account of the parliamentary proceedings tells him about the intentions of those who first passed the law. Rather, he has to take account of the change in circumstances and hence define afresh the normative function of the law." Hans-Georg Gadamer, *Verdade e Método*, trans. Flávio Paulo Meurer (Petrópolis, RJ: Vozes, 1997), 485.

59. "The judge who adapts the transmitted law to the needs of the present is undoubtedly seeking to perform a practical task, but his interpretation of the law is by no means merely for that reason an arbitrary revision. Here again, to understand and to interpret means to discover and recognize a valid meaning." Gadamer, *Verdade e Método*, 487.

60. William N. Eskridge Jr., "Gadamer/Statutory Interpretation," 613.

61. William N. Eskridge Jr., "Dynamic Statutory Interpretation," 1482.

62. Dworkin, *Law's Empire*, 229.

63. Consider Gadamer's concerns with "tradition": "Actually 'prejudice' means a judgment that is rendered before all the elements that determine a situation have been finally examined. In German legal terminology a 'prejudice' is a provisional legal verdict before the final verdict is reached. For someone involved in a legal dispute, this kind of judgment against him affects his chances adversely." Gadamer, *Verdade e Método*, 407.

64. William N. Eskridge Jr., "Dynamic Statutory Interpretation," 1550.

65. For Hart, Dworkin's "noble dream" would be particularistic and holistic, as it seeks ways to limit the discretionary power of judges by using the resources of specific legal systems. The "nightmare," in turn, would be represented by the realists and their vision of the impossibility of limiting judges' discretionary power, and the resulting lack of clarity in decisions. "So for Dworkin, even in the hardest of hard cases where each of two alternative interpretations of a statute or two conflicting rules seems to fit equally well the already clearly established law, the judge is never to make law. So Oliver Wendell Holmes was, in Dworkin's view, wrong in claiming that at such points the judge must exercise what he called 'the sovereign prerogative of choice' and must legislate even if only 'interstitially.' According to the new theory, the judge, however hard the case, is never to determine what the law *shall* be; he is confined to saying what he believes *is* the law before his decision, though of course he may be mistaken. This means that he must always suppose that for every conceivable case there is some solution which is already law before he decides the case and which awaits his discovery. He must not suppose that the law is ever incomplete, inconsistent, or indeterminate; if it appears so, the fault is not in *it*, but in the judge's limited human powers of discernment, so there is no space for a judge to make law by choosing between alternatives as to what shall be the law." Hart, *Essays in Jurisprudence and Philosophy*, 138.

66. William N. Eskridge Jr., "Dynamic Statutory Interpretation," 1554.

67. William N. Eskridge Jr., "Dynamic Statutory Interpretation," 1554.

68. "I call a 'policy' that kind of standard that sets out a goal to be reached, generally an improvement in some economic, political, or social feature of the community (though some goals are negative, in that they stipulate that some present feature is to be protected from adverse change). I call a 'principle' a standard that is to be observed, not because it will advance or secure an economic, political, or social situation deemed desirable, but because it is a requirement of justice or fairness or some other dimension of morality." Dworkin, *Taking Rights Seriously*, 22.

69. Dworkin, *Law's Empire*, 263.

70. William N. Eskridge Jr., "Dynamic Statutory Interpretation," 1553.

71. Such as, for example, Gadamer: "Again, the initial meaning emerges only because he is reading the text with particular expectations in regard to a certain meaning. Working out this fore-projection, which is constantly revised in terms of what emerges as he penetrates into the meaning, is understanding what is there." Gadamer, *Verdade e Método*, 402. Eskridge explicitly assumes Gadamer's influence on his theory. In regard to Dworkin: "My view is that Dworkin is influenced by Gadamer and Habermas but seems to depart from their metaphor of interpretation-as-conversation by taking the position that interpretation is constructive—the interpreter's *making* the text the best it can be." William N. Eskridge Jr., "Gadamer/Statutory Interpretation, 647. See: Dworkin, *Law's Empire*, 51–52.

72. Eskridge recalls that the dichotomy between "subject" and "interpreter" cannot be accepted uncritically: "Interpretation is a social process of construction, not a scientific process of Discovery. Method can channel the argumentation and suggest information to be considered, but it cannot dictate all that goes on in statutory, or any,

interpretation." William N. Eskridge Jr., "The New Textualism," *UCLA Law Review* 37, no. 100 (1990): 691.

73. Vermeule and Sunstein list different authors from different historical moments, noting that they are "blind" or "insensitive" to institutional aspects in interpretation. William Blackstone, Jeremy Bentham, Herbert Hart, Ronald Dworkin, William Eskridge, John Manning, and Richard Posner would not have been able to produce a satisfactory theory that combined aspects of interpretation with an analysis of institutional capacities. Cass R. Sunstein and Adrian Vermeule, "Interpretation and Institutions," *John M. Olin Program in Law and Economics Working Paper*, no. 156 (2002), 5–23. "*Institutional capacity* involves determining which branch is best qualified to produce the best decision for a given matter. Legal judges may not be the most qualified arbiter for subjects involving very complex technical or scientific aspects, due to a lack of information or specific knowledge. As well, the risk of unpredictable and undesirable *systemic effects* may recommend a position of caution and deference by the judiciary. The judge, by vocation and training, will normally be prepared to mete out justice in the concrete case—micro-justice—often without being able to evaluate the impact of their decisions on an economic segment or on the provision of a public service." Luís Roberto Barroso, "Constituição, Democracia e Supremacia Judicial: Direito e política no Brasil contemporâneo," in *Tratado de direito constitucional: constituição no século XXI* 2, ed. Felipe Dutra Asensi and Daniel Giotti De Paula (Rio de Janeiro: Elsevier, 2014), 765.

74. Sunstein and Vermeule, "Interpretation and Institutions," 2.

75. In the economic sphere, the "second-best" theory deals with situations in which optimal conditions cannot be met. If ideal distribution conditions are not available, the second-best available alternative must be sought to distribute wealth. "Given those assumptions, the basic reasoning strategy of those who take 'institutional capacities' seriously is that it does not involve seeking some kind of ideal solution and recommending that the decision-making bodies get as close to it as they can, but rather, comparing the costs associated with each possible state of affairs linked to the implementation of different alternatives in a given scenario, they should seek to adopt the 'second-best' solution. Along these lines, our main hypothesis is that the key to understanding the specificity and relevance of an argument based on institutional capacities lies in incorporating what economists call 'second-best reasoning' in discussions on the appropriateness of institutional attitudes and decision-making methods. The removal of any of the assumptions or structures described above nullifies the argument of institutional capacities." Diego Werneck Arguelhes and Fernando Leal, "O Argumento das 'Capacidades institucionais' entre a banalidade, a redundância e o absurdo," in *Tratado de direito constitucional: Constituição no século XXI* 2, ed. Felipe Dutra Asensi and Daniel Giotti De Paula (Rio de Janeiro: Elsevier, 2014), 404. "So far, however, very little attention has been given to some of the implications of problems of the second best for institutional design. Such problems concern the optimal policy when all the conditions required for a first best solution are not present." Bruce T. Coram, "Second Best Theories and the Implications for Institutional Design," in *The Theory of Institutional Design*, ed. Robert E. Goodin (Cambridge, UK: Cambridge University Press, 1996), 90.

76. Sunstein and Vermeule, "Interpretation and Institutions," 23.

77. "Institutional analysis is necessary, even if not sufficient, to an adequate evaluation of interpretive methods." Sunstein and Vermeule, "Interpretation and Institutions," 24.

78. According to that theory, consensus is formulated about the outcome, but the explanations that led up to it are left open for other theorizations, and thus, more far-reaching arguments to explain the case under discussion are put to the side. This is because, as a rule, it is easier to produce an agreement on specific topics than on abstract and generic ones. Those characteristics coincide with the initial critiques of institutional capacity, regarding how difficult it is for judges to produce decisions based on very abstract values. Cass R. Sunstein, "Incompletely Theorized Agreements," *Harvard Law Review* 108, no. 7 (1995).

79. According to José Rodrigo Rodriguez, formalism can mean "a) The vision of law that puts the mechanical application of positivist law at its center. 'Mechanical' is understood as application using logical-formal reasoning, i.e., the subsumption of the specific case to the abstract rule. A formalist is thus someone who sees the law as being characterized by applying rules through subsumption. To identify this position more accurately, it will be called *legalism*. b) We will also use the term formalist to describe the view of law that thinks of its categories as being endowed with truth that transcends positive law, either because of its roots and historical origin or because of its logical or rational value. This mode of being formalist implies the naturalization of dogmatic categories and will be called *conceptual absolutism*." José Rodrigo Rodriguez, *Como decidem as cortes? Para uma crítica do direito (brasileiro)* (Rio de Janeiro: Editora FGV, 2013), 119. Also see: Duncan Kennedy, "Legal Formalism," in *Encyclopedia of the Social and Behavioral Sciences* 13, no. 13, ed. Neil Smelser and Paul Baltes (New York: Elsevier, 2001), 8634–8638; Frederick Schauer, "Formalism," *Yale Law Journal* 97, no. 4 (1988); Daniel A. Farber, "Legal Formalism and the Red-Hot Knife," *University of Chicago Law Review* 66, no. 3 (Summer 1999).

80. Sunstein and Vermeule, "Interpretation and Institutions," 27.

81. Adrian Vermeule, *Judging under Uncertainty: An Institutional Theory of Legal Interpretation* (Cambridge, MA: Harvard University Press, 2006), 1.

82. "My premises are thus firmly consequentialist. Indeed they are rule-consequentialist: judges should interpret legal texts in accordance with rules whose observance produces the best consequences overall." Vermeule, *Judging under Uncertainty*, 5.

83. Vermeule acknowledges that there are at least two types of formalism; he refuses the formalism that seeks to deduce legal rules from legal "essences" without moral and political considerations being made. Vermeule, *Judging under Uncertainty*, 5. "Formalism cannot be justified (or opposed) by an appeal to self-evident constitutional principles, by an appeal to the nature of democracy or lawmaking, or by an appeal to a definition of law." Sunstein and Vermeule, "Interpretation and Institutions," 28.

84. Sunstein and Vermeule, "Interpretation and Institutions," 29.

85. Sunstein and Vermeule, "Interpretation and Institutions," 36.

86. "Many of the most well-known arguments on behalf of judicial review, including those in *Marbury* itself, are blind to institutional considerations. . . . Indeed, what

is most striking about Marshall's arguments for judicial review is that they depend on a series of fragile textual and structural inferences, ignoring the institutional issues at stake." Sunstein and Vermeule, "Interpretation and Institutions," 36.

87. "We have argued that issues of legal interpretation cannot be adequately resolved without attention to institutional issues." Sunstein and Vermeule, "Interpretation and Institutions," 46.

88. Sunstein and Vermeule, "Interpretation and Institutions," 47. The agencies now have the authority to produce regulations based on laws enacted by U.S. Congress. On certain occasions, the U.S. president may delegate portions of presidential authority to an agency. Normally, when Congress passes a law creating an agency, it is accompanied by legislative authority, to ensure that agencies can regulate certain specific activities. Congress may also pass a law that more specifically directs the agency's activity towards solving a problem or completing a certain activity. An agency may not act beyond the limits of its authority, established by law, or contrary to the Constitution. As well, they must observe a public process in the legislative process, which follows the Administrative Procedure Act. Federal agencies have long had the authority to enact regulations regarding almost every aspect of life in society.

89. Vermeule, *Judging under Uncertainty*, 11.

90. "These considerations suggest that interpretive doctrine should move in the direction of a minimalist set of principle, cheap, and manageable interpretive sources and doctrines—that is, in the direction of interpretive formalism." Adrian Vermeule, "Interpretive Choice," *New York University Law Review* 75 (2000): 81. Vermeule, *Judging under Uncertainty*, 254.

91. Cass Sunstein, "Second-Order Perfectionism," *University of Chicago Law and Economics, Olin Working Paper*, no. 319 (2006).

92. "The goal of political liberalism, as opposed to comprehensive liberalism, is to bracket foundational disputes about human nature, the good, and the like, and to seek general commitments on which diverse people can converge from their different stating points. Minimalists are sympathetic to this goal, but they attempt to go one step further. They seek incompletely theorized agreements—particular judgments and low-level rationales that people can accept notwithstanding their disagreements or uncertainties about foundational questions." Sunstein, "Second-Order Perfectionism," 17–18.

93. Vermeule, *Judging under Uncertainty*, 17.

94. "Theorists should design their proposals in light of the capacities of the implementing institutions, rather than by imagining that the institutions are just like the theorists themselves." Vermeule, *Judging under Uncertainty*, 36. "The frequent disregard for institutional capacity and systemic effects means that traditional theories of legal interpretation assume an idealized and romantic view of judicial capacities, according to which judges would have all the knowledge and time necessary to obtain optimal results or, in other words, to construct the 'correct interpretation' (first-best theories) even for very complex issues." Rodrigo Brandão, *Supremacia judicial versus diálogos constitucionais: A quem cabe a última palavra sobre o sentido da constituição?* (Rio de Janeiro: Lumen Juris, 2012), 186.

95. Ran Hirschl, "The Judicialization of Politics," in *Oxford Handbook of Political Science* (Oxford, UK: Oxford University Press, 2008). "Institutions such as Congress, the President and regulatory agencies—the argument goes—would generally be in a position to offer *better* answers than those that judges would tend to produce. In this regard, we find references to the judiciary's 'institutional capacities' to be a justification for adopting a more self-restrained stance when acting in areas in which there is great need for technical expertise or an equal weighing of multiple and complex political variables." Arguelhes and Leal, "O Argumento das 'Capacidades institucionais,'" 401.

96. "From this perspective, the constitution can be compared to the plan drawn up by an 'institutional architect,' who distributes competencies and powers among institutions created specifically to promote certain objectives while also providing each institution with specific conditions capable of increasing the efficiency with which those powers will be exercised by them." Arguelhes and Leal, "O Argumento das 'Capacidades institucionais,'" 407.

97. "Comparing the advantages and disadvantages of different institutions capable of offering different responses to the same types of problems—without expressly violating rules and functions of the institutional design—is a legitimate and useful way of guiding the composition of inter-institutional tensions. Comparative analysis guided by the definition of institutional capacities begins from this assumption and attempts to provide a specific argumentative scheme to support the selection of attitudes and decision-making methods that are most appropriate for each institution, given their merits and functional and material constraints." Arguelhes and Leal, "O Argumento das 'Capacidades institucionais,'" 426.

98. Adrian Vermeule, "Collective Wisdom and Institutional Design," in *Collective Wisdom: Principles and Mechanisms*, ed. Hélène Landemore and Jon Elster (Cambridge, UK: Cambridge University Press, 2014), 351.

99. Jeff A. King, "Institutional Approaches to Judicial Restraint," *Oxford Journal of Legal Studies* 28, no. 3 (2008): 430.

100. "The question arises in a number of contexts: statutory interpretation, judicial review of administrative discretion, review of tribunal findings, adjudication of human rights claims and in the interpretation of international law to mention a few. In all of these contexts, judges have identified certain questions as being inappropriate for judicial resolution, or have refused on competency grounds to substitute their judgment for that of another person on a particular matter." King, "Institutional Approaches to Judicial Restraint," 409.

101. Robert Post, "Theorizing disagreement: Reconceiving the relationship between law and politics." *California Law Review* 98, no. 4 (2010): 1319–1350. "Between the skepticism of legal realism and critical theory, which equate the law with voluntarism and politics, and the idealized view of legal formalism, with its belief in the existence of a dividing wall between the two, this study will demonstrate what already seemed to be the intention: in the real world, there is neither equivalence nor a complete separation. In the creation of legal rules—particularly constitutional rules—law and politics coexist and influence each other, in an interaction that

has complexities, subtleties and variations." Luís Roberto Barroso, "Constituição, Democracia e Supremacia Judicial," 759.

102. King, "Institutional Approaches to Judicial Restraint," 411. Also see: T. R. S Allan, *The Sovereignty of Law: Freedom, Constitution, and Common Law* (Oxford, UK: Oxford University Press, 2013), 279.

103. See the considerations on "banality," "redundancy," and "absurdity" presented by: Arguelhes and Leal, "O Argumento das 'Capacidades institucionais,'" 419–423.

104. Vermeule, *Judging under Uncertainty*, 44.

105. "Note, for example, that critiques regarding excess abstraction in Dworkin's theory contain a basic error: Dworkin's philosophical orientation is towards a pragmatic analysis of reality. That accusation could be directed towards argumentative and epistemic procedural theories but not towards Dworkin or philosophical hermeneutics." Lenio Luiz Streck, "O problema da decisão jurídica em tempos pós-positivistas," *Novos Estudos Jurídicos* 14, no. 2 (2009): 10.

106. Henry Hart Jr. and Albert M. Sacks, *The Legal Process: Basic Problems in the Making and Application of Law* (New York: Foundation Press, 1994).

107. "Courts must police inhibitions on expression and other political activity because we cannot trust elected officials to do so: ins have a way of wanting to make sure the outs stay out." Ely, *Democracy and Distrust*, 106.

108. Antonin Scalia, *A Matter of Interpretation: Federal Courts and the Law* (Princeton, NJ: Princeton University Press, 1998); "The new textualism posits that once the Court has ascertained a statute's plain meaning, consideration of legislative history becomes irrelevant." William N. Eskridge Jr., "The New Textualism," 623.

109. "Yet he offers little empirical or theoretical reason to think that unmonitored agencies will be good for the country, and the book as a whole suffers from 'agency nirvana.'" William N. Eskridge Jr., "No Frills Textualism," *Harvard Law Review* 119, no. 7 (May 2006): 2046. There is nothing to ensure that the interpretations made by agencies will effectively reflect public interests better than legal decisions. Vermeule does not consider the fact that certain agencies can be "captured" by private interests and that their actions will be shaped by that "capture." In turn, judges who have a lifetime appointment may be considered to have an interesting institutional position for reviewing the legislative interpretations made by agencies.

110. Vermeule, *Judging under Uncertainty*, 33.

111. In Lenio Luiz Streck's terms: "Since the law is no longer subordinated to policy as if it were an instrument of it, *policy becomes an instrument of the law*, subordinated to the bonds imposed on it by constitutional principles: negative bonds, such as those generated by the rights to freedoms that cannot be violated, and positive bonds, such as those generated by social rights, which must be satisfied." Lenio Luiz Streck, *Jurisdição Constitucional e Hermenêutica: uma nova crítica do direito* (Rio de Janeiro: Forense, 2004), 182.

112. Eskridge Jr., "No Frills Textualism," 2042.

113. "A state that arrests and detains a tricycle-riding girl under a statute not aimed at her is a state whose legitimacy is potentially in peril. If that state followed with further arrests of skateboarders, roller skaters, and even parents pushing baby carriages (all of which could be justified under a no-frills textualism), the legitimacy of the

criminal law and perhaps of the rule of law itself would decline over time." Eskridge Jr., "No Frills Textualism," 2053.

114. The emphasis on deference to interpretations offered by agencies seems to be sufficient: "So far as agency deference goes, no high-level choice of interpretive values over time, no high-level theory of the legitimacy of statutory drift, seems necessary" (Vermeule, *Judging under Uncertainty*, 226). For Streck: "not every law is valid and legitimate, only a law that has passed the test of 'hermeneutical reason,' i.e., legal *application*. That moral content is woven into the space of judicial decision-making. This means that when it is argued that discretionary decisions cannot be accepted—that they are nothing more than decisions that absolve the judge of the duty to decide correctly—the moral element has already been introduced, as well as the greatest proof of the autonomy of the law, at the moment when that correctly-made decision will be *recognized* by the entire legal community *as* law." Streck, "O direito como um conceito interpretativo," 510.

115. Streck, *Jurisdição Constitucional e Hermenêutica*, 210–211.

116. Streck, *Jurisdição Constitucional e Hermenêutica*, 165.

117. Streck, *Jurisdição Constitucional e Hermenêutica*, 171. "Thus, *the constitution is not an objective element, separate from the interpreter, outside the hermeneutic circularity; it is impossible to 'deduce' 'another' 'objective' element from it.*" Streck, *Jurisdição Constitucional e Hermenêutica*, 229.

118. Lenio Luiz Streck, *Hermenêutica Jurídica e(m) Crise: Uma exploração hermenêutica da construção do Direito* (Porto Alegre: Livraria do Advogado, 2000), 164.

119. Streck, *Hermenêutica Jurídica e(m) Crise*, 166.

120. Streck, *Hermenêutica Jurídica e(m) Crise*,182.

121. Jonathan R. Siegel, "Judicial Interpretation in the Cost-Benefit Crucible," *Minnesota Law Review* 92 (2007): 389.

122. "In offering such a stingy view of the courts' potential value, Vermeule gives too little weight to the courts' vital role of checking the executive. This role arises not merely from the courts' political insulation, but from their status as a separate branch of government that does not participate in the primary formulation or execution of policy. If that role were removed, executive agencies would have a greatly enhanced ability to set the limits of their own power." Siegel, "Judicial Interpretation in the Cost-Benefit Crucible," 425–426.

123. Siegel notes situations where the courts may have an advantage in decision-making: "Courts act at the moment the statutory text is actually applied to a particular case. In contrast to legislatures, which act generally and in advance, and thus cannot anticipate every circumstance to which statutes will apply, courts are better positioned to use certain interpretive techniques. . . . Legislatures are institutionally disadvantaged when it comes to appreciating the potential absurdity of what they write. No matter how much work they do in advance, they will make some mistakes that come to light only afterwards. Courts, on the other hand, are in a position to see the statute after the drafting process, when its absurdity may be apparent in light of the particular case in which it arises." Siegel, "Judicial Interpretation in the Cost-Benefit Crucible," 420–421.

124. "It is usually far easier for most people—whether ordinary citizens or law professors—to criticize the Court rather than the Constitution itself. The idea of 'judges on a rampage' is a familiar element of our standard narratives of American constitutional history, even if different persons will offer conflicting examples of exemplary rampages." Jack M. Balkin and Sanford Levinson, "13 Ways of Looking at Dred Scott," *Chicago-Kent Law Review* 82 (2007): 79.

Chapter 3

Institutional Dialogue

Structure and Legitimacy

The proposal to maintain a productive conversation among the branches is one of the theoretical and practical projects involved in pursuing a solution to the dilemma over which an institution has the best conditions to respond to controversial cases. The process of resolving complex cases, which requires sophisticated institutional responses, must be established dialogically, as an ongoing conversation between the parties involved in their construction and subsequent oversight.

That solution is underpinned by concerns regarding the legitimacy of the activities performed by the branches. The collection of arbitrary historical facts that marked the twentieth century is a key indicator that any decisions made by public bodies require some type of democratic support. The construction of a democratic rule of law is carried out "brick by brick," as an ongoing process, in a social orchestration that does not have a predetermined end on its horizon but, rather, focuses on the necessary exchange between the potential aspects and limitations of each branch of government.

The theoretical origin of the proposal for dialogue is the separation of the activities pertaining to each branch. Influenced by this idea, the classic schism between law and politics was articulated as follows: the political sphere would be determined by popular sovereignty and the majoritarian principle, while the legal sphere would be determined by the idea of rule of law and respect for fundamental rights.[1]

In terms of its production, the law cannot be separated from politics, as it is the product of the majoritarian will of society and political disputes that are stabilized through the formulation of rules with a claim to universality. In the context of its application, however, the separation between law and politics is held to be possible and is intended to prevent the legal from being colonized by the political.[2] In application, for example, the schism aims to protect the principle of legality. It should not, however, be made absolute, to the point of advocating for a certain "neutrality" or the pure instrumentalization of the legal phenomenon, as if it were possible to completely eliminate the presence of ideological elements in decision-making processes.

The definition of the concept of the constitution's supremacy also aids in understanding the proposal of institutional dialogue. Without that being predicated, the tension between constitutionalism and democracy would lose its force. The supremacy of the constitution is a "distinctive feature" that places it in a higher position than the other rules in the system.[3] A constitution is expected to be the result of the confluence of a superqualified political manifestation of the popular will[4] and to stand above the legally established majoritarian will. This is historical constitutional drafting or "high-level" constitutional production (higher lawmaking).[5]

Conversely, constitutional supremacy is the initial factor that allows constitutional oversight to occur. This is because the rules must be compatible with the precepts enshrined in the charter,[6] which had a new role to play in defining the organization of the state:

> Constitutions are now normative documents of the state and society. The constitution represents a redefinition of the political and social relations developed within a given social formation. It not only regulates the exercise of power, transforming *potestas* into *auctoritas*, but also imposes specific guidelines on the state, indicating the vector (meaning) of its action as well as its interaction with society. The constitution has normative force, always connecting—positively or negatively—the public powers. Today, citizens have direct access to constitutional rules, including seeking protection from the will or omission of the legislature.[7]

As a result, the notion that the constitution is the Fundamental Law requires recognition of its privileged position in the legal system as well as legal instruments that guarantee the preservation of that status.[8] Those mechanisms are related to the attempt to establish a democratic rule of law, with the guarantee of fundamental rights for citizens and procedural structures that establish democratic conditions for deliberation.

It is thus understood that the government must treat everyone with equal consideration and respect. The correct conception of equality advocates for *equal treatment*, understood as the same distribution of goods and opportunities for everyone and that *everyone is treated equally*, that is, equal consideration and respect in terms of the political decision-making that facilitates the distribution of goods and opportunities.[9] In this context, decisions in controversial cases now have normative beacons that guide political actors in defining legitimate institutional responses.[10]

Constitutions ultimately create institutions that can implement the basic commitments of constitutionalism, among them, that the government must operate according to a previously established list of rules and principles and that these must guarantee fundamental rights.

Different institutional arrangements can be used to observe the main characteristics of constitutionalism, which are usually set out in the constitutional text. The latter, in turn, is the tool that is often used to restrict the field of majoritarian choices. The guardianship of the constitution and a series of majoritarian decisions that define the self-government of a people are thus the binary elements of the tension between constitutionalism and democracy.

Furthermore, questions about the legitimacy of constitutional oversight are no longer an "external issue." Brazil is now experiencing a rising wave of criticism of judicial activism.[11] Some of those considerations, however, end up reproducing the same misconception as the emphasis on a "final word," forgetting the institutional structure that contains the branches of government.

Some argue that the executive branch has better conditions for assessing specific cases and that the judiciary should defer to decisions by government agencies.[12] In popular constitutionalism, the people would be the ideal agent for resolving conflicts.[13] There are also those who argue that judicial review should be reduced as much as possible in favor of debates held in the houses of parliament.[14] Those constructions, based on different ideological references, which seek to maximize different modes of institutional arrangements, are guided by a concern for the legitimacy of constitutional jurisdiction.

Rather than romanticizing or painting an inaccurate portrait of one of the branches (or political agents) involved in litigation processes on issues that provoke significant disagreements, in the steps suggested by Justice Ruth Bader Ginsburg, judges have an interdependent role in democracy; they alone do not define the legal doctrine but participate in a dialogue with other government bodies as well as with the people.[15]

THE STRUCTURE OF DIALOGUES: THE BEGINNING OF THE CONVERSATION

The practice of reproducing past categories that seek to justify the current state of affairs of institutions has an early and recurrent author in the legal field. Montesquieu, with his doctrine on the separation of powers, provides a foundation for all manner of discourses and has been used in different historical and cultural contexts.[16] The crucial eighteenth-century philosopher and the advances he made in Aristotelian formulations regarding forms of government should not be forgotten but, rather, refined and tested in a reality in which government institutions are now performing hybrid and multiple functions, as a way of responding to the increasing complexity of the social world.[17]

Based on Jorge Miranda's lessons, it is evident that the separation of powers was enshrined in all the constitutional charters of the eighteenth and nineteenth centuries, by virtue of Article 16 of the Declaration of the Rights of Man and the Citizen of 1789; it was not, however, uniformly adopted. As a mechanistic perspective prevailed in France and the rejection of constitutional oversight reigned in the United States, the separation of powers took on a "coordinative" sense, of checks and balances, which judicial review was acknowledged as being from the outset: "It is no coincidence that the 1787 Constitution has produced the clearest distinction between *pouvoir de statuer* and *pouvoir d'empecher*."[18]

Consequently, we have the contemporary question of institutional design, rather than merely replicating the formula of the tripartite separation of powers. The creation of new branches of government cannot be done inadvertently based on their structure and normative guidelines—their powers within government and their aims. Moreover, dealing with a branch also means addressing its limits, recalling that—in general terms—if a branch is granted a certain authority, it is expected to exercise it to justify its existence; however, the potential consequences of the malfunctioning of a certain institution must also be considered.[19]

For Conrado Mendes, distributing the ability to enact and veto to different public agents leads to an institutional design with a distribution of powers, establishing the objectives and channels of communication among them. In this architecture, constitutional oversight would be an additional veto in the network of abilities that makes up the separation of powers.[20]

The modeling processes of institutions represent an important step in defining—not only theoretically and normatively—what the idealized functions of each of the branches should be. They invite reflection on the inadequacy of the traditional view of the separation of powers and indicate that the attempt to establish insurmountable boundaries between them is not only impractical but undesirable.

Rather than a traditional reading of the separation of powers, the practice of institutional dialogue seeks to highlight at least two aspects of the formulation of decisions in controversial cases. First, decisions—made by any of the branches—become *partially* definitive, as they can be challenged in other public bodies. Second, each space of power has characteristics that strengthen or inhibit it in decision-making processes; this reaffirms the need for channels of dialogue between institutions, as one may have better conditions than the other to address the specific case in question. Just as the legislature usually adopts a political discourse to build consensus, the judiciary therefore must translate political demands into legal terms. Those differences will complement the set of discourses produced on the subject thus far and will lead to new rounds of deliberation on the matter.

Constitutional oversight is a structure that is embedded in the tension and dialogue among the branches and can be justified—from an institutional perspective—as a "counterpower"[21] or, in terms of the protection of fundamental rights, as "trump cards" against inappropriate majoritarian political practices.[22]

Take the emblematic Canadian case, highlighted as an important milestone in the practice of institutional dialogue. Following the enactment of the "Charter of Rights and Freedoms" in 1982, the democratic legitimacy of judicial review was questioned. The answer to that challenge was that review would be part of the *dialogue* between judges and legislators;[23] in cases where the judicial ruling is open to corrections from the legislature, an interinstitutional dialogue is thus taking place.

On Canadian soil, there has been a series of institutional decisions in which the judicial provision can be reversed, modified, or circumvented by a new law. Institutional dialogue could be a restriction of the democratic process. It is understood, however, that the practices of revising enacted laws and accommodating decisions on constitutional jurisdiction are important characteristics of the democratic game itself.[24]

In this sense, the Canadian Charter of Rights ended up acting as a catalyst for exchanges between the judiciary and the legislature. The idea of institutional dialogue thus did not originate in a normative demand for institutions to engage in dialogue. In Canada, they did indeed exchange experiences, and this occurred in cases where judicial review was followed by an action brought by the responsible legislative body.[25]

Judicial review in Canada is based on levels of scrutiny or standards of review; Section 1 of the Charter of Rights states that the guaranteed rights must observe the reasonable limits defined by law and that they can be justified in a free and democratic society.

The levels of scrutiny in Section 1 were established in *R v. Oakes* (1986), which provides that 1) the law must pursue an important objective; 2) the law must be rationally connected to its objective; 3) the law must not limit the right beyond what is necessary to achieve its objective; and 4) the law must not have a disproportionately severe effect when applied to its subjects.[26] Most legal disputes focus on point 3; that is, the law is declared unconstitutional because it does not pursue its objective through the least restrictive means of a right protected by the Charter.[27] Section 1 also enables the institutional response of the legislature, which can advocate for maintaining the law on the grounds of point 4, by arguing that the legislation seeks to achieve certain objectives through the least restrictive means possible.

The solution pursued by the Canadians does not focus on direct popular participation as a way to correct decisions made by the court but, rather, on the institutional structure itself and on the ongoing dialogic tradition established among the branches.[28] The decisions resulting from constitutional jurisdiction are seen as provocations for dialogue, as they bring controversial topics that might lie dormant in the public arena and force a new discussion to be held on the matter. In the case of old laws, the new round of debates serves to restore legitimacy to a law that may be declared unconstitutional.[29]

The idea of interinstitutional dialogue does not attempt to prevent discussions from exceeding the scope of constitutional jurisdiction, ensuring that the dialogue can continue beyond the courts. In the case of Canada, decisions open up space for a legislative response; in that scenario, judicial review does not become a veto on political decisions but, rather, the *beginning of the conversation*, aimed at reconciling the values of the Charter of Rights and the social and economic policies enacted by Parliament.[30]

The thesis of institutional dialogue has passed beyond the walls of universities and is now being used in decisions by constitutional courts. Given the weak model of judicial review adopted in Canada, it does not signify the final word; in this approach, the idea of dialogue would involve opening up space after the judicial decision for responses from the legislature.

In *Vriend v. Alberta* (1998), Justice Iacobucci expressly mentioned the thesis of dialogues: "As I view the matter, the *Charter* has given rise to a more dynamic interaction among the branches of governance. This interaction has been aptly described as a 'dialogue.'"[31] Moreover, the Justice sought to move away from the simplistic reading of democracy as majority rule, particularly in cases where the interests of minority groups are affected.[32]

The democratic appeal of Canada's judicial review has a specific logic. Once the unconstitutionality of the law has been declared, the task of reconstructing it falls to the legislature—this is what is meant by dialogue. The advantage of parliament is that it is democratically elected and is able to prevent constitutional oversight by using Section 33 of the Charter of Rights, which supersedes any judicial review by suspending the protections of the Charter for a limited period of time. The final form of the law is up to the legislature, if they so wish.[33]

The thesis of dialogue thus presents a number of reasons for reconsidering the legitimacy of judicial review and the role of the courts in legislative oversight. In cases where the court believes that the legislature is in a more advantageous institutional position for deciding on the contentious issue, an opportunity may open up for parliament to speak or take a deferential stance towards the law.[34]

That does not mean, however, that the court is relinquishing its supervisory responsibility; it merely decides that other branches may first offer remedies to correct the constitutional violation. If that opportunity is not used, the law is declared unconstitutional.

The dialogical stance, which guarantees the opportunity for expression by the legislature, was also taken up in Brazil by the STF, although with quite distinct characteristics. Justice Luís Roberto Barroso explicitly endorses a change in the rationality of the Court's stance.[35] This can be observed on different occasions when the Justice requested a statement from the legislature, guaranteeing certain periods of time for it to issue an opinion.

In the ruling on the loss of the parliamentary mandate, Question of Order in Criminal Action 606, Justice Rapporteur Roberto Barroso, j. 08.12.2014, *DJe* 09.18.2014, the Justice asserted:

> For all those reasons, it is a time to revive a desirable practice of institutional dialogue between the STF and the legislative branch. Remember that in the recent past, given the difficulties posed by the constitutional text as regards the loss of parliamentary mandate due to criminal conviction, the Federal Senate, in due time, approved a proposed constitutional amendment to resolve the confusing approach to the matter in the Constitution.

In General Repercussion (*Repercussão Geral - RE*) 661,256, on October 9, 2014, the Rapporteur stated:

> Finally, the decision made here, without relinquishing the proper role of the courts, which is the protection of rights, made a point of opening up an institutional dialogue and respecting the separation of powers. The solution proposed here stems from the systematic and teleological interpretation of the Constitution and the legislation, but it is certainly innovative in that it fills a gap concerning the legal treatment of unretirement. Along those lines, a period of 180 (one hundred and eighty) days has been set for it to come into effect, allowing the legislative and executive branches to address the matter, filling the gap in different ways, if they so desire.

In the ruling on ADI 4357, Justice Rapporteur Ayres Britto, j. 03.14.2013, *DJe* 09.26.2014, which addresses the special regime for court-ordered debt payments by the states, Federal District, and municipalities, Minister Luiz Fux argued the following:

> It seems to me that this Supreme Court cannot claim to judge the robustness of parliamentary debate beyond the forms expressly required by the Federal Constitution. As regards what goes beyond the constitutional limits, it is necessary to recognize a kind of deference to the action of the legislative branch in the area of the formal acts that are part of the political process that have an intrinsic value due to democratic baptism, also as regards the interpretation of the Constitution. There is indeed a fine line between the judicial defense

> of the values of the Constitution—a mission that the STF cannot relinquish by virtue of the 1988 Charter (CF, art. 102, caput)—and a dangerous type of judicial supremacy, through which this Court ends up denying any voice to the other political powers in the construction of the meaning and scope of constitutional rules.

There is, however, a significant difference between the Brazilian and Canadian legal cultures. In Brazil, due to the theoretical approach of certain STF Justices, dialogues are a goal to be pursued to refine institutional arrangements, while in Canada, dialogues are part of the ongoing practice within the limited action of the constitutional court, which waits for responses from the legislature and even rules on laws that have been corrected by parliament after judicial review (second look cases).[36] While in Brazil institutional dialogue is discovered, in Canada, it has become a recurrent instrument in the interaction among the branches.[37]

THE (NORMATIVE) PROMISE OF DIALOGUE

The justification for judicial review—if there is some concern about the legitimacy of constitutional oversight—cannot be provided solely by the theory of institutional dialogue. The fact that constitutional courts effectively offer an opportunity for a conversation with the legislature, or should do so, is not sufficient to resolve the counter-majoritarian difficulty. Moreover, arguments critical of the thesis of institutional dialogue indicate other points of disagreement on the issue.

Would the theory make sense when the final word in constitutional interpretation lies with the courts? For critics, the problem would lie in assuming a judicial monopoly on correct interpretation, while the legislature would not have the effective means to assert its interpretation.[38] They note that decisions made by constitutional courts can distort policies and take control of the legislative agenda.[39] Additionally, the theory was used to both defend judicial deference and to legitimize judicial review.[40]

The series of questions is important because it ultimately raises fundamental issues regarding the relationship between constitutionalism and democracy. The question about the final word is linked to the topic of constitutional supremacy and the need for a group of agents with the power to state the meaning of the rights protected by the constitution.

Another relevant aspect concerns the institutional arrangement determined by each country's constitution. In some contexts, judicial review is not a tool that prevails over legislative activity; in others, however, judicial review is strong and definitive.[41] Proposals that aim to modify those constructions must simultaneously transform the institutional design and justify revision in the governmental tradition.

Additionally, given the existence of judicial review, the legislature may be compelled to pay greater attention to appeals from minority groups that are unjustifiably excluded from the public arena or do not receive due protection. Moreover, according to the institutional aspects of each country, the decisions made by the constitutional court could be reversed by the competent legislators when they deem the outcome unacceptable.[42]

On the question involving the possibility of usurping the political agenda, the proposal of dialogues seems institutionally interesting, as politics should not be thought of as a one-way street or as exclusive to parliament. The existence of mechanisms that can serve to provoke the other branches of government into offering an institutional response on a given topic is not only consistent with democratic terms but also a way to enrich the material produced in those dialogues.

The maturation of democracies thus involves translating disagreements into appropriate spaces for deliberation, as a way to safeguard democracy itself. Dialogues are not necessarily intended to lead to a consensus, nor is the party with the best reasons expected to prevail. After all, there are a number of compelling factors that can lead to consensus-building and case-by-case decision-making beyond the bounds of rationality. What is being challenged are the "majoritarian monologues"[43]; disagreements are inevitable in a democracy, but the institutions that allow people to continue to disagree must be preserved.

The criticism that the thesis of dialogues can be used to justify both an active and deferential stance by the judiciary when it is carrying out judicial review has a dual response. Although this only reaffirms the insufficiency of dialogues for justifying constitutional oversight, the criticism is misplaced, as the plethora of ways in which a theory is used by a certain institution cannot represent the death of the theory itself,[44] that is, the practice of and need for interinstitutional dialogue remain important, even if used in a distorted manner by the courts. Nonetheless, their use does not imply an active or deferential stance in judicial review.

Deliberative democracy manages to be better suited to understanding the problems of constitutional jurisdiction beyond the simple majority derived from counting votes in parliament. The issue of lack of legitimacy in the decision-making process of the Courts can be improved with the participation of amicus and public hearings, for example. It even allows the Court to function, at certain times, in a counter-majority way.[45]

It is important to highlight the attempt to elaborate a complementary argument for the legitimacy of constitutional courts based on their supposed deliberative qualities and abilities; the legitimacy can be assessed on the basis of deliberative performance; deliberation is not something that can be assumed, on the otherwise, is an achievement and should be reached in each case.[46]

In judicial review, the dialogic theory does not seek to emphasize the interpretative aspects that should be utilized by magistrates when making their decisions but, rather, the institutional function occupied by constitutional oversight. It is thus no longer (only) a question of emphasizing the importance of the fundamental moral values guarded by the constitution but how to define the structures of power to ensure that the production of decisions is not the result of "monologues."

The production of the constitution's meaning is therefore a task that involves the collaboration of political agents outside the judiciary.[47] The theory wagers that the aggregation of knowledge from different sources will alleviate the counter-majoritarian difficulty, as the other branches and the people themselves would participate in constructing the constitutional meaning.[48] Dialogue would be a guarantee that the branches of government that are required to periodically report on their activities to their voters would respond to the judicial decisions with which they do not agree.[49]

The premise that the final word becomes relative is based on the possibility that the branches subject to accountability will contest the political space eventually occupied by the judiciary. Because the institutional structure created for establishing a democratic rule of law eventually results in the judicialization of politics—which can be observed in Brazil after the 1988 Constitution, as well as in other countries[50]—there is hope that there may be institutional mechanisms through which judicial decisions can be reformed by the legislature.

It is not a question of condoning a difficult notion that political decisions should only be made in the parliamentary sphere, for the legislature itself has turned to the judiciary to continue discussions where they had ultimately been defeated. The difference, however, is that once the threshold of justice has been crossed, a necessary grammatical adjustment must be made to the conflict, which had previously flowed within the confines of the fundamental guarantee of the parliamentarians' freedom of lawmaking.

There is a set of rules to be observed, just as there is a different rationality that governs the judiciary. Explicitly political discourses should give way to arguments based on rules, jurisprudence, doctrine, and opinions rather than being based on the opinions of the people's representatives. This does not, however, eliminate the potential for vigorous disagreements between politically polarized parties nor strategic action by the court to prevent its decisions from being attacked by the legislature.[51]

In general terms, notes Christine Bateup, the more normative the dialogic theory, the less it is able to address issues related to the legitimacy of judicial review in an appropriate way. The theories that advocate for institutional dialogue can thus be divided into at least three types. First, at one end of the spectrum are those that offer a positive assessment of the institutional contexts in which each branch operates, and they develop their normative proposals based on this approach. Next, there are theories that recognize that judicial decisions do not need to have the "final word," and they offer proposals for how institutional dialogue should occur based on this fact. At the other end of the spectrum are the theories that depart from a clear focus on the positive dynamic among the branches and emphasize the ideal conditions under which dialogue should take place.[52]

Bateup thus suggests what she calls a "dialogical fusion," in which the best theories of dialogue—found in "equilibrium" and "partnership"—are synthesized.[53] The "equilibrium" theories propose a different way of thinking about the judiciary's privileged position in constitutional dialogue, to avoid overshadowing the legislature. The role of the magistrates is focused on encouraging broad constitutional discussions in society, leading to an equilibrium regarding the constitutional meaning under discussion.[54] The "partnership" theories are based on the recognition that the different branches of government can make different contributions to the constitutional dialogue, so as to ensure that the judiciary alone is not privileged. In this case, each of the branches learns from the contributions of the others, and judicial or external actors are thus conceived as equally legitimate in the constitutional decision-making process.[55]

The dialogical fusion, presented by Bateup, would have the potential to solve the problem of legitimacy and would offer a comprehensive view of the social and institutional aspects of constitutional dialogue. On the one hand, it advocates for expanding constitutional debates, with the judiciary as a proponent and facilitator of those discussions, seeking to include the people as a partner in the construction of constitutional meanings and the changes that have occurred in society. On the other, it seeks to resolve the counter-majoritarian difficulty by proposing that both judges and legislators have unique institutional perspectives, due to their separate but interconnected positions. Consequently, if the branches of government are open to listening and learning from perspectives different from their own, there is hope that better answers will be formulated to the problems related to the constitutional meaning being contested.[56]

INSTITUTIONAL DIALOGUE IN BRAZIL

As mentioned above, in Brazil, effective institutional dialogue among institutions is a project that must be consolidated by altering the understanding that the duties of the branches are ironclad. Nonetheless, the Brazilian institutional design has mechanisms that can contribute to the dialogic functioning of institutions.

Examining the series of reforms promoted in the Brazilian judiciary over the past two decades, it is clear that Brazilian constitutional jurisdiction has acquired "concentrating" and "binding" aspects, characteristics that were coupled with the advent of binding precedent and the need to demonstrate the general repercussions to hear extraordinary appeal.[57]

As for the type of deliberation—external or internal—Virgílio Afonso da Silva argues that the Brazilian model of judicial review can be considered an extreme model of external deliberation.[58] In the STF, there is no practice of exchanging votes among the justices, such that the chance of votes being combined or reconsidered is minimal; the justices "are not there to hear arguments from their colleagues at the court."[59] Moreover, there is no "decision-making institutional unit," that is, the STF simply aggregates the votes of the justices and, as a consequence, there is a "lack of clear, objective decisions that convey the court's opinion."[60] That makes it difficult, for example, to distinguish between the aspects of the decision that are merely ancillary arguments for the vote, the *obiter dicta* and the reasons that actually led to the decision—the rationale for making the decision (*ratio decidendi*).

Refining the internal deliberation in the STF would thus require greater interaction among its justices, such as exchanging votes and establishing an institutional position that is not limited to a gathering of votes. Those modifications could be made through procedural changes and would not require amendments to the Constitution. However, more than anything, they would require changes to the justices' institutional understanding of the Court, as they would need to accept the counter-productivity of institutional monologues.[61]

Beyond the intrainstitutional scope, as concerns dialogue with the other branches, there are mechanisms for overruling decisions by the STF. As Rodrigo Brandão notes, to bypass concentrated judicial review, the National Congress typically issues amendments to the Constitution.[62] Nonetheless, it is also possible to observe the Court's contribution to refining constitutional interpretations in the legislative sphere:

> The Brazilian experience essentially confirms the consequentialist and epistemic merits of the theory of constitutional dialogues. In effect, the ability to approve constitutional amendments made it possible to override decisions by the STF, which despite being grounded in technical and textual elements, produced extremely adverse practical effects. The STF, in turn, contributed significantly to resolving constitutional problems in which the National Congress simply could not fulfill its constitutional duty to legislate or in which the rule

> that had been issued could not rise above the influence of interest groups, particularly articulated in the parliamentary arena.[63]

Furthermore, with regard to the interaction between the STF and the people, the mechanisms of the public hearing and the *amicus curiae* are potential instruments for substantively refining the development of the public reasons that must be presented by the justices on the grounds of their decisions.

In line with the concern about the democratic legitimacy of judicial review, those mechanisms open up the STF to direct contributions from interested parties in the cases under discussion, lending greater reality to the production of decisions, as the cases begin to acquire real faces and narratives; although this is not a cornerstone of decisions, it is fundamental to their epistemic enrichment.[64]

There are also cases in which the STF seeks to prompt dialogue, as there are indeed matters that, in principle, would be better addressed with the participation of the legislature. So far, this is an isolated initiative, embraced by a certain number of justices, who are concerned with giving greater legitimacy to judicial review.

FINAL CONSIDERATIONS

Recognizing that the relationship among the branches can take many forms, the aim was to outline the central aspects related to the theory of institutional dialogue. The considerations on the institutional positions occupied by each of the branches can no longer be used as a synonym for insurmountable boundaries. As an alternative, the importance of intra-and interinstitutional dialogue is posited.

The boundaries between law and politics have been blurred by the ability to refer political issues to the judiciary. In terms of that phenomenon, little can be done to return to an idealized place where the judiciary strictly rules on technical matters and the legislature only deliberates on political issues. The judicialization of politics indicates that other paths can be sought by parties who demand their rights beyond the traditional relationship between representatives and the represented. This is a sign of the maturation of democratic institutions, which now hear disagreements between citizens and translate them into the appropriate institutional terms to address the matter.

In turn, with the exception of the strictly procedural perspective, the notion that the judiciary must have the final word to resolve constitutional conflicts must be tempered. The judiciary may be the final *locus* of a conflict, but not necessarily. The alternative that considers the importance of maintaining institutions—without this implying a self-referential conservatism—should be complemented by opening up those institutions to epistemic contributions from the other branches and from the parties affected by the decisions.

Thinking about the judiciary as having the final word is important for preventing standstills and maintaining an unjustifiable status quo. In light of the demand for parliamentarians to observe fundamental rights when formulating their legislative proposals, it is also possible to demand that judges respond to the conflicts presented to them in a dialogic manner. Given the unique perspective that judges can bring to cases and the expectation that their responses to constitutional issues will be more enduring, it is essential to consider—more broadly—the necessity of continuing the conversation among the branches of government and the people (i.e., maintaining public spaces for deliberation):

> Using the concepts of the "provisional final word" and "procedural rounds," I seek to indicate the exact dimension and limitation of that question. Theories of dialogue, by observing the fact of continuity (of "legislative sequences," and so on), place the simple existence of judicial review in a new light. The final word and dialogue, in this sense, are complementary. Just as law and politics need "provisional final words," they also need continuity.[65]

Politics is therefore perceived as a complex social form, which implies not only that disagreements must be resolved through established institutional means but also that political actors will continue to disagree about their political agendas and objectives. The law, in turn, is guided by the presumption of the establishment of agreements, but not necessarily the fact that consensuses will be reached.[66]

The maturation of the democratic rule of law is tested by its capacity to maintain an institutional arrangement over time and, equally, its ability to update those institutions, to make structural changes that will accommodate the tension between law and politics. Although the institutional structure of the judicial decision requires the parties to defend their cases with arguments as if they could have definitive answers,[67] the search for consensus in the legal space cannot overshadow the judiciary in regard to the political facts that drive social life and animate life in society. Hence, disagreement over judicial decisions can always rekindle political controversies, and to our best knowledge, the most sophisticated ways of resolving tensions between law and politics occur through institutional dialogue.

NOTES

1. Luís Roberto Barroso, *O novo direito constitucional brasileiro: Contribuições para a construção teórica e prática da jurisdição constitucional no Brasil* (Belo Horizonte: Fórum, 2012), 252. In terms of what one of the authors stated earlier: "The attempt to restore politics to the law is the most interesting—albeit ambitious—epistemic proposal of critical thinking focused on 'jus.' It is not a question of positing a new legal theory to replace the traditional legal schools. On the contrary, it seeks to create a renewed dimension for legal discourse, such that in addition to instrumental concerns, it can understand its object as something belonging to history." Clèmerson Merlin Clève, *O direito e os direitos: elementEs para uma crítica do direito contemporâneo* (Belo Horizonte: Fórum, 2011), 139.

2. Ran Hirschl, "The Judicialization of Politics," in *Oxford Handbook of Political Science* (Oxford, UK: Oxford University Press, 2008); Barroso, *O novo direito constitucional brasileiro*, 252–253.

3. Luís Roberto Barroso, *Curso de direito constitucional contemporâneo: Os conceitos fundamentais e a construção do novo modelo* (São Paulo: Saraiva, 2009), 299.

4. The statement is made in a normative sense, as it does not discount that constitutional changes may occur via a coup or other undemocratic forms: "Constitutions . . . are drafted in four major scenarios: creation or emancipation of a state, restructuring of the state after a war, following a revolutionary movement or the culmination of some process of negotiated political transition." Barroso, *Curso de direito constitucional contemporâneo*, 161.

5. "The Founders were clever fellows, but they made serious mistakes, moral no less than instrumental. And so will every generation. In a democracy, the People of today must have the chance to change their minds about the fundamental choices made by preceding generations. The object of higher lawmaking design is not to frustrate this process, but structure it—so that it occurs when a mobilized citizenry wants it to occur, so that it will proceed in a deliberate and focused fashion, so that changes in constitutional identity will occur, when they occur, in a deliberate and weighty fashion that will gain respect as a *considered* judgment of We the People." Bruce Ackerman, *We the People*: *Foundations* (Cambridge, MA: Harvard University Press, 1993), 279.

6. "In Brazil, this review is carried out through two different rites: a) *incidental*, by which the unconstitutionality of a rule may be invoked in any judicial proceeding, before any court or tribunal, and the judicial body must no longer apply the rule to the specific case if it considers the claim to be founded; and b) *principal*, for which some persons, bodies or institutions, listed in article 103 of the Federal Constitution, may file a direct action before the STF, which will discuss the constitutionality or unconstitutionality—in principle—of a certain law or normative act." Barroso, *Curso de direito constitucional contemporâneo*, 299.

7. Clèmerson Merlin Clève, *A Fiscalização Abstrata de Constitucionalidade no Direito Brasileiro* (São Paulo: Revista dos Tribunais, 2000), 22.

8. Clève, *A Fiscalização Abstrata de Constitucionalidade no Direito Brasileiro*, 29.

9. "Government must treat those whom it governs with concern, that is, as human beings who are capable of suffering and frustration, and with respect, that is, as human beings who are capable of forming and acting on intelligent conceptions of how their lives should be lived. Government must not only treat people with concern and respect, but with equal concern and respect." Ronald Dworkin, *Taking Rights Seriously* (Cambridge, MA: Harvard University Press, 1978), 272–273.

10. "In the plural context in which we live, the political community is only fully legitimate when it ensures the equal right of every individual to live according to their own plans and existential choices; when it provides the basic material means for this; and when it respects and values the particular identities of each of its members. Democratic constitutions are responsible for guaranteeing those elements, which are vital to the feeling of belonging to the political community becoming widespread among citizens." Cláudio Pereira Souza Neto and Daniel Sarmento, *Direito Constitucional: Teoria, história e métodos de trabalho* (Belo Horizonte: Fórum, 2012), 238.

11. On judicial activism, see: Carlos Alexandre de Azevedo Campos, *Dimensões do ativismo judicial do Supremo Tribunal Federal* (Rio de Janeiro: Forense, 2014).

12. Adrian Vermeule, *Judging under Uncertainty: An Institutional Theory of Legal Interpretation* (Cambridge, MA: Harvard University Press, 2006); Diego Werneck Arguelhes and Fernando Leal, "O Argumento das 'Capacidades institucionais' entre a banalidade, a redundância e o absurdo," in *Tratado de direito constitucional: Constituição no século XXI*, ed. Felipe Dutra Asensi and Daniel Giotti de Paula (Rio de Janeiro: Elsevier, 2014).

13. Larry D. Kramer, *The People Themselves: Popular Constitutionalism and Judicial Review* (Oxford, UK: Oxford University Press, 2004); Marianna Montebello Willeman, "Revisão parlamentar no controle de constitucionalidade, constitucionalismo popular e humildade institucional," *Revista Brasileira de Direito Público* 43 (2013); Rodrigo Mendes Cardoso, "As teorias do constitucionalismo popular e do diálogo na perspectiva da jurisdição constitucional brasileira," *RECHTD* 6, no. 2 (2014). For a critical perspective, see: Bruno Meneses Lorenzetto, *Os Caminhos do Constitucionalismo para a Democracia* (Phd diss., Universidade Federal do Paraná, 2014).

14. Jeremy Waldron, *Law and Disagreement* (Oxford, UK: Oxford University Press, 1999); Jeremy Waldron, "The Core of the Case against Judicial Review," *Yale Law Journal* 115 (2006). "For Waldron, however, justifying the judicial review of constitutionality on the grounds that rights should function as a trump card against majoritarian legislative decisions would ignore the moral disagreement that exists in plural societies, that is, would ignore the fact that people have different conceptions of their most basic rights (just as they have different conceptions of social justice and public policies). As a result, given broad disagreement about fundamental rights, the decision about the question 'who should make decisions about those rights'? should be made on equal terms by citizens in a community, which does not occur when that decision is restricted to a judicial elite." Virgílio Afonso da Silva, "O STF e o controle de constitucionalidade: Deliberação, diálogo e razão pública," *Revista de Direito Administrativo* 250 (2009): 204.

15. Ruth Bader Ginsburg, "Speaking in a Judicial Voice," *New York University Law Review* 67 (1992): 1198.

16. Charles de Secondat Montesquieu, *O Espírito das Leis*, trans. Cristina Murachco (São Paulo: Martins Fontes, 2000).

17. "A 'new separation of powers' is emerging in the twenty-first century. To grasp its distinctive features will require us to develop a conceptual framework containing five or six boxes—or maybe more. And so we must say a fond farewell to Montesquieu." Bruce Ackerman, "Adeus, Montesquieu," *Revista de Direito Administrativo* 265 (2014): 15. The institutional expansion that can be observed in the brief history of the National Justice Council (*Conselho Nacional de Justiça-CNJ*) in Brazil is an example of the insufficiency of the tripartite canon for explaining contemporary phenomena.

18. Jorge Miranda, *Manual de Direito Constitucional* Tomo III (Coimbra: Coimbra Editora, 2004), 383.

19. According to Jorge Miranda: "The principle of the separation of powers will therefore remain a principle of an optimal organization of state functions, a functionally appropriate organizational structure, legitimacy for the decision and responsibility for the decision, hence a *positive* dimension, along with a *negative* dimension, of control and the limitation of power. And, consequently, there is a recognition of the need for an *essential core* of each body's authority, determined by the appropriateness of its structure for the type or nature of the authority in question." Miranda, *Manual de Direito Constitucional*, 385.

20. Conrado Hübner Mendes, *Controle de Constitucionalidade e Democracia* (Rio de Janeiro: Elsevier, 2008), 132.

21. "This veto is not justified by its content, which will necessarily be controversial, but by the prudential reason of cautioning the political system against majoritarian upheavals. It therefore does not guarantee the ethical minimum of the democratic regime but, rather, delays the decision-making process, hoping that time might contribute to a decision with more intense deliberations." Conrado Hübner Mendes, *Direitos fundamentais, separação de poderes e deliberação* (São Paulo: Saraiva, 2011), 27.

22. Ronald Dworkin, "Rights as Trumps," in *Theories of Rights*, ed. Jeremy Waldron (Oxford, UK: Oxford University Press, 1984).

23. Peter W. Hogg and Allison A. Bushell, "The Charter Dialogue between Courts and Legislatures (Or Perhaps the Charter of Rights Isn't Such a Bad Thing After All)," *Osgoode Hall Law Journal* 35 (1997): 79.

24. "The dialogue that culminates in a democratic decision can only take place if the judicial decision to strike down a law can be reversed, modified, or avoided by the ordinary legislative process." Hogg and Bushell, "The Charter Dialogue between Courts and Legislatures," 80.

25. Hogg and Bushell, "The Charter Dialogue between Courts and Legislatures," 82.

26. Hogg and Bushell, "The Charter Dialogue between Courts and Legislatures," 84–85; Saulo Tarso Rodrigues, Paulo Bonavides, Nuria Belloso Martín, and Alexandre Fernandes Silva, *Teoria da decisão judicial e teoria da justiça: Jusfilosofia e novos paradigmas constitucionais* (Curitiba: Juruá, 2015), 624.

27. On the levels of scrutiny in the United States, see: Clèmerson Merlin Clève and Bruno Meneses Lorenzetto, "Constituição, Governo Democrático e Níveis de Intensidade do Controle Jurisdicional," *Revista Jurídica Luso Brasileira* 1 (2015).

28. To such an extent that cases where dialogue between the court and the legislature was not possible are extremely rare. Hogg and Bushell, "The Charter Dialogue between Courts and Legislatures," 96.

29. On the notwithstanding clause, see: Bruno Meneses Lorenzetto and Tanya Kozicki de Mello. "Revisão legislativa dos atos jurisdicionais," in *Direito Constitucional Brasileiro* II, ed. Clèmerson Merlin Clève (São Paulo: Revista dos Tribunais, 2014).

30. Hogg and Bushell, "The Charter Dialogue between Courts and Legislatures," 105. The thesis was maintained by the authors in a later article: Peter Hogg, Alisson A. Bushell Thornton, and Wade K. Wright, "Charter Dialogue Revisited—Or 'Much Ado about Metaphors,'" *Osgoode Hall Law Journal* 45 (2007).

31. "In reviewing legislative enactments and executive decisions to ensure constitutional validity, the courts speak to the legislative and executive branches. As has been pointed out, most of the legislation held not to pass constitutional muster has been followed by new legislation designed to accomplish similar objectives (see: Hogg and Bushell, "Charter Dialogue Revisited," 82). By doing this, the legislature responds to the courts; hence the dialogue among the branches." *Vriend v. Alberta* (1998).

32. The case addressed a legislative omission in the province of Alberta. The province's code included all the protections typical of Canadian codes protecting fundamental rights but did not address protection from discrimination on the basis of sexual orientation. Delwin Vriend brought the case before the constitutional court because he had been dismissed from a university due to his sexual orientation and could not find support in Alberta's legislation for his claim. The court's decision was that the legislative omission represented a violation of the guarantee of equality protected by the Charter of Rights and Freedoms.

33. Hogg, Thornton, and Wright, "Charter Dialogue Revisited," 13.

34. Hogg, Thornton, and Wright, "Charter Dialogue Revisited," 15–16.

35. Luís Roberto Barroso, "Retrospectiva 2014," *Consultor Jurídico*, December 31, 2014, accessed on July 7, 2015, http://www.conjur.com.br/2014-dez-31/roberto-barroso-ano-sinaliza-mudancas-supremo-tribunal-federal. Along the same lines: "In some cases, I have adopted a doctrinal position that is called 'institutional dialogues,' which is an interaction between the judiciary and the legislative branch, known as the appeal to the legislator." Luís Roberto Barroso, "Óleo na engrenagem," *Consultor Jurídico*, July 2, 2015, accessed on July 7, 2015, http://www.conjur.com.br/2015-jul-02/entrevista-luis-roberto-barroso-ministro-stf-parte.

36. "The notion of dialogue that we proposed in '*Charter* Dialogue' was descriptive rather than normative. We described how legislatures *did* behave—rather than how they *should* behave—following a court decision striking down one of their laws on *Charter* grounds." Hogg, Thornton, and Wright, "Charter Dialogue Revisited," 26.

37. "In Brazil, there was an attempt to approve PEC 33, which would allow the legislature to overrule the STF's decisions, in a model very similar to that established in Canada. However, the effects in Brazil, as we understand it, would be disastrous

(. . .)" Rodrigues, Bonavides, Martín and Silva, *Teoria da decisão judicial e teoria da justiça*, 624.

38. "The third, and most crucial, flaw in the normative argument is its assumption of a judicial monopoly on correct interpretation." Christopher Manfredi and James B. Kelly, "Six Degrees of Dialogue: A Response to Hogg and Bushell," *Osgoode Hall Law Journal* 37 (1999): 523.

39. F. L. Morton and Rainer Knopff, *The Charter Revolution and the Court Party* (Peterborough: Broadview Press, 2000), 157.

40. "When dialogue is invoked to support activism in one case and its opposite in another, it is difficult to conclude that principles matter to the Court. Decisions appear instead to follow a political barometer that tells the judges either that the legislature has been progressive and that its law should be upheld, or that the legislature has acted regressively, in which case the *Charter* can be enforced. Though the institutions may be placated, the concept of *constitutional* rights is certain to be compromised." Jamie Cameron, "Dialogue and Hierarchy in Charter Interpretation: A Comment on R. V. Mills," *Alberta Law Review* 38 (2001): 1063.

41. "The design differences are significant and should be studied, but the idea that there should be dialogue between courts and legislatures with respect to the treatment of rights seems to be gaining ground." Kent Roach, "Dialogic Judicial Review and Its Critics," *Supreme Court Law Review* 23 (2004): 50.

42. In the case of Canada, there is even the possibility of including the nonbinding clause. Hogg, Thornton, and Wright, "Charter Dialogue Revisited," 40.

43. Roach, "Dialogic Judicial Review and Its Critics," 75.

44. The authors identify five distinct moments in which the theory was used: "First, some judges have invoked the idea of dialogue in seeking to justify judicial review. Second, some judges have invoked the idea of dialogue in opposing the reading down of legislation in a *Charter* case. Third, some judges have invoked the idea of dialogue as a reason for suspending declarations of invalidity in *Charter* cases. Fourth, some judges have invoked the idea of dialogue in the context of a case considering the exercise of remedial discretion under section 24 of the *Charter*. And finally, some judges have invoked the idea of dialogue in second look cases, at times as a reason for deferring to the legislative judgment, and at other times to remind legislatures that the courts will not automatically defer to the legislature simply because it has revised and re-enacted an invalid law." Hogg, Thornton, and Wright, "Charter Dialogue Revisited," 52–53.

45. Carlos Santiago Nino, *The Constitution of Deliberative Democracy* (New Haven, CT: Yale University Press, 1996).

46. Conrado Hübner Mendes, *Constitutional Courts and Deliberative Democracy* (Oxford, UK: Oxford University Press, 2013).

47. Richard Fallon understands that constitutional courts have an institutional advantage over other branches of government for discussing matters of principle. However, the courts cannot be understood as merely a forum of principle because they also have a duty to enforce the constitution. That activity is a collective function involving other government bodies, and, in fact, the initial responsibility for implementing the constitutional provisions belongs to the political branches of the

government. Richard H. Fallon Jr., *Implementing the Constitution* (Cambridge, MA: Harvard University Press, 2001).

48. "The *fundamental idea of democracy* is as follows: a normative determination of the type of coexistence of a people, by the people themselves. Because self-government cannot be achieved—it is almost impossible to do so in practice—the intention is to ensure at least the self-codification of the current regulations based on free competition between opinions and interests, with manageable alternatives and effective possibilities for public sanctioning." Friedrich Müller, *Quem é o Povo? A questão fundamental da democracia*, trans. Peter Naumann (São Paulo: Max Limonad, 1998), 57.

49. Christine Bateup, "The Dialogic Promise: assessing the normative potential of theories of constitutional dialogue," *Brooklyn Law Review* 71 (2006): 1118.

50. John Ferejohn, "Judicializing Politics, Politicizing Law," *Law and Contemporary Problems* 65, no. 3 (2002).

51. For Bateup: "In addition, the political branches of government can, and frequently do, challenge judicial decisions by enacting new legislation that tests or attempts to restrict court rulings. . . . Given the existence of these institutional constraints that serve to keep judicial decisions within democratic limits, the overwhelming reliance on objective interpretative theories in constitutional scholarship thus appears to be misplaced." Bateup, "The Dialogic Promise," 119.

52. Bateup, "The Dialogic Promise," 1121.

53. Bateup, "The Dialogic Promise," 1112.

54. Bateup, "The Dialogic Promise," 1157. Along those lines, see: Barry Friedman, "Dialogue and Judicial Review," *Michigan Law Review* 91 (1993); Robert C. Post, "Fashioning the Legal Constitution: Culture, Courts, and Law," *Harvard Law Review* 117 (2003).

55. Bateup, "The Dialogic Promise," 1168. See: Keith E. Whittington, "In Defense of Legislatures," *Political Theory* 28 (2000); Janet Hiebert, *Charter Conflicts: What Is Parliament's Role?* (Montreal: McGill-Queen's University Press, 2002).

56. Bateup, "The Dialogic Promise," 1174–1175.

57. Silva, *O STF e o controle de constitucionalidade*, 216.

58. In internal deliberation, there is an exchange of information between the members of an institution, while in external deliberation, the concern is focused on convincing external actors.

59. Silva, *O STF e o controle de constitucionalidade*, 217.

60. Silva, *O STF e o controle de constitucionalidade*, 217.

61. "If a court, when exercising judicial review, has to be a privileged *locus* of deliberation and public reason and if its legitimacy depends on the quality of its decision, it is essential to reconsider the STF's form of deliberation. Additionally, it seems clear to me that an institutional unit is a prerequisite for dialogue, as constitutional dialogue does not take place between people but between institutions." Silva, *O STF e o controle de constitucionalidade,* 219.

62. Rodrigo Brandão, *Supremacia judicial versus diálogos constitucionais: A quem cabe a última palavra sobre o sentido da Constituição?* (Rio de Janeiro: Lumen Juris, 2012), 289–290.

63. Brandão, *Supremacia judicial versus diálogos constitucionais*, 299.

64. Vanice Lírio do Valle and Cecília de Almeida Silva accurately note: "The focal point of all this is to deepen the reflection on what the defining element of this dialogical openness—or the denial of it—actually is in the exercise of constitutional jurisdiction in the Brazilian system. After all, if the *amicus curiae* and the public hearing legitimize the decision, as they make it possible to open up the debate on constitutional meaning, removing either of them would be recommending, at the very least, a more substantive decision in terms of their determining reasons." Vanice Lírio do Valle and Cecília de Almeida Silva, "Abertura dialógica no controle abstrato de constitucionalidade: Um olhar ainda preceitual," *A & C Revista de Direito Administrativo & Constitucional* 43 (2010): 126–127.

65. Mendes, *Direitos fundamentais, separação de poderes e deliberação*, 238.

66. Robert Post, "Theorizing Disagreement: Reconceiving the Relationship between Law and Politics," *California Law Review* 98 (2010): 1323.

67. Post, *Theorizing Disagreement*, 1347.

Chapter 4

Fundamental Rights

Revisions and New Paths

This chapter not only summarizes the theoretical elements that have shaped the recent history of discussions on fundamental rights but also identifies the dilemmas that are rekindling the most current debates on the subject. To that end, it begins by presenting the central characteristics of the doctrine of effectiveness,[1] emphasizing social fundamental rights. Then, it briefly discusses the objections to judicial activism. Finally, it maps out new horizons of the search for an ever-greater effectiveness of fundamental rights.

RETURNING TO THE DOCTRINE OF EFFECTIVENESS

It has become routine for us to reconstruct a narrative trajectory about fundamental rights that begins with the current Constitution and its drafting and strives to navigate through the subsequent decades as a continual series of accomplishments. There is no reason to think differently, at least on the legal plane. Those achievements, however, were not necessarily linear or smooth. In contrast, at different times, they have been plagued by tensions and attempts to reduce the list of constitutional guarantees.

Looking at the latest developments in fundamental rights in Brazil, the new challenges have at least two dimensions: first, the continued pursuit of the achievement of fundamental rights and second, and directly related to the former, ensuring that the institutional design established by the Constitution, in a broad sense, is compatible with the definition of the structures of power and government as well as the list of fundamental rights. While the practical challenge of the first dimension is permanent and (in principle) never-ending, the theoretical questions of the second require the governmental machine and its procedures to be reconciled with the commitments that give substance to the Constitution, to its reserve of justice.

The doctrine of effectiveness, which contributed to constructing the narrative around fundamental rights following the restoration of democracy, proposed the recognition of the normative force of constitutional provisions. The *Brazilian doctrine of effectiveness* sought to place a particular importance on the position the Constitution occupies—from a legal perspective—in the organization of the country's legal system. Constitutional supremacy was coupled with the demand for the direct and immediate implementation of rules on fundamental rights. The first step was thus to privilege the role of the judiciary in the protection of fundamental rights.[2]

The adoption of a specific interpretative strategy was proposed, namely to identify the *subjective rights*[3] enshrined in the Constitution, which became enforceable—albeit differently, for both individuals and the government—by refining the constitutional and infra-constitutional jurisdictional mechanisms.[4] One of the important advances promoted by the constitutionalism of effectiveness was an emphasis on the understanding that the Constitution was a normative document that should be taken seriously. Beyond being simply a political declaration or a discursive set of abstract objectives, the normative force of the constitutional provisions should be recognized.[5]

Accordingly:

> Under the aegis of the 1988 Federal Constitution, the state—a political space par excellence—will also have to be understood as a kind of institutional skeleton designed by the constituent assembly to satisfy the principles, objectives and fundamental rights by updating the legislature, seeking to implement the constitutional provisions, including social rights granted by the state, through the action of the judiciary, which must be expressed through hermeneutics committed to constitutional principles and through the action of the executive responsible for developing public policies to achieve rights and public services for the same purpose (health, education, housing, etc.).[6]

To fulfill the commitment to effectiveness, it was necessary to reconstruct the legal dogma, establishing an appropriate theory to resolve the possible tensions between rights, freedoms, and guarantees that emerge based on the substantive purposes established by the legal system. At this point, in addition to the doctrinal advances, there was also an attempt to refine the civic aspects of republicanism and the demands of democracy (strengthening the necessary political participation of the subjects of laws), with the sphere of rights of liberal modernity.[7]

It was therefore necessary to confront the challenges inherent to the achievement of social rights and the public policies that corresponded to them, given the many political, economic, and institutional obstacles that exist on the realm of factuality. Another significant characteristic thus concerned the convergence and correspondence between policies and law, focusing on the possibility of them being achieved through governmental institutional practices. It was a question of measuring the limits of the constitutional normative discourse; although the thesis of the constitutionalization of all the branches of law was already beginning to have an effect in the legal realm, there was still a *lack* of correspondence between constitutional statements and political practices in the social, economic, and cultural spheres.[8]

The alternative encountered was to transform the foundations of the state of law. The formal adoption of a Charter of Rights was not enough, as the discourses set out within it needed to be transformed into reality. There were thus proposals to include citizens in the state's political decision-making processes, beyond occasional elections, as well as their right to a set of basic material goods for a dignified life and, along the same lines, their access to justice in a substantive dimension.

This involved constructing instrumental conditions aimed at protecting rights, which could be observed—at least in the constitutional realm—through the refinement of the techniques of constitutional jurisdiction. However, along the same lines, the objective was to produce the consequences envisaged by the normative provisions.[9] The ideal *locus* for this was thus the judiciary. The demand for efficacy was presented as effectiveness, the "social efficacy of the rule,"[10] its practical action in the life-world, such that it was possible to reconnect the abstract provisions of the *should be* with the *is* of the social reality.

By revealing the multipotential capacity of rules and, in particular, principles, they could authorize factual changes in life in society. The (re)discovery of the importance of the law was coupled with an emphasis on the judiciary as a space for achieving fundamental rights (particularly social rights) and modifying power relations.[11] Although there was no profound redefinition of the social structures, there was at least a recognition that the law would not only be a stabilizing space but also—in its political dimension—a space of democratic tensions and disputes.

ADVANCES IN THE THEORIZATION OF FUNDAMENTAL RIGHTS

Concomitantly with the doctrine of effectiveness, there have been renewed discussions on fundamental rights in Brazilian society, resulting in a refinement and *aggiornamento* of the constitutional discourse on the matter.

In terms of the development of theories, the dual dimension of fundamental rights—subjective and objective—is now recognized. A subjective right inherent to a person who could be its bearer was identified; as for its objective aspect, the multiple functions that fundamental rights exercise in the legal system were emphasized.

The "multifunctionality of fundamental rights" was also acknowledged.[12] The democratic rule of law, however, should remain open to different ways of understanding fundamental rights, which are clearly derived from different ways of understanding a good life.

In the wake of those developments, the specific legal framework of social rights has become more important. Moving beyond the conception that the state would only be a rights-violating agent,[13] demands were made for the state institution to take an active stance, to fulfill the promises in the constitutional pact. Once they were integrated into the legal system, social rights needed to be complemented by procedures, policies, and instruments that could actually bring to light the set of promises the constitution was proclaiming.

It was then possible to perceive the fragility of mechanisms that are created without an intimate relationship with the life-world. Fundamental rights had entered a new chapter in Brazil, stepping into a new paradigm. Their adoption in the political sphere, however, was still lacking, in the absence of which social rights would remain merely a promise. Ultimately, the greater or lesser degree to which they were achieved[14] did not depend only on what would be produced on the jurisdictional plane but—to a larger extent—on the factual plane, through public policies.

However, social rights, like all fundamental rights, have a social and defensive dimension,[15] hence the need to formulate public policies, defining objective indicators to measure the evolution of their effectiveness, all for the best and most transparent verification of the achievement of the reserve of justice defined by the constituent assembly.

Although we cannot advocate for different legal frameworks for freedoms and social rights—as exists, for example, in Portugal—it is impossible to deny the peculiarities that affect different types of rights.[16] Regardless of how similar the starting point is, the factors that serve as criteria for distinguishing between rights of freedom and social rights are more clearly placed on the plane of the factual, for while the conditions for producing the effects of individual rights have a considerable advantage—because they have greater historical, argumentative, institutional, and normative support—social rights still encounter, here and there, institutional resistance and precarity in regard to producing their effects.

Furthermore, the renewed understanding of the rules that make up the legal order, which identifies the non-absolute character of principles, implying the impossibility of an anticipated prevalence for specific situations,[17] also leads to the recognition that they may be restricted.[18] Constitutional rules addressing fundamental rights are generally subject to some process of specification or a greater or lesser restriction, respecting the essential core, through normative formulations. It is thus possible to deduce the limited usefulness of differentiating between rules for fundamental rights that may or may not be restricted.[19]

Another important facet to be considered in terms of fundamental rights concerns their cost. The identification of rules with limited effectiveness—asserting that they would require positive action by the state, which would entail expenditures—has been reformulated in the sense that even the most elementary rights, which are imagined as not involving state intervention, require—even if indirectly—some type of public spending.[20]

As a result, rather than seeking to reduce the potential achievement of fundamental rights, particularly social rights, other effects arising from those rights have been targeted, such as a) horizontal effects, which concern relations between individuals; b) the effects of protection rights, which include constitutional remedies to guarantee behaviors intended to preserve the sphere of freedoms as well as the possible correction to be made through the dimension of equality; and c) the effects arising from rights to procedures, affirming their necessity not only as instruments of constitutionalism and means of limiting power but also as a guarantee, recognizing that it is impossible to preserve fundamental rights without a set of procedures that guarantee, for example, democracy itself.[21]

REVISIONS AND NEW PATHS

Having concluded the affirmation of rights and the recognition of the necessary constitutionalization of all legal disciplines, the dilemmas no longer concern only effectiveness but also the limits of the judiciary in the achievement of fundamental rights.

Judiciary Between Deference and Intervention

The new era in the theory of effectiveness now involves questioning its epistemological foundations, following the emergence of possible excesses resulting from jurisdictional activity.[22] Although its main foundations—related to the process of achieving fundamental rights—had not been modified, they needed to be reexamined in light of new historical and conceptual frameworks.

Perhaps the judiciary might take on a more modest role, once it is acknowledged that rights must also be guaranteed by the other branches, which are sometimes more in touch with the social reality and have democratic legitimacy. It is important to recognize that there have been a growing number of objections to possible excesses in judicial decisions in recent years.[23]

The different and related phenomena of the judicialization of politics and judicial activism have become commonplace in critiques regarding the stance of judges in rulings on controversial cases, for example, the important considerations raised by Oscar Vilhena Vieira, who indicated that one reason for *Supremocracy* was the architecture of the Brazilian constitution, which, in a singular manner, ended up giving the STF broad powers as a constitutional guardian; it has the role of a constitutional court but is also a specialized judicial forum and a court of last resort.[24]

Those considerations, along with others on the judicialization of public policies,[25] have led to intense reflections on fundamental rights, in particular, considerations focused on studying the institutional design established in the Federal Constitution and the challenges in the processes intended to achieve those rights.

The judicialization of politics in our reality must therefore be treated as a historical phenomenon, resulting from the institutional structure designed by the constituent assembly, which in turn made it possible to channel demands repressed in society during the dictatorship into the constitutional text.[26] As a result, there is a great profusion of rules in the Brazilian constitutional text, while the principles largely reside in Titles I and II, in the part concerning the "reserve of justice," which addresses fundamental rights.[27]

Before the 1988 Federal Constitution, the most common form of Brazilian judicial review was diffuse; from that moment on, abstract review became more prominent. That is a consequence of the provision of new actions that trigger review in theory, an increase in the list of legitimate assets and the provision of mechanisms that enhance abstract review.

Constitutional jurisdiction in Brazil must therefore seek a difficult balance between the separation of powers and the STF's need to uphold the Constitution.[28] As noted above, the Constitution has an expansive nature, which implies a broader scope for the STF's activity as a "constitutional guardian."[29]

In Brazil, there has been a gradual bringing together of the US model, which prefers diffuse judicial review,[30] and the European model,[31] which emphasizes concentrated review operated by a constitutional court. The STF, contemporaneously, despite favorable declarations in this direction, has not yet taken on the role of a true body restricted to "guarding the Constitution," or a constitutional court.[32]

There is thus convergence between the diffuse-incidental and concentrated-primary forms of review. Ultimately, both are oriented towards the protection of substantive rights referenced in the fundamental rights established in the Constitution. It can therefore be argued that abstract review is not limited to defending the objective constitutional order.[33]

There are thus no doubts about the gradual strengthening of the judiciary, particularly the STF, following the democratic stabilization of Brazil. That observation does not attempt to divert attention to the eminently agonistic, adversarial aspect that characterizes democracy.[34] In contrast, the stabilization and constancy of a certain set of elementary processes guaranteeing democracy during the last two decades resulted in a deepening of political discussions and the inclusion of new problems for deliberation in the public arena. However, despite the constitutional commitment to representative democracy and the role of the legislature, the inertia of the latter on certain occasions ends up leaving power vacuums that are filled by the judiciary, to such an extent that some justifications for judicial activism are woven around the omissions of the other branches.[35]

That reality, which has recently seen progressives defending other spaces for legal production beyond the Court, implies the return of the unending problem of judicial review. Given the counter-majoritarian difficulty,[36] is it more productive to defend only one of the different forms of democracy and abandon constitutionalism or, alternatively, to confront the tension between them, defending the need for a commitment?

In our reality, it is not possible—given the role assigned to the STF by the Constitution—nor would it be desirable for the judiciary to be purely deferential to the other branches. Such an arrangement would reduce the judiciary to playing a formal and symbolic role in Brazil's institutional design and would have direct implications for the protection of fundamental rights. As a result, the practice of institutional dialogue has gained momentum as a way of easing tensions and forming dialogic spaces for resolving conflicts, which—as is widely recognized—cannot be limited to decisions by one branch alone, particularly given the multifaceted nature of fundamental rights.[37]

Considering the institutional complexity involved in the achievement of fundamental rights, new theoretical approaches began to indicate other paths that would need to be followed in the attempt to implement the fundamental axioms of the Brazilian Republic. Without abandoning the guidelines that had previously been established in the sense of guaranteeing the normative force of the constitutional provisions, the dangers of focusing exclusively on one of the branches began to be identified, in cases of both commissive acts violating fundamental rights and omissive acts with the same outcome.[38]

Unconstitutional State of Affairs?

An omission by the state that violates fundamental rights, specifically, took on greater prominence following the STF's declaration in ADPF n. 347, which recognized the ECI in a preliminary ruling, based on the systemic violation of fundamental rights that occurs in the Brazilian penitentiary system.[39]

At this point, it is necessary to ask whether the ECI would justify a continuation—with noteworthy technical refinements—of the developments of the doctrine of effectiveness.

At first glance, the grounds of the ECI bear a similarity to the assumptions that had been made by the doctrine of effectiveness. However, the technical sophistication—the instrumental refinement of the ECI—is laudable but with due precautions to not commit the excesses already alleged in terms of judicial activism.[40] Thus, while the set of internal procedures for identifying systematic violations of fundamental rights and pursuing an institutional solution requires an intricate network of active and deferential stances by the judiciary, nothing would prevent it from taking on greater significance and being used as a mechanism to replace the other constitutional bodies. In that scenario, the ECI would become a justification for paternalistic actions by the judiciary when there are omissions by the other branches.

It is essential, however, to move beyond concerns about the risk of trivializing the ECI. A closer examination indicates that it cannot be used as a generic mechanism for any problem that may exist in the social environment; it requires the massive violation of fundamental rights, which is the result of structural flaws.

The Constitutional Court of Colombia pioneered the recognition of the "unconstitutional state of affairs," which involved adopting structural measures to combat those factual circumstances.[41] To remedy omissions by the state, such as the insufficient production of public policies, the Court sought to base the use of that concept on the achievement of constitutional values, with the intention of guaranteeing the constitutional project: "The concern is with the effectiveness of fundamental rights, with the insufficient protection of rights regardless of the normative typologies of the constitutional provisions involved."[42] It is therefore a measure that may intensify the judicialization of politics.[43]

Nonetheless, this does not involve any prevarication; the ECI is a concept grounded in recurrent activism (the Colombian Constitutional Court),[44] and based on early signs, it will become yet another argument for the STF to adopt an active stance when it understands that the factual situation demands judicial intervention to correct it.

Moreover, it belongs to a field that is still being developed in Brazil: structural decisions. Inspired by structural injunctions, formulated in the United States, structural decisions aim to go beyond the binary logic—the foundation of traditional procedural law—and seek to solve collective issues, using gradual responses and measures, which are intended to guide a *state of affairs* in the future, identifying that there is a systemic problem beyond the case presented.[45]

Within the scope of infra-constitutional procedural law, for example, it is understood that a pecuniary fine has a limited spectrum for impeding the continued violation of the rights in question. This occurs, among other reasons, because of the way the state internalizes its costs but specifically because of the greater capacity for institutional remedies in terms of awarding or not awarding injunctive relief and structural injunctions.

As Juliana Pondé Fonseca explains:

> Structural injunctions, in turn, reform an institution in order to prevent it from continuing to violate citizens' rights, in reality comprising a series of complex decisions that may last for many years—decades even (*Brown* was closed in 1999). In addition to the phase when the measure is issued, there is an implementation phase, in which the judge assesses compliance with the orders and adapts them if necessary. A structural measure therefore involves cycles of supplementary orders. In each cycle, the orders become more specific.[46]

The establishment of structural reform often depends on the creation of an ad hoc committee formed by groups of people who have had their rights violated, the parties' lawyers, public agents involved in the institutions that cause the violation of rights, as well as people with specific technical knowledge on the subject. To that end, agreements are signed to implement the structural reforms (consent decrees).[47]

An important aspect in structural reforms is that although they have not become widespread, there are—albeit tentative—initiatives prior to the ECI that have already been adopted in Brazil.[48] In the field of public-interest civil action, steps have been established for correcting rights violations, along the lines of what—in the case of the ECI—ends up being implemented on an exponential scale.

The "unconstitutional state of affairs" should not be confused with unconstitutional omissions that can be combated through Direct Action of Unconstitutionality (*Ação Direta de Inconstitucionalidade – ADI*) by Omission. The ADI by Omission is filed when there is a demonstration of normative omissions by both the legislature and the executive, providing a remedy for the "inertia of the public authorities as regards the issuing of normative acts and the implementation of measures of a predominantly legal nature."[49]

In the case of the ECI, the objective is much more ambitious, involving the factual recognition of a certain "state of affairs" and the adoption of a set of measures—both material and legal—that could disrupt the continued violation of rights.[50] Thus, within the context of the STF, the unconstitutional state of affairs will demand the filing of a Claim of Non-Compliance with a Fundamental Precept (*Arguição de Descumprimento de Preceito Fundamental – ADPF*).

The difference in relation to Colombia is that the ECI seems to have been designed by the jurisprudence of the court to resolve the collective procedural void in that country. In Brazil, however, there is a strong tradition of defending fundamental rights, particularly diffuse and collective rights, through collective actions, particularly public-interest civil actions. As a result, for us, the "unconstitutional state of affairs" within the context of the STF, will take on a particular configuration, which is different from that found in Colombia.

Faced with a paternalistic or authoritarian provision, granting little deference to the other branches, the STF's action in cases that involve recognizing an unconstitutional state of affairs should be oriented towards institutional dialogue. Incidentally, the need for dialogue seems to be one of the most laudable aspects guiding the set of procedures that make up the ECI.[51] This indicates that a heroic and solitary activity by the judiciary is insufficient for repairing the violation of fundamental rights.[52]

In short, it is clear that the dilemmas concerning the efficacy of fundamental rights are becoming increasingly complex as time goes by and that this is not only the moment to acknowledge *what should be done* but also to determine *how to do it*, proposing—if the functional organization of the state and the democratic and republican postulates are respected—an appropriate way to achieve the constitutional promises, particularly in hard cases involving differing and legitimate conceptions of a dignified life or challenges requiring structural solutions.[53]

FINAL CONSIDERATIONS

There has thus been a clear shift over the past few decades in Brazil, from a situation where the judiciary failed to act in terms of its important role in determining the institutional paths of the state to a situation where it is a fundamental actor—with the duty to protect fundamental rights—that now finds the boundaries of its activity under discussion.

While in the past, constitutional supervision was thought about in the limited terms of controlling the normative, commissive or omissive actions of the state, it is impossible to deny that there has been a change in the meaning of the analyses, to incorporate factual matters requiring structural decisions.[54] Two aspects can therefore be linked to the ECI.

First, there is a positive aspect, as the STF, in the case of the ECI, "took responsibility" for factual matters. While the Court is indeed responsible for condemning the inaction of the other branches, particularly in terms of developing appropriate public policies and assessing their actions and results using objective indicators, judicial intervention cannot attempt to replace the other branches in the execution of tasks. In this regard, institutional dialogue can be very useful.

The ECI may—if it is used properly—become a surplus instrument, occasionally used in cases where the violation of fundamental rights is systemic. Unlike in Colombia, where the ECI was created, Brazil already has other remedies that can be used to develop structural decisions capable of offering appropriate solutions outside the context of the STF. Nonetheless, it is also possible that activist measures, which are difficult to justify in terms of their democratic legitimacy, may be adopted.

It must be acknowledged, however, that the first case brought before the STF, which questioned the state of affairs in Brazilian prisons, may recommend more active measures by the Court, due to its exceptional nature. This is because it involves both systemic violations of fundamental rights declared in the constitutional document and recurrent cases of simple—albeit unjustifiable and serious—illegality, arising from the recurrent failure to comply with the current legislation on the execution of the sentence.

As noted by the rapporteur in the case, Justice Marco Aurélio, there would be a lack of institutional coordination in which the responsibility for the unconstitutional state of affairs could not be attributed solely to one branch, in the sense of formulating and implementing public policies but also applying and interpreting criminal law. Structural omissions could be identified in the judiciary, with the temporary custody of prisoners, and in the other branches, in terms of effective administrative, legislative, and budgetary formulas. This ultimately involved repeated violations of rights and the deterioration and continuation of the situation in the prison system.

There is an issue that deserves consideration: even problems in the prison system—such as overcrowding—do not appear to be solved only by recognizing the unconstitutional state of affairs. There is a serious risk that if the judiciary adopts the ECI in a less careful manner, it will lose its legitimacy to act as a provocateur for the other branches, given future confirmation of the ineffectiveness of its measures. The alternative must be to continue monitoring, extending, and periodically assessing the measures, as well as, of course, maintaining the spaces for deliberation.[55]

Criticism aimed at activism will also be directed at the ECI. This is not an attempt to dismiss the importance of structural injunctions in Brazil. As observed above, structural injunctions result from overcoming binary procedural logic and understanding the inadequacy of conventional decisions. The question is how structural decisions will be handled in the judiciary, particularly in the STF, once a systemic violation of fundamental rights is recognized.

The struggle to achieve fundamental rights has clearly advanced. With new challenges and the intensification of institutional debates, there is still much to be done, particularly in terms of adjusting the roles of the branches. In any case, it is important to remember that the responsibility for achieving fundamental rights cannot be entrusted to only one of them.

NOTES

1. On this topic, see: Clèmerson Merlin Clève, *Para uma dogmática constitucional emancipatória* (Belo Horizonte: Fórum, 2012); Luís Roberto Barroso, *Interpretação e aplicação da Constituição: Fundamentos de uma dogmática constitucional transformadora* (São Paulo: Saraiva, 2009).

2. Luís Roberto Barroso, "Da Falta de Efetividade à Judicialização Excessiva: Direito à Saúde, Fornecimento Gratuito de Medicamentos e Parâmetros para a Atuação Judicial," in *Direitos Sociais: fundamentos, judicialização e direitos sociais em espécie*, ed. Cláudio Pereira Souza Neto and Daniel Sarmento (Rio de Janeiro: Lumen Juris, 2008), 877.

3. "If subjective rights are understood as legal positions and relations in the sense presented above, it is possible to distinguish between (a) reasons for subjective rights, (b) subjective rights as legal positions and relations and (c) the legal enforceability of subjective rights." Robert Alexy, *Teoría de los Derechos Fundamentales*, trans. Ernesto Garzón Valdés (Madrid: Centro de Estudios Constitucionales, 1993), 178.

4. On the topic, Luis Roberto Barroso explained: "The theory of effectiveness, which has been crucial to the scientific affirmation of constitutional law for the last ten years, uses a concept traditionally explored in the field of private law but that is actually part of the general theory of law: the *subjective right*. A subjective right, in short, means the power to act, based on the objective right, and is intended to satisfy an interest. More relevant for the purposes here are the essential characteristics of subjective rights, namely a) it always corresponds to a *legal obligation* by another; b) it is *inviolable*, i.e., there may be a situation when the party who had the legal obligation to render a certain service does not do so; and c) if the legal obligation is violated, its holder now has a *claim* and can use the coercive and punitive mechanisms of the state, notably through a lawsuit." Luís Roberto Barroso, *Temas de Direito Constitucional* (Rio de Janeiro: Renovar, 2001), 83–84.

5. According to Cláudio Pereira de Souza Neto and Daniel Sarmento: "It is now understood that the plane of effectiveness and the plane of grounds must not only be complementary but also interrelated. This is intended to establish material—and not solely formal—criteria linked to the text, in order to affirm the effectiveness of the Constitution." Cláudio Pereira Souza Neto and Daniel Sarmento, *Direito constitucional: História e métodos de trabalho* (Belo Horizonte: Fórum, 2012), 200.

6. Clève, *Para uma dogmática constitucional emancipatória*, 20.

7. José Joaquim Gomes Canotilho, *Estudos sobre direitos fundamentais* (São Paulo: RT; Coimbra: Coimbra Editora, 2008), 30–31.

8. "Consider the following starting points: (1) direct applicability does not mean that the rules protecting rights, freedoms and guarantees are *subjective rights*, in the classic sense of absolute rights, but (2) in any case, they give the individual the *right* to invoke these rights-granting rules, and in this sense, fundamental rights usually convey subjective rights; (3) direct applicability does not preclude a sufficient degree of determinability, i.e., legal-constitutional content, which defines the scope of protection of a fundamental right and its legal effects, as well as the fundamental dimensions of the restrictions necessary to harmonize conflicting rights." Canotilho, *Estudos sobre direitos fundamentais*, 146–147.

9. "Effectiveness therefore means the implementation of the law, the concrete achievement of its social function. It represents the creation—in the world of facts—of legal precepts and symbolizes the convergence—as intimate as possible—between the normative *should be* and the *is* of the social reality." Barroso, *Interpretação e aplicação da Constituição*, 254–255.

10. Luís Roberto Barroso, *Temas de Direito Constitucional* (Rio de Janeiro: Renovar, 2001), 83.

11. "The normative data of the constitution—not just any constitution, but a Fundamental Law such as the Constitution of 1988—must be strengthened by a democratic and emancipatory constitutional dogma. If the constitution normatively enshrines values essential to the exercise of citizenship, nothing is more important than the (political, yes, but also) legal pursuit of its affirmation (achievement, implementation, application). *How* to draft this, legally, is a task for a new constitutional dogma, the challenge of which is to make the constitution a synthesis of comprehensive rule-making. One cannot run the risk of making it a *normative constitution* in the section that addresses the interests of the hegemonic classes and a *nominal constitution* in the section that addresses the interests of the classes seeking emancipation." Clèmerson Merlin Clève, *A Fiscalização Abstrata da Constitucionalidade no Direito Brasileiro*, (São Paulo: RT, 2000), 312.

12. Ingo Wolfgang Sarlet, Luiz Guilherme Marinoni and Daniel Mitidiero, *Curso de Direito Constitucional* (São Paulo: RT, 2012), 299. In other terms: "Fundamental rights, as human rights posited in a given constitution, are polymorphic, endowed with core content conducive to openness and variation, only revealed in specific cases and in interactions between them or when they are related to other values enshrined in the constitutional text. The rules of a fundamental right are endowed with a considerable degree of openness and dynamism when they are presented for their social achievement." Clèmerson Merlin Clève, *Temas de Direito Constitucional* (Belo Horizonte: Fórum, 2014), 27.

13. "It has twice been shown that the *individual* is fundamentally dependent on state measures, institutions, distributions and redistributions and that their freedom has social and governmental conditions that they themselves cannot ensure. Rather than the fiction of the autocratic individual in bourgeois society, what has emerged is the image of an individual who is both needed and responsible in the social community. The idea that the state of law could, as a liberal state, intervene as little as possible in the freedom of the individual was coupled with the idea that, as a social state, it first had to *create and ensure the conditions of freedom*." Bodo Pieroth and

Bernhard Schlink, *Direitos Fundamentais*, trans. António Francisco de Sousa and António Franco (São Paulo: Saraiva, 2012), 68.

14. Ingo Wolfgang Sarlet, "Os direitos sociais como direitos fundamentais: seu conteúdo, eficácia e efetividade no atual marco jurídico-constitucional brasileiro," in *Direitos Fundamentais e estado constitucional: estudos em homenagem a J. J. Gomes Canotilho*, ed. George Salomão Leite and Ingo Wolfgang Sarlet (São Paulo: Revista dos Tribunais; Coimbra: Coimbra Editora, 2009), 215.

15. "Social rights (whether or not they are considered fundamental) also encompass both social (positive) and defensive (negative) rights, based here on the criterion of the nature of the legal-subjective position recognized for the rights-holder as well as the circumstance that negative rights (notably the rights to non-intervention in personal freedom and the fundamental goods protected by the Constitution) have a 'positive' dimension (as their implementation calls for positive action by the state and society), whereas rights to benefits (positive) also underlie 'negative' subjective positions, particularly when they are protected from undue interference from state bodies but also from social organizations and individuals." Sarlet, "Os direitos sociais como direitos fundamentais: Seu conteúdo, eficácia e efetividade no atual marco jurídico-constitucional brasileiro," 218.

16. "Conversely, the recognition of a substantially uniform legal system (particularly as regards material openness, direct applicability and protection) for all fundamental rights reveals that there is no need to speak about a distinct treatment of social rights, in the sense that they are subject—in general—to a different and less robust legal system than other fundamental rights, in particular civil and political rights." Sarlet, "Os direitos sociais como direitos fundamentais: seu conteúdo, eficácia e efetividade no atual marco jurídico-constitucional brasileiro," 232–233.

17. Konrad Hesse, *Elementos de Direito Constitucional da República Federal da Alemanha*, trans. Luis Afonso Heck (Porto Alegre: Sergio Antonio Fabris, 1998), 62.

18. "Indeed, interpretation is present when resolving conflicts between fundamental rights as a procedure intended to give meaning to the development of a decision rule. In that situation, the weight is placed on the task of balancing the rights that are in a state of tension. The interpretative activity begins with reconstructing and classifying the opposing interests, giving meaning to the decision rule. However, placing that weight encourages a sorting between the facts and the rule, thus providing criteria for obtaining a constitutionally appropriate decision." Clève, *Temas de Direito Constitucional*, 34.

19. Virgílio Afonso Silva, *Direitos Fundamentais*: Conteúdo essencial, restrições e eficácia (São Paulo: Malheiros, 2010), 223.

20. "*Every rule, from that point of view, has limited effectiveness*—but some of them, for extrinsic reasons, have better conditions for producing effects." Silva, *Direitos Fundamentais*, 232. See: Stephen Holmes and Cass Sunstein. *The Cost of Rights: Why Liberty Depends on Taxes* (New York: W. W. Norton & Company, 1999).

21. "1 – The procedure is a system of rules and/or principles; 2 – These rules and principles are intended to achieve a certain result; 3 – The fair conformation of the procedure, within the scope of fundamental rights, allows at least the presumption that the result obtained by observing *iter procediemental* is, with reasonable probability

and to a sufficient extent, appropriate for fundamental rights; 4 – The *right to procedure* implies, fundamentally (1) the right of the legislator to issue certain procedural rules and (2) the right of a judge to interpret and apply the procedural rules and principles in practice." Canotilho, *Estudos sobre direitos fundamentais*, 75–76.

22. "The efficacy of constitutional rules thus requires the role of the jurist and the judiciary (particularly the constitutional court) to be redefined within that complex interplay of forces, insofar as the following paradox arises: *a Constitution rich in rights (individual, collective and social) and a legal-judicial practice that repeatedly (only) denies the application of those rights*." Lenio Luiz Streck, *Jurisdição Constitucional e Hermenêutica* (Rio de Janeiro: Forense, 2004), 15.

23. "In many situations involving social rights, . . . the judiciary can and should intervene. That observation, however, does not make that intervention immune from different objections, particularly when it is excessively invasive into the deliberations of other branches." Luís Roberto Barroso, "Da Falta de Efetividade à Judicialização Excessiva: Direito à Saúde, Fornecimento Gratuito de Medicamentos e Parâmetros para a Atuação Judicial," 891.

24. Oscar Vilhena Vieira, "Supremocracia," *Revista Direito GV* 4, no. 2 (2008): 447.

25. Vanice Regina Lírio do Valle, *Políticas públicas, direitos fundamentais e controle judicial* (Belo Horizonte: Editora Fórum, 2009).

26. "The first major cause of judicialization was the country's *redemocratization*, which culminated in the enactment of the 1988 Constitution. In the last few decades, with the restoration of judicial guarantees, the judiciary has ceased to be a specialized technical department and has become a true political power, capable of enforcing the Constitution and the laws, even when it involves confronting the other branches. . . . The second cause was *comprehensive constitutionalization*, which included countless matters in the Constitution that had previously been left up to the majoritarian political process and to ordinary legislation. . . . The third and final cause of the judicialization, which will be examined here, is the *Brazilian system of judicial review*, one of the most comprehensive in the world." Luís Roberto Barroso, "Judicialização, Ativismo Judicial e Legitimidade Democrática," *Revista de direito do estado* 13 (January/March 2009): 73–74.

27. One example of this lies in the possible dichotomy that can be drawn from the constitutional text, both in the sense of heteronomous philosophical perspectives as well as others that seek to guarantee the greatest autonomy for individuals. Those philosophical perspectives collide in situations involving hard cases (or tragic decisions).

28. Per Conrado Mendes: "In the separation of powers, interaction is inevitable. Deliberative interaction is a gain; purely adversarial interaction—if it is not a loss—wastes its epistemic potential. . . . Judicial review does not need to be seen as solely a dike or a containment barrier but also as a driving mechanism for better deliberations. It not only serves to (try to) protect us from politics when it succumbs to panic or irrationality but also to challenge it to excel in quality." Conrado Hübner Mendes, *Direitos fundamentais, separação de poderes e deliberação* (São Paulo: Saraiva, 2011), 211–212.

29. The normative critique of the STF's role as a "guardian" does not change its structural function, but it is relevant because it points to other forms of institutional interaction, seeking to move beyond the tricky question of the "final word": "The deliberative type of interaction is the ideal that permeates, hence that exercise. It provides a conditioned justification for the STF's role while simultaneously taking it down from its pedestal as a 'guardian.' . . . But it also does not reject the STF's legitimacy to practice strong activism in certain circumstances. This is in line with the concept of the separation of powers outlined in the previous chapter, according to which there are no (and never will be) abstract and preset recipes that exhaust the definition of functions." Mendes, *Direitos fundamentais, separação de poderes e deliberação*, 214.

30. *Marbury v. Madison* (1803).

31. H. Kelsen, *Jurisdição constitucional*, trans. Alexandre Krug (São Paulo: Martins Fontes, 2007).

32. Clèmerson Merlin Clève, *A Fiscalização Abstrata de Constitucionalidade no Direito Brasileiro* (São Paulo: RT, 2000), 413.

33. "The three dimensions analyzed above—legality, constitutionality, fundamental rights—indicate that the principle of the rule of law is informed by two ordering ideas: (1 the idea of subjective ordering, guaranteeing a legal status to individuals that is essentially anchored in fundamental rights, and (2 the idea of objective ordering, based on the principle of constitutionality, which in turn embraces the principle of the separation of powers as an objectively structuring principle. These two dimensions are not divorced from one another, but the stress accent will now fall on the objective functional ordering of the rule of law." J. J. Gomes Canotilho, *Direito Constitucional e Teoria da Constituição* (Coimbra: Almedina, 2003), 250.

34. Chantal Mouffe recalls that democracy is fragile and must constantly be defended. Chantal Mouffe, *El retorno de lo político* (Barcelona: Paidós, 1999).

35. With regard to activism, Carlos Campos notes its multi-dimensionality: "Those decisions have different dimensions rather than solely a single form of expression, which means that judicial activism involves decision-making practices, generally multifaceted, and therefore cannot be reduced to unique identification criteria. There are multiple indicators of judicial activism, such as the expansive interpretation of constitutional texts, the lack of institutional deference to the other branches of the government, the judicial creation of general and abstract rules, etc." Campos, *Dimensões do ativismo judicial do Supremo Tribunal Federal*, 163.

36. Alexander Bickel, *The Least Dangerous Branch: The Supreme Court at the Bar of Politics* (New Haven, CT: Yale University Press, 1986), 16.

37. On institutional dialogue, see: Rodrigo Brandão, *Supremacia Judicial versus Diálogos Constitucionais: A quem cabe a última palavra sobre o sentido da Constituição?* (Rio de Janeiro: Lumen Juris, 2012).

38. "Making the Constitution a comprehensive *Fundamental Law* involves constructing—through constitutional dogma—sufficient categories to account not only for the violation of the Constitution by a normative act but also for noncompliance with it by virtue of an omissive act. It would then be necessary to recognize as unconstitutional any acts—commissive or omissive—that are in violation of the

constitutional rules." Clève, *A Fiscalização Abstrata de Constitucionalidade no Direito Brasileiro*, 312.

39. STF. Plenary Session. ADPF 347 MC/DF, Justice Rapporteur Marco Aurélio, heard on 09.09.2015, Bulletin 798. The ADPF was filed by the Socialism and Liberty Party (*Partido Socialismo e Liberdade-PSOL*), and the hearing concluded on September 9, 2015. Among the eight requests made, two were judged to be well-founded: to hold custody hearings and to cease funding the National Penitentiary Fund (*Fundo Penitenciário Nacional-FUPEN*). In addition, an *ex-officio* injunction was granted by Justice Luís Roberto Barroso, who ordered that a diagnosis be made within one year of the situation for the STF to rule on the merits.

40. In contrast to the ECI, see: Lenio Luiz Streck, "O que é preciso para (não) se conseguir um Habeas Corpus no Brasil," *Conjur*, September 9, 2015, accessed on October 10, 2015, http://www.conjur.com.br/2015-set-24/senso-incomum-preciso-nao-obter-hc-brasil.

41. Carlos Alexandre de Azevedo Campos, "Da Inconstitucionalidade por Omissão ao 'Estado de Coisas Inconstitucional'" (PhD diss., Universidade do Estado do Rio de Janeiro, 2015). The first case of an ECI, in *Sentencia SU.559/97*, addressed the unequal distribution of teachers across regions by the administration. The Court therefore decided to declare "the *state of affairs* that originated the actions for protection that are the subject of this revision are not in accordance with the Political Constitution, for the reasons set forth in this ruling. As the situation described appears to be present in many municipalities, the competent authorities are advised that the *state of affairs* must be corrected within the framework of the functions assigned to them by law, within a reasonable period of time." The following year, the Court addressed a case analogous to one recently heard in Brazil, involving the situation of penitentiaries in *Sentencia T-153/98*, as grounds for declaring the unconstitutional state of affairs of penitentiaries in Colombia. The Court stated: "This Institution has used the concept of the unconstitutional state of affairs in order to seek a remedy for situations involving the violation of fundamental rights of a general nature—insofar as they affect a multitude of people—and whose causes are of a structural nature—in other words, they do not typically originate exclusively in the defendant authority, and therefore, their solution requires joint action by different bodies. Under these conditions, the Court has considered that given that thousands of persons are in the same situation and that if all of them were to resort to the action of protection they could needlessly overwhelm the administration of justice, the most appropriate action is to issue orders to the competent official institutions to use their powers to eliminate this unconstitutional state of affairs." In 2004, it heard the case of associations of "displaced" persons: victims of forced displacement within the country due to the violence of armed conflicts. In *Sentencia T-025/04*, the Colombian Court defined the state of affairs as follows: "The concept of an unconstitutional state of affairs has evolved jurisprudentially since 1997, when it was first declared. In the most recent rulings on this phenomenon, in accordance with the doctrine of this Institution, a state of affairs is unconstitutional when '*(1) there is a recurrent violation of the fundamental rights of many persons—who then have recourse to an action of protection in order to obtain the defense of their rights and thus complete the judicial process—and (2) where*

the cause of that violation is not attributable solely to the defendant authority but is based on structural factors.' Among the factors assessed by the Court for determining whether an unconstitutional state of affairs exists are as follows: (i) the massive and widespread violation of different constitutional rights affecting a significant number of persons; (ii) the prolonged failure of the authorities to fulfill their obligations to guarantee the rights; (ii) the adoption of unconstitutional practices, such as the incorporation of the action of protection as part of the procedure to guarantee the violated right; (iii) the failure to adopt the necessary legislative, administrative or budgetary measures to prevent the violation of the rights; (iv) the existence of a social problem whose solution involves intervention by different bodies, requires the adoption of a complex and coordinated set of actions and necessitates a level of resources that demands a significant additional budgetary effort; and (v) if all the persons affected by the same problem were to resort to the action of protection to obtain the protection of their rights, there would be greater judicial gridlock."

42. Campos, "Da Inconstitucionalidade por Omissão ao 'Estado de Coisas Inconstitucional,'" 209.

43. "The Court has interfered in most of the government's political and economic decisions, justifying the full fairness of social rights, above all because of its 'doctrine of connectedness': the social right must be protected when its violation implies the non-respect of a fundamental right with an immediate application, such as, the right to life." Campos, *Dimensões do ativismo judicial do Supremo Tribunal Federal*, 125.

44. "The main political attacks on the Court were the set of proposals to amend the Constitution in order to expressly eliminate the possibility of this controversial judicial review. But those threats did not materialize, and the Constitutional Court has revived this specific activist judicial stance. . . . The second and most important aspect of the Colombian Constitutional Court's judicial activism has been the practice of achieving fundamental, social and economic rights. The Court has played a fundamental role in advancing the protection and promotion of rights in the country, either by directly protecting those rights or by guiding the legislation and decisions of the lower courts." Campos, *Dimensões do ativismo judicial do Supremo Tribunal Federal*, 124.

45. Owen M. Fiss, "Foreword: The Forms of Justice," *Harvard Law Review* 93 (1979): 1; Sérgio Cruz Arenhart, "Decisões estruturais no direito processual civil brasileiro," *Revista de Processo* 225 (2013): 7.

46. Juliana Pondé Fonseca, "O (des)controle do Estado no Judiciário brasileiro" (PhD diss., Universidade Federal do Paraná, 2015), 206.

47. Fonseca, "O (des)controle do Estado no Judiciário brasileiro," 209.

48. "Structural reform already exists in Brazil. One of the greatest examples is the public-interest civil action involving coal; this action addresses the environmental damage caused by coal mining in Santa Catarina between 1972 and 1989. It was filed in 1993 and is still being executed—a detailed plan for the region's recovery that was prepared by the defendants over the course of six months is now being implemented. The ruling was handed down in 2014, but the long execution (which can be divided into four major phases) began in 2000, following the provisional order. In 2002, a public-interest civil action was filed by the Public Prosecutor's Office of the State

of Rio de Janeiro, seeking to supply medications to low-income individuals. The lawsuit was filed against the state and the municipality, and an initial hearing resulted in an agreement to create a service center to organize the distribution. Finally, in 2014, the Federal Public Prosecutor also filed a public-interest civil action against the Union and the state of Paraná, demanding a plan to end the detention of prisoners in degrading conditions in the Federal Police Precinct of Londrina. The defendants were ordered to draw up a plan to solve the problem and to implement it within eight months." Fonseca, "O (des)controle do Estado no Judiciário brasileiro," 213–214.

49. Clève, *A Fiscalização Abstrata de Constitucionalidade no Direito Brasileiro*, 323.

50. "ADPF 347 is based on the thesis of the 'unconstitutional state of affairs,' originally used by the Colombian Constitutional Court to protect fundamental rights in situations involving a structural violation. Rather than the STF examining the law or the normative act, it is required to rule on the unconstitutionality of a factual situation, created by actions and/or inactions of the public authority. The judiciary is called upon to coordinate a dialogue among the branches to ensure that the factual situation is corrected. This involves thinking about the Constitution beyond its written rules, in order to understand it in its concrete form." Egon Bockmann Moreira and Heloísa Câmara, "Quem pode dar cabo deste estado de coisas?" *Gazeta do Povo*, September 29, 2015, accessed on February 10, 2015, http://www.gazetadopovo.com.br/opiniao/artigos/quem-pode-dar-cabo-deste-estado-de-coisas-2vz9g0a4fd4hj1yjq4pswibpw.

51. "The process for reviewing public policies requires an appropriate procedure with open, consecutive, coordinated and dialogue-based commands, as it seeks to resolve—in coordination with all those involved—a matter of public interest that requires a structural solution and takes place over time." Ada Pellegrini Grinover and Paulo Henrique dos Santos Lucon, "ADPF 347 e o controle judicial de políticas públicas," *Folha de São Paulo*, September 28, 2015, accessed on October 19, 2015, http://www1.folha.uol.com.br/opiniao/2015/09/1686769-adpf-347-e-o-controle-judicial-de-politicas-publicas.shtml.

52. In the case of Colombia, "dialogic activism" was adopted, in which the Court sought to unblock channels of deliberation and coordinate the planning and execution of public policies in the case of displaced persons (*deplazados*). See: César Rodriguez Gravito and Diana Rodriguez Franco, *Cortes y cambio social: como la Corte Constitucional transformo el desplazamiento forzado en Colombia* (Bogotá: Centro de Estudios de Derecho, Justicia y Sociedad, 2010).

53. "The line of action follows this schematic: (a) identification and proof of systematic violations of rights, through inspections, reports, surveys, witnesses, etc. → (b) declaration of the ECI → (c) notification of the ECI to the relevant bodies, particularly those at the top and those responsible for adopting administrative and legislative measures to solve the problem → (d) establishment of a timeframe for presenting a proposed solution, to be developed by the institutions that are directly responsible → (e) presentation of the proposed solution with deadlines and goals to be met → (f) execution of the proposed solution by the institutions involved → (g) monitoring of compliance with the plan by institutions indicated by the judiciary → (h) after the end of the timeframe granted, analysis of compliance with the measures and the resolution of the ECI → (i) if the ECI was not resolved, a new diagnosis, with an attribution

of responsibilities in relation to what was not done → (j) new declaration of an ECI and repetition of the schematic, this time with more intense judicial action." George Marmelstein Lima, "O Estado de Coisas Inconstitucional—ECI: apenas um nova onda do verão constitucional?" *Direitos Fundamentais*, February 10, 2015, accessed on May 10, 2015, http://direitosfundamentais.net/2015/10/02/o-estado-de-coisas-inconstitucional-eci-apenas-uma-nova-onda-do-verao-constitucional/.

54. Owen M. Fiss, "Foreword: The Forms of Justice," *Harvard Law Review* 93 (1979): 1. "The current scenario confirms the 'counterdiagnosis' of this work, which emphasizes that the courts can do little on their own and that the success or failure of the judiciary's attempts to implement rights depends on the context and configuration of other political factors. The fact is that structural reforms continue to motivate the courts and influence jurists all over the world, including in Latin America." Fonseca, "*O (des)controle do Estado no Judiciário brasileiro*," 213.

55. "The judiciary's role in implementing wide-ranging solutions cannot be overestimated. The judiciary has a limited capacity to enforce fundamental rights, particularly when we are faced with important decisions, such as ruling on the cessation of violations of prisoners' rights or achieving economic, social and cultural rights." Lima, "O Estado de Coisas Inconstitucional—ECI: apenas um nova onda do verão constitucional?"

Chapter 5

Notes on Tolerance

Foundations, Distinctions, and Limits

> "The time is out of joint.
> O cursèd spite,
> That ever I was born to set it right!"
>
> —Shakespeare

The closing moments of the second decade of the twenty-first century have led us to the realization that although our society seemed to be on track, it has been thrown out of order. Someone embracing a more skeptical reading of the world will insist that it was a mistake for us to have placed our hopes in rationality, democracy, plurality, tolerance, and justice as the values underpinning our society and that there are not many reasons to be surprised; phenomena such as populism, irrationality, single-mindedness, intolerance, and injustice continue to fill the news every day and to be present in our lives, even if, in the end, we did not have sufficient knowledge about them.

A more optimistic person could use data and point out that we live a better life than our ancestors in a number of areas; although the problems are new and require new tools and techniques to resolve them, the correct path has already been mapped out, and all we have to do is continue along it.

Between those two extreme versions, we understand that the source of surprise is not only the challenges of new technologies and the immeasurable capacity to process information (real and fake)—which could potentially lead to madness, understood here as the inability to process data—but also the fact that a door we had imagined to be closed has now been reopened: the door that reintroduced the possibility of a disrespect for institutions and a rupture of the constitutional order into the Brazilian political grammar as practices for carrying out activities in the political arena.

Reopening this door raises concerns; the unwritten agreements that we thought had been firmly established in the domestic political game were challenged, and we began to observe and—dangerously—grow accustomed to formulating new ways of articulating activities that bear the mark of destruction, converging with a latent death drive, which has become a defining factor of the national political agenda.

It is difficult not to recognize that we are now guided by acts and statements that cause discomfort (*Unbehagen*); they are guided by a mass death drive, mediated by representatives who no longer obscure or are deterred from making political proposals with the explicit aim of carnage, which began to organize life for death, for the undoing of what—until that point—had been understood as the march of culture and civilization, linked to the values present in the redemocratization and reconstruction of the Brazilian political community since 1988.

According to Amin Maalouf, the world has become disordered environmentally, intellectually, financially, geopolitically and ethnically. This is due to retrograde movements that threaten to undo what successive generations have struggled to build.[1] He argues that we are adrift in a ship, lost, with no destination or visibility and that we need something to "shake us up" to avoid a shipwreck.

With the fall of the Berlin Wall and the end of a bipolar world, we entered a world where the divisions are not predominantly ideological but identity-based, with little room for deliberations. Each person proclaims their affiliations to others, mobilizes those around them and demonizes their enemies. The world seems to have chosen a path of "decline," that is, in the direction of belittling values such as universalism, rationality, and secularism, which ultimately had a negative influence on an important element in our social structure: the free debate of ideas.

Given this state of affairs, there is a duty to remember. This is always extremely valuable at times when things seem to be "off course." Disordered times demand a renewal of our commitment to freedom.[2] We therefore have to recognize that forgiveness (*amnesty*) should not be confused with forgetting (*amnesia*) and that there is no mythical past, which can be selectively chosen, to advance the fascist politics of unthinking praise of the nation's glory.[3]

At this point, we would like to recall a concept, extremely precious to liberalism and an important element that, although not stated explicitly in our 1988 Constitution, is present as a reserve of justice, entrenched as a supra-constitutional clause:[4] tolerance. It is expressed in the fundamental objective of the Republic, in terms of the prohibition of prejudice and other forms of discrimination. The connection is evident in the effort to promote the good of all, in a tolerant society with no discrimination, basic aspects of our "minimum consensus,"[5] immune to changes caused by momentary passions.

FOUNDATIONS

One way of referencing liberalism is by referring to its political influence. Not without reason, Judith Shklar warned that liberalism seemed to have completely lost its identity and had become so amorphous that it could serve any purpose. It became essential to insist that liberalism was a political doctrine with the sole purpose of guaranteeing the political conditions necessary for people to exercise their personal freedoms.[6]

From that perspective, liberalism would not be a proactive political doctrine; its sole mandate would be to not interfere in other people's lives. Furthermore, it would not provide any specific guidance on people's ways of life, on who they should be or how they should behave, the lives they should lead or the choices they should make. Shklar argued that liberalism had appeared only rarely in both theory and practice over the past two hundred years; in her 1989 text, she was already warning that those who believed fascism was dead—in one way or another—should think again.[7]

For Shklar, liberalism was a "latecomer," as its origins were in post-Reformation Europe, in the grave tension with Christianity; the cruelties of the religious wars thus led to an important shift in the perspective of many Christians, who began to perceive tolerance as an expression of Christian charity.[8]

While the understanding that people must make ethical decisions about their lives and take responsibility for those decisions lies at the core of liberalism, the principles of tolerance cannot be treated as equivalent to political liberalism; this demand for not only personal autonomy but also its theorization is thus incomplete without any mention of a limited and responsible government.[9]

Liberalism's deepest roots, however, are anchored in the condemnation presented by the first advocates of tolerance, such as John Locke and Pierre Bayle, following the horrors of the religious wars, which led them to the formulation that cruelty was an offense to God and humanity.

Shklar understands that Thomas Hobbes cannot be considered the father of liberalism, for the singular reason that no theory that gives the authorities unconditional power to impose a belief and even a vocabulary can be considered even remotely liberal.[10] Tolerance, in contrast, is presented as limiting public agents and as the factor that will support the line drawn between the public and the private, a separation that is not ironclad but that is fundamental to liberalism.

Shklar's liberalism warns us that we must always repudiate abuses of power, in any regime, and be concerned about the excesses of public agents at all levels of government; those who are likely to suffer most from those measures are precisely the most vulnerable: the weak and the poor.[11] Government agents will behave in that manner—more or less blatantly—unless they are prevented from doing so. A limited government is thus a necessary but insufficient condition for political liberalism.

Locke's legacy for liberalism is the idea that governments—with their enormous powers to kill, maim, wage war, and indoctrinate—should not be trusted unconditionally and that any trust that might be developed in their agents must be guided by skepticism.[12] In that perspective, even mistakes made by people who hold other opinions should be tolerated, as long as they do not revert to perpetrating domination over others.

One of Locke's central concerns is thus the separation between the functions of the civil government and religion. Religion should not be a matter for the state, as the government was not an appropriate instrument for saving souls. Matters of faith and affairs of state would, according to his interpretation, be perfectly distinct and infinitely different, such that the difference between people's religions would not allow someone to take away someone else's goods or their freedom.[13]

However, that was not all; it would not be enough for people of one religion to refrain from violence and all forms of persecution against others. Those who longed to be a "successor of the apostles" should teach the duties of peace and good will to all people, including those who "err" and those who differ in faith and worship.[14] In Locke's view, pagans, Muslims, and Jews should therefore not have their rights taken away because of their religion, as that was not stipulated in the Gospel, and civil society should embrace—in an indiscriminate manner—all those who are peaceful, honest, and hardworking.[15]

His tolerance did not extend, however, to atheists; those who deny the existence of God would not be able to make commitments and promises, activities considered fundamental to the whole of human society.[16] Nor should tolerance extend to Roman Catholics, who adopted destructive doctrines of the society in which they lived and were subordinate only to the Pope. They should therefore not be tolerated, unless it were guaranteed that those dangerous opinions would be separated from their religious worship, which would be very difficult to accomplish.[17]

For Locke, tolerance of Jews, Muslims, and pagans is categorical, although he hopes that they will convert. On this point, there is a particular concern regarding the procedure for that conversion; in contrast to the violent means observed in his time, he understood that charity and kindness towards different opinions would be the central factors of Christian unity and would contribute more to conversion than confusion and discussions about the union of Christians.[18]

Religion should be adopted in people's hearts, and thus charity would be central to faith, which would be derived from love rather than force. Based on this, Locke "appeals" to the conscience of those who persecute, torment, destroy, and kill others because of their religion, questioning whether they do so in the name of friendship and kindness towards them, as it would be contrary to the principles of charity and love to practice cruelties and take another person's life due to religion.[19]

Persecution would be extremely inefficient; coercion could not, as a rule, achieve the objective of bringing people together around a belief. Violent conversion practices would be more opposed to the glory of God than any dissent, insofar as those who are cruel to people with different opinions would not be promoting the values of the Church.[20]

Conversation and peace would be the appropriate means for engaging with difference, while instruments of force such as the "sword" were rejected as being inconsistent with the Gospel. Tolerance as a value would therefore be similar to the true "reason of humanity," such that it seemed monstrous to Locke that people did not understand its benefit and necessity. It would thus be impossible to settle disputes between those who genuinely have an interest in the salvation of souls and in the safety of the community.[21] The function of society would be to preserve the betterment of the civil goods of its members, and therefore, even if someone so desired, no one could be granted the power to impose their beliefs on others; faith would be a private activity and should be immune from the violence expressed in the public sphere.

Everyone would have the right to try to convince others of their reasons, persuading them through arguments. The judge, however, would be responsible for enforcing "with the sword," and civil law would not be appropriate for prescribing articles of faith. If penalties were not attached to them, the force of laws would disappear, and even if penalties were created for that behavior, they would clearly be inadequate, as they would lead to the error of forcing people to adopt a religion in which they do not believe. The tolerance in question is primarily religious tolerance, although what was said about it could be expanded to political forms and other types of tolerance.

As Luís Roberto Barroso explains: "The sixteenth century was marked by the effects of the Reformation and the reception of Luther and Calvin's ideas; it became the stage for a long and violent period of conflict between Catholics and Protestants. Henry IV's ascension to the French throne in 1594, following his conversion to Catholicism, ushered in a phase of religious tolerance."[22] In 1598, Henry IV issued the Edict of Nantes, which granted equal political rights to Protestants.

Another question is whether someone who has sincere beliefs and is perceived to be in "error" should be forced to change his or her position. For Bayle, in the case of an "error of conscience," coercion—even understood to be in the individual's interest—was not justified.[23] The relevance of that question in the context in which the author lived, pervaded by persecutions of the Huguenots (French Protestants persecuted by Louis XIV, as in the case of the Edict of Fontainbleu of 1685, which ordered the destruction of Huguenot churches and the closure of Protestant schools) was fundamental.

For liberalism, the use of coercive means and threats to prevent the spread of ideas with which we disagree is a moral issue. In Bayle's time, many Christians believed that God had ordered the use of violence to prevent the spread of "religious error," and even outside the religious realm, it seemed natural to prevent the spread of dangerous ideas through the use of force, if that were the most effective means. However, for liberal thought, even if it eventually becomes the most effective means, it is morally wrong.

In the late seventeenth century, Bayle presented a broad defense of religious tolerance that can be understood as a defense of different beliefs and political practices. He writes in opposition to the perspective of St. Augustine, for whom the use of force as a tool for conversion would be an acceptable practice.

Augustine relied on his interpretation of a passage from the Bible, more specifically Luke 14:23, in which the use of force was permitted to compel people to participate in a banquet of the Kingdom of God; several guests had previously given excuses for not attending the event.

The Augustinian objective was the conversion of the Donatists, against whom violence could be used as a "disciplinarian" form; the purpose of conversion was not their (physical) destruction but their re-education, that they might be saved from their own "error"[24] by saving what was truly most important: their souls.

Augustine argued that Christians had an obligation to compel people of other religions and heretics into believing, while also understanding that the use of violence was a possible method for "opening up" recalcitrant people to the truth of Catholicism. The use of violence against heretics for the purpose of "opening their eyes" to the truth was not only admissible but—in some cases—mandatory behavior.

Bayle criticized Augustine's argument against tolerance for two reasons: first, he asserted on an interpretative level that Augustine's literal interpretation of the gospels ran counter to the spirit of the Bible; second, that coercion in religious matters was neither useful in practical terms nor acceptable in the moral sphere.

Bayle thus suggests the following experiment: let us suppose, for a moment, that the Church of Rome is the true Church. We must then examine the results of compulsory conversion to it, as in the case of the Edicts of the King of France. What would the consequences have been? Bayle answers that the removal of Protestants' rights has only resulted in an increase in religious fervor, more than ever before.[25] He goes on to say that if a Protestant prince eventually did the same to Roman Catholic subjects, they would become more devoted to the Pope, just as "Turks" would become more obstinate in "Mohammedanism" and Jews in Judaism.[26]

From that perspective, persecution would have the potential to ignite passions rather than encourage proper conversion; if people fear being tortured, they will not suddenly become aware of a particular idea. In this respect, the conscious has a crucial role. This is because decisions must be made according to people's conscious; they have an obligation to themselves and to God to follow them, even in cases where they are wrong.[27] That "error" makes the projection of the connection established by the conscience more prevalent, such that it does not depend on factual truthfulness.

Thus, if it were permitted by law that those who hold an opinion that they believe to be right may coerce those who are wrong through the use of force, this would create a number of problems; that right would be abused by everyone, even those who hold wrong opinions—they would be influenced by the truthfulness of their beliefs, which would authorize them—in the same manner—to use coactive power to affirm them.

Bayle also asserts that people should not interfere with certain behaviors by others, for that interference would be morally wrong, and not only because it has unwanted consequences for those who experience the interference. Tolerant people would therefore have an aprioristic moral reason for not interfering in other people's lives.

An argument that was widely used to defend an official religion was that it would bring stability to the government. In addition to Locke's reasons and the importance of the separation between state and religion, advocates of intolerance could raise a number of grievances stemming from disagreement over religious plurality. Bayle, for his part, stated that there would be no danger in religious tolerance by governments, as the danger would instead be that different religions would seek to destroy one another through methods of persecution.[28]

In that scenario, we would have a game that everyone loses, in which one religion would have the ability to coerce others using state power. Consequently, those who advocated for intolerance would have to consider the foreseeable losses that were associated with their perspective.

At the historic moment in which Bayle was living, intolerance included brutal acts of violence, such as punishment with fire, banishment, imprisonment in dungeons and quartering. Coercion in religious matters would make the practice of intolerance inherently problematic. The moral reason advocated by Bayle was thus the following: because it is predictable that the command to not tolerate will result in crimes, the command to not tolerate other religions would be immoral.[29]

DISTINCTIONS

For Ira Katznelson, tolerance is a deeply important concept because it concerns the most complicated and persistent characteristics of human relations.[30] Its importance can be observed among groups who understand that plurality is integral to them and that they must develop skills to live in a community. As an alternative to oppression, suffering, and violence, tolerance emerges in situations where respect, cooperation, and social peace are difficult to achieve.[31]

For this to occur, there is a liberal assumption at the very core of social relations: the idea that people should be free to make ethical decisions as they see fit, in order to pursue their understanding of a good life, as long as it does not involve the violation of rights.

This idea is thus projected into a society potentially teeming with different forms of conflict, dissension, and controversy; what is desired is the coexistence of social practices and beliefs that are not widely accepted by all and that deserve to be accommodated (i.e., circumstances should be established that make them possible and reasons should be given to make them desirable).[32]

Forms and strategies for producing and reproducing tolerance are plural. It is therefore important to draw conceptual distinctions. Tolerance should not be confused with indifference; it requires an intentional decision to allow groups, practices, and beliefs considered repugnant to continue to exist.[33] Tolerance is necessary when certain expressions generate more than mere discomfort or antipathy; being tolerant thus requires that we do not react to behaviors that embarrass us, outrage us, or fill us with disgust.

Those forms of intentional omission, deliberate silence, or self-restraint posit that a community should be shared by people with different visions of the world. To that end, in the political sphere, the deliberative arena must be organized with spaces for the entry of otherness. Tolerance thus works with the material substrate that at least one group perceives the ideas and actions of another group of people as inappropriate, and it is therefore a question of patience with the other(s).

Katznelson argues that tolerance does not necessarily conflict with the capacity to not tolerate (i.e., to reject intolerance). While tolerance constrains the activities of those who are able to repress others, it does not require that the beliefs motivating the aversion to those behaviors be abandoned.[34]

There is also a recognition that historical contingencies exist in situations that require tolerance. This can be interpreted as an act of self-denial, for example, of group A deciding not to harm group B, even though it has the power to do so. Similarly, tolerance can be an interrogative category in which people will question what should be done in different cases. Prior to the Reformation, questions about tolerance were primarily religious, while after the Reformation, they were transferred to the political arena. As a result, when that transfer occurred, tolerance increased, becoming deeper, taking on the status of moral virtue. In this guise, it was eventually translated into the legal sphere, as seen in a number of normative documents, such as our own Constitution of 1988.

Furthermore, it is important to differentiate between tolerance (religious or secular) and simple patience or indulgence. While tolerance involves an act of willingness to tolerate, a decision to allow the physical presence of others from different cultures, patience concerns a limited circumstance in which others are treated in a tolerant manner temporarily; they are allowed, for example, to access certain material goods or humanitarian aid. Those differences are important because they concern the possibility of access to rights and belonging (in the sense of citizenship) to the community, which are not subject to the restrictions of patience, although patience may be a starting point for broadening more sophisticated forms of recognizing and guaranteeing rights.

For that reason, a lack of appreciation for the broad spectrum of ways of life within a community can produce a potential trap. This is because the diversity of ways of life can lead to high value being placed on decisions that give greater prominence to the community than to the individual. It is thus essential to consider multiculturalism, as well as the shortcomings of the Western concept of tolerance.

In Western cultures, tolerance has become confused with freedom of conscience, to such the extent that in our Constitution of 1988, in Article 5, VI, freedom of belief appears alongside freedom of conscience. Then, the impossibility of denying rights because of religious belief appears in Article 5, VIII, a provision that allows people to embrace, spread, change, or renounce a certain religion. Along those lines, Barroso stated: "I believe, ultimately, in tolerance. The world is characterized by pluralism and diversity: racial, sexual, religious, political. The truth has no master, and there is no single formula for a good life."[35]

Will Kymlicka explains that in addition to the model based on freedom of conscience, there is a second perspective on tolerance that is grounded in the idea of the rights of groups, rather than individual freedom.[36] The idea of group rights has become a latent issue in many democracies, as ethnic or religious groups have come to demand the power to restrict the freedom of their own members as a way to preserve their traditional practices.[37]

The problem in those cases lies in a certain ambiguity: while the groups seek protection from potential external oppression to maintain their practices, they want to be free to repress the internal dissent of the group without having to answer for it,[38] in terms of the legal protection of individualized fundamental rights.

What alternatives exist for that problem? From a liberal perspective, fundamental rights could answer those questions. One path might be constructed through the right to education, enabling children to learn about different opinions, cultures, histories, religions, and societies, as well as to develop the capacity for critical reflection about reality. Another path might be traced through the right to freedom of expression and information, allowing the circulation of plural knowledge in a democratic society, and would work with the fundamental right to education in a complementary way, helping people make decisions about all areas of their lives, including what kind of life they would like to live.

It is not surprising that those two fundamental rights are often lacking in authoritarian countries and that they can also serve as barriers for preventing sporadic anti-democratic upheavals, which unfortunately tend to reappear from time to time in different parts of the world.

Under the liberal model, granting access to information allows people to review and reflect on their ways of life, and guaranteeing education empowers people to learn how to judge, determine, and seek the means to guarantee their rights.

Those aspects of a liberal society make sense, according to Kymlicka, if we assume that we have an interest in not only pursuing our conception of an existing good but evaluating and revising those conceptions.[39] Accordingly, people's goals in life do not always deserve to be pursued; the assessment and revision of life plans demands the ability to make informed judgments about what is truly worthwhile.

This shows that tolerance does not strive to acquire the status of an absolute value. It is available in potential competition with other values that people have and wish to achieve. It can be a virtue longed for by many and placed on the list of values shared by a democratic society, but it can also be retracted and strained by its limits, in the presence of intolerant and profoundly aversive expressions or the spiral of fears and insecurities.

Conversely, Katznelson asserts that when tolerance is reciprocal, it can encourage true cultural, social, and political heterogeneity as well as create possibilities for broader and more welcoming forms of respect and recognition; similar to purgatory, tolerance is a space with paths that lead in more than one direction.[40]

LIMITS

Jürgen Habermas explains that the term *Toleranz* appeared in German later than it did in other languages, borrowed from Latin and French in the sixteenth and seventeenth centuries; the notion of tolerance as tolerance of other religions also emerged during this period, as well as the construction of its legal aspect.[41] In those centuries, governments issued decrees that ordered people to be tolerant of religious minorities. Just as the Portuguese language makes no distinction between religious tolerance and tolerance in the sense of patience, the term *Toleranz* is used in German for the willingness to treat others with generosity but also for the political virtue of dealing with people who are different.[42]

Another element to be considered is the possibility of a conceptual convergence between the universalist foundation of the right to religious freedom and the normative foundations of a democratic rule of law (i.e., one governed by democracy and fundamental rights).[43] That model of the state would thus envision the judiciary as the branch that is capable of distinguishing the abuses of the theocratic order that may violate democratic freedoms.

In this perspective, tolerance seeks to preserve a plural political community, proposing that it should not be fragmented by different visions of the world. Accordingly, given the importance of religion as a source of values and an element of a people's culture, the separation between state and religion proposed by Locke must not be broken.

For Habermas, tolerance is practiced within the limits of the democratic principle of secularity, in which the state must be guided by impartiality, caution, and the preservation of the constitutional order.[44] Intolerant practices, in turn, would be incompatible with the state of law. Fundamentalist expressions and interpretations of the world that demand exclusivity for a privileged way of life also conflict with the state of law and thus lack awareness of the fallibility of their claims.[45]

The democratic process for the achievement of subjective rights can therefore be opened up to include the coexistence of equal rights for ethnic groups and specific ways of life, hence: "The identity of the individual is interwoven with collective identities and can be stabilized only in a cultural network that cannot be appropriated as private property any more than the mother tongue itself can be."[46] The protection sought by forms of life and traditions that constitute people's identity should thus be aimed at the recognition of its members, rather than the "preservation of species by administrative means."[47]

Democracy therefore represents the possibility of articulating the coexistence of heterogeneous societies. The definition of the concept of tolerance is often the definition provided by public authorities, such that tolerance must be established in a democratic society, which guarantees equal consideration and respect for all.

In his normative conceptualization of the state, Habermas understands that the democratic formation of opinions and wills are the result of deliberations, whether they are held in the general political arena or in the parliamentary sphere, but for this to occur in an appropriate manner, there would be underlying conditions of communication to guide the political process of a deliberative policy, which must consider "the multiplicity of forms of communication"[48] to construct a common will.[49]

Plurality can thus be produced within the democratic state and goes hand in hand with religious tolerance, both of which foster the multiplicity of forms of life and communication. This is demonstrated by the central role that tolerance has come to have in political culture, which can be observed in the origins of liberalism.

In this context, tolerance has the function of "negotiating" conflict between assertions of opposing "truths," that is, it becomes necessary based on the rejection of other people's convictions, of the cognitive conflict between beliefs and attitudes,[50] and tolerance therefore cannot be confused with indifference. Just as the answer to intolerance is not simply more tolerance, in the struggle for equal rights, a racist expression is not expected to simply be tolerated; rather, the racist must overcome their prejudices.

According to Habermas, the first element to be considered is the inclusion of all citizens in the political community. Without the inclusion of everyone, we cannot be expected to have tolerance for one another, and thus, the prohibition of discrimination provides moral and constitutional grounds for tolerance.[51] Moreover, a line must be drawn to demarcate what cannot be tolerated, but this cannot be done in an authoritarian manner, or else a paradox will be produced. Political deliberation is the path that enables the construction of legitimate rules, accepted by all those involved in the deliberative arena, and it also applies to the definition of tolerance.

Proportionally, one might imagine that the increased complexity of a particular political community will eventually result in an expansion of people's different forms of life. For this reason, the foundations of society—previously constructed as outpourings of divine will—are supported by different pillars; although we may still see the influence of those perspectives, they are no longer portrayed as resulting from the natural order of things but, rather, as human constructions, reflections of interactions between people and political structures, artifices resulting from the general agreements that organize society and that are bound up, for example, in constitutional rules.

There has been a departure from theories that proclaim a (questionable) idea of totality that is structured by (small or large) parts, such as Hobbes' Leviathan.[52] In Habermas' understanding, the life-world is organized as a network of communicative actions in different branches, which are propagated in certain specific spaces and times, for they are nourished by aspects of cultural traditions but also by the identities of the people who belong to society: "Socialized individuals could not maintain themselves as subjects at all if they did not find support in the relationships of reciprocal recognition articulated in cultural traditions and stabilized in legitimate orders—and vice versa."[53]

Here, as Barroso asserts: "truth has no master"[54]; i.e., "comprehensive doctrines,"[55] which claim to have the authority to structure a form of life in its entirety, as proclaimed by certain religions, began to be viewed—following the secularization of the state—as simply one possibility for reading the world, among many other options. According to this perspective, they should abandon the pretense of comprehensively shaping the entire society's way of life.[56]

The tension arises from the fact that certain religions end up being intrinsically intolerant of other religious expressions and ways of perceiving the world. To avoid those types of internal contradictions, forced conversions or the use of violence should not be permitted, as Bayle had previously criticized. In fact, the purpose of constructing a democratic rule of law is to ensure that conflicts are mediated argumentatively and guided by democratic institutions, not by the use of force or violence.

It is impossible to ignore, however, that in the context of specific human relations, what often prevails is intolerance, aggression, and hatred. This discussion does not focus on those areas, although they may appear in the background of discussions on their historical relevance, more remote or close to us in time. We are concerned with defining the limits of the state and people's actions in the normative realm, that is, what the appropriate means for stabilizing expectations and mediating conflicts should be in a society defined not by fear and destruction but by the constitutional order, which includes fundamental rights and democracy as the main vectors of intersubjective relations.[57]

Habermas recognizes that antagonistic preferences will not always be defused on the discursive plane; it is enough to observe that on certain topics, controversial interests are connected with the way the collectivity understands itself, and thus, ethical-political questions "pose themselves from the perspective of members who, in the face of important life issues, want to gain clarity about their shared form of life and about the ideals they feel should shape their common life."[58]

The tension between the individual and collective identity is established in the following way: while people may identify with a collectivity and be part of the "we," their lives are not reduced only to their community identity, such that they may change their religion, country, culture, gender, employment, family, etc. In Habermas' terms: "How we make our native traditions and forms of life our own by selectively developing them determines who we recognize ourselves to be in these cultural transmissions—who we are and would like to be as citizens."[59] Culture is not ironclad, and neither are the identities articulated and shaped by it.

Between the fluidity and stability of ethical values, another question that emerges concerns the limits of tolerance. It arises from the controversy over the definition of the criteria used to define tolerance. For Rainer Forst, the limits must be established at the onset of intolerance; because tolerance implies reciprocity, it can only be demanded for those who are tolerant.[60]

Where does tolerance begin? There is a potential danger here: stripping the concept of its meaning could lead to the conclusion that any attempt to achieve it could itself end up being intolerance.[61] While that warning is an important reminder of the problematic way in which the lines that define tolerance have been drawn, it also leads to a dangerous generalization: anyone who wants to delineate the limits of intolerance would inevitably do so arbitrarily, constituting a "destructive paradox," to which Forst responds, arguing that a critique of intolerance should not be equated with another form of intolerance.[62]

To define the concept of intolerance, Forst presents the following characteristics: the context of toleration must be established; the tolerated practices and beliefs must be condemned to a certain degree; the condemnation must be minimally balanced with some type of acceptance, which establishes rudimentary positive reasons for its defense; the limits of toleration must be defined; toleration cannot be the result of coercion; and toleration as a practice is different from tolerance as a virtue or attitude.[63]

According to Forst, while toleration is articulated as a demand for justice, its obverse is a specific form of injustice.[64] There is also a mark of humility that aligns with the practice of tolerance, that is, the perception that a certain ethical conception defended by a person is good for them as individuals and for others to eventually share. However, they are not sufficient to prevent other people from developing separate ethical conceptions and are thus insufficient for permitting the moral rejection of others.

Finally, tolerance may, in different cases, be lacking and inadequate. While it can be the axiological starting point for a society that desires to be open and plural, tolerating otherness without recognizing equal citizenship and the enjoyment of rights can be deceptive. This is evident with the victims of intolerant actions, such as reactionary expressions aimed at excluding minority groups from society because they belong to a particular ethnic group. Here, a line can be drawn that, according to Forst, represents an action of justice towards those who have been victims of intolerance, as those who cross the line and violate the basic right to respect and justice cannot, without contradiction, demand tolerance.[65]

FINAL CONSIDERATIONS

Disjunctive times demand answers, put social relations back on track, demonstrate that the state of affairs in Denmark or Brazil is "disordered" and point out alternatives. We have focused on remembrance and a reaffirmation of tolerance. Political confusion and expressions that attempt to displace the centrality of institutions and the institutional mediation of relations between the people and the government must be rejected. It is not the purpose to argue, however, that there is an ideal profile for a judge. In fact, it points out alternatives for facing the issues that arise in view of the possibilities of argumentation, for example, between the paradox of rules and principles.[66]

Perhaps, in particular, we also see the present as being somewhat confusing, which is why tolerance appears to be a possible light in the midst of the storm. Its contribution is, simply, not allowing those who are different to be eradicated because of their otherness; more broadly, a contribution is made by plurality to the epistemological enrichment of democracy. Finally, confronted by the many paths through purgatory, we press on in the terms mentioned above by Barroso: "there is no single formula for a good life"[67]; all we have are partial decisions about how to live, and we must always have the ability and responsibility to reflect on and revise our ways of life as well as have institutional channels open to make mistakes, learn from mistakes and pursue life.

NOTES

1. Amin Maalouf, *O mundo em desajuste: quando nossas civilizações se esgotam*, trans. Jorge Bastos (Rio de Janeiro: DIFEL, 2011).

2. Thimothy Snyder, *Sobre a tirania: Vvinte lições do século XX para o presente* (São Paulo: Companhia das Letras, 2017).

3. Jason Stanley, *How Fascism Works: The Politics of Us and Them* (New York: Random House, 2018), 33.

4. Oscar Vilhena Vieira, "A Constituição como reserva de justiça," *Lua Nova* 42, (1997): 53–97.

5. "The constitution of a democratic state has two primary functions. First, it is responsible for expressing a minimum consensus, which is essential for the dignity of people and the functioning of the democratic regime and which should not be affected by occasional political majorities. . . . Second, the constitution must guarantee space for political pluralism, ensuring the proper functioning of democratic mechanisms."

Luís Roberto Barroso, *Curso de Direito Constitucional contemporâneo: os conceitos fundamentais e a construção do novo modelo* (São Paulo: Saraiva, 2017), 116.

6. Judith Shklar, "The Liberalism of Fear," in *Liberalism and the Moral Life*, ed. Nancy L. Rosenblum (Cambridge, MA: Harvard University Press, 1989), 21.

7. Shklar, "The Liberalism of Fear," 22.

8. Shklar, "The Liberalism of Fear," 23.

9. Shklar, "The Liberalism of Fear," 23.

10. Shklar, "The Liberalism of Fear," 24. For example, for Hobbes: "It is therefore manifest enough by this one place that by the kingdom of God is properly meant a Commonwealth, instituted (by the consent of those which were to be subject thereto) for their civil government and the regulating of their behavior, not only towards God their king, but also towards one another in point of justice, and towards other nations both in peace and war." Thomas Hobbes, *Leviatã, ou, A matéria, forma e poder de um estado eclesiástico e civil* (São Paulo: Ícone, 2000), 289.

11. Shklar, "The Liberalism of Fear," 28.

12. Shklar, "The Liberalism of Fear," 30.

13. John Locke, *A Letter Concerning Toleration and Other Writings* (Indianapolis, IN: Liberty Fund, 2010), 45.

14. Locke, *A Letter Concerning Toleration and Other Writings*, 45.

15. Locke, *A Letter Concerning Toleration and Other Writings*, 63.

16. Locke, *A Letter Concerning Toleration and Other Writings*, 60.

17. Locke, *A Letter Concerning Toleration and Other Writings*, 96.

18. Locke, *A Letter Concerning Toleration and Other Writings*, 74.

19. Locke, *A Letter Concerning Toleration and Other Writings*, 36.

20. Locke, *A Letter Concerning Toleration and Other Writings*, 37.

21. Locke, *A Letter Concerning Toleration and Other Writings*, 38.

22. Barroso, *Curso de Direito Constitucional contemporâneo*, 50.

23. Pierre Bayle, "A Philosophical Commentary on These Words of the Gospel," in *Compel Them to Come In, That My House May Be Full*, Luke 14.23 (Indianapolis, IN: Liberty Fund, 2005), 412.

24. Lucas Jorge de Freitas, "Estudo da Construção do Ethos Retórico Donatista e suas Implicações no Cristianismo Africano do Século IV e V" (PhD diss., Universidade de São Paulo: São Paulo, 2013), 57–58.

25. Bayle, "A Philosophical Commentary," 176.

26. Bayle, "A Philosophical Commentary," 176–177.

27. Bayle, "A Philosophical Commentary," 299.

28. Bayle, "A Philosophical Commentary," 245.

29. Bayle, "A Philosophical Commentary," 457.

30. Ira Katznelson, "A Form of Liberty and Indulgence: Tolerance as a Layered Institution," in *Boundaries of Toleration*, ed. Alfred Stepan and Charles Taylor (New York: Columbia University Press, 2014), 38.

31. Katznelson, "A Form of Liberty and Indulgence," 38.

32. Katznelson, "A Form of Liberty and Indulgence," 39.

33. Katznelson, "A Form of Liberty and Indulgence," 40.

34. Katznelson, "A Form of Liberty and Indulgence," 41.

35. Luís Roberto Barroso, "Bem, justiça e tolerância," *Folha de São Paulo*, June 26, 2013.

36. Will Kymlicka, "Two Models of Pluralism and Tolerance," *Analyse & Kritik* 13 (1992): 34.

37. Kymlicka, "Two Models of Pluralism and Tolerance," 39.

38. Kymlicka, "Two Models of Pluralism and Tolerance," 39.

39. Kymlicka, "Two Models of Pluralism and Tolerance," 43.

40. Katznelson, "A Form of Liberty and Indulgence," 45.

41. Jürgen Habermas, "Intolerance and Discrimination," *International Journal of Constitutional Law, Oxford* 1, no. 1 (2003): 2.

42. Habermas, "Intolerance and Discrimination," 3.

43. Jürgen Habermas, *Entre naturalismo e religião: Estudos filosóficos*, trans. Flávio B. Siebeneichler (Rio de Janeiro: Tempo brasileiro, 2007), 282.

44. Habermas, *Entre naturalismo e religião.*

45. Jürgen Habermas, *A inclusão do outro: Estudos de toeria política*, trans. Denilson Luís Werle (São Paulo: Editora Unesp, 2018), 373.

46. Habermas, *A inclusão do outro*, 368.

47. Habermas, *A inclusão do outro*, 370.

48. Habermas, *A inclusão do outro*, 408.

49. "Weaving together *negotiations and discourses of self-understanding and of justice*, this *democratic procedure* grounds the presumption that under such conditions reasonable or fair results are obtained. According to this proceduralist view, practical reason withdraws from universal human rights or from the concrete ethical life of a specific community into the rules of discourse and forms of argumentation that derive their normative content from the validity-basis of action oriented to reaching understanding, and ultimately from the structure of linguistic communication." Habermas, *A inclusão do outro*, 410.

50. Habermas, "Intolerance and Discrimination," 3.

51. Habermas, "Intolerance and Discrimination," 3–4.

52. Hobbes, *Leviatã, ou, A matéria, forma e poder de um estado eclesiástico e civil.*

53. Jürgen Habermas, *Direito e Democracia: Entre facticidade e validade*, trans. Flávio Beno Siebeneichler (Rio de Janeiro: Tempo brasileiro, 1997), 111.

54. Barroso, "Bem, justiça e tolerância."

55. See: John Rawls, *Political Liberalism* (New York: Columbia University Press, 1995).

56. Regarding the concept of tolerance in law, Néviton Guedes explains: "The discourse of law does not ignore natural truth or formal logic but is and always will be more than that. It opens itself up with tolerance to the possibility of disagreements and is content with verisimilitude. In the field of law, particularly in 'hard cases,' knowledge is not imposed through irrefutable logical judgments but only convinces through the logic of argumentation. Admittedly, it is based on the truth of the facts and does not overlook formal logic, but it has the obligation to not always stop there." Néviton Guedes, "Luís Roberto Barroso e a tolerância no direito," *Revista Consultor Jurídico*, June 27, 2013, accessed November 27, 2019, https://www.conjur.com.br/2013-mai-27/constituicao-poder-luis-roberto-barroso-tolerancia-direito.

57. Bruno Meneses Lorenzetto, *Os caminhos do constitucionalismo para a democracia* (Belo Horizonte: Arraes Editores, 2014).

58. Habermas, *Direito e Democracia*, 201.

59. Habermas, *Direito e Democracia*, 201.

60. Rainer Forst, "Os limites da tolerância," trans. Mauro Victoria Soares, *Novos Estudos—CEBRAP* 84 (2009): 16.

61. "That is why although I spend a great deal of time demonstrating how liberal theorists are always performing the exclusionary acts for which they stigmatize others, I do not fault them for so performing, but for thinking and claiming to be doing something else." Stanley Fish, "Mission Impossible: Settling the Just Bounds between Church and State," *Columbia Law Review* 97, no. 8 (1997): 2256–2257.

62. Forst, "Os limites da tolerância," 18.

63. Forst, "Os limites da tolerância," 19–20.

64. Forst, "Os limites da tolerância," p. 22.

65. Forst, "Os limites da tolerância," p. 27.

66. Marcelo Neves, *Constitutionalism and the Paradox of Principles and Rules: Between the Hydra and Hercules* (Oxford, UK: Oxford University Press, 2021).

67. Barroso, "Bem, justiça e tolerância."

Bibliography

Ackerman, Bruce. *Adeus, Montesquieu. Revista de Direito Administrativo* 265 (2014): 13–23. https://doi.org/10.12660/rda.v265.2014.18909.

———. "Beyond Carolene Products." *Harvard Law Review* 98, no. 4 (1985): 713–746.

———. *We the People: Foundations*. Cambridge, MA: Harvard University Press, 1993.

———. *We the People: Transformations*. Cambridge, MA: Harvard University Press, 1998.

Alexy, Robert. *Teoría de los Derechos Fundamentales*. Translated by Ernesto Garzón Valdés. Madrid: Centro de Estudios Constitucionales, 1993.

Allan, T. R. S. *The Sovereignty of Law: Freedom, Constitution, and Common Law*. Oxford, UK: Oxford University Press, 2013.

Arendt, Hannah. *The Origins of the Totalitarianism*. San Diego, CA: Harcourt Brace, 1976.

Arenhart, Sérgio Cruz. "Decisões estruturais no direito processual civil brasileiro." *Revista de Processo* 225 (2013).

Arguelhes, Diego Werneck, and Fernando Leal. "O Argumento das 'Capacidades institucionais' entre a banalidade, a redundância e o absurdo." In *Tratado de direito constitucional: Constituição no século XXI*, edited by Felipe Dutra Asensi and Daniel Giotti de Paula. Rio de Janeiro: Elsevier, 2014.

Aristotle. *Politics*. London: William Heinemann, 1932.

Ávila, Humberto. *Teoria dos Princípios: Da definição à aplicação dos princípios jurídicos*. São Paulo: Malheiros, 2004.

Balkin, Jack M., and Sanford Levinson. "13 Ways of Looking at Dred Scott." *Chicago-Kent Law Review* 82 (2007): 49–95.

———. "Understanding the Constitutional Revolution." *Virginia Law Review* 87, no. 6 (2001): 1045–1109.

Barroso, Luís Roberto. "Bem, justiça e tolerância." *Folha de São Paulo* (2013).

———. "Constituição, Democracia e Supremacia Judicial: Direito e política no Brasil contemporâneo." In *Tratado de direito constitucional: Constituição no século XXI*, edited by Felipe Dutra Asensi and Daniel Giotti de Paula. Rio de Janeiro: Elsevier, 2014.

———. *O controle de constitucionalidade no direito brasileiro: Exposição sistemática da doutrina e análise crítica da jurisprudência*. São Paulo: Saraiva, 2011.

———. *Curso de direito constitucional contemporâneo: Os conceitos fundamentais e a construção do novo modelo*. São Paulo: Saraiva, 2009.

———. *Curso de direito constitucional contemporâneo: Os conceitos fundamentais e a construção do novo modelo*, 6th ed. São Paulo: Saraiva, 2017.

———. *A dignidade da pessoa humana no direito constitucional contemporâneo: A construção de um conceito jurídico à luz da jurisprudência mundial*. Belo Horizonte: Fórum, 2012.

———. *O direito constitucional e a efetividade de suas normas: Limites e possibilidades da Constituição brasileira*. Rio de Janeiro: Renovar, 2006.

———. "Da Falta de Efetividade à Judicialização Excessiva: Direito à Saúde, Fornecimento Gratuito de Medicamentos e Parâmetros para a Atuação Judicial." In *Direitos Sociais: Fundamentos, judicialização e direitos sociais em espécie*, edited by Souza Neto, Cláudio Pereira, and Daniel Sarmento. Rio de Janeiro: Lumen Juris, 2008.

———. *Interpretação e aplicação da Constituição: Fundamentos de uma dogmática constitucional transformadora*. São Paulo: Saraiva, 2009.

———. "Judicialização, Ativismo Judicial e Legitimidade Democrática." *Revista de direito do estado* 13 (January/March 2009).

———. "Não tenho nenhum orgulho do volume de processos que o Supremo julga." *Os Constitucionalistas*, February 23, 2015, http://www.osconstitucionalistas.com.br/entrevista-luis-roberto-barroso-nao-tenho-nenhum-orgulho-do-volume-de-processos-que-o-supremo-julga.

———. *O novo direito constitucional brasileiro: Contribuições para a construção teórica e prática da jurisdição constitucional no Brasil*. Belo Horizonte: Fórum, 2012.

———. "Óleo na engrenagem." *Consultor Jurídico*, accessed July 7, 2015, http://www.conjur.com.br/2015-jul-02/entrevista-luis-roberto-barroso-ministro-stf-parte.

———. "A razão sem voto: O Supremo Tribunal Federal e o governo da maioria." *Revista Brasileira de Políticas Públicas* 5, (2015).

———. "Retrospectiva 2014." *Consultor Jurídico*, accessed on July 7, 2015, from http://www.conjur.com.br/2014-dez-31/roberto-barroso-ano-sinaliza-mudancas-supremo-tribunal-federal.

———. *Temas de Direito Constitucional*. Rio de Janeiro: Renovar, 2001.

Bayle, Pierre. *A Philosophical Commentary on These Words of the Gospel, Luke 14: 23, "Compel Them to Come In, That My House May Be Full."* Edited by John Kilcullen and Chandran Kukathas. Indianapolis, IN: Liberty Fund. 2005.

Bickel, Alexander. *The Least Dangerous Branch: The Supreme Court at the Bar of Politics*. New Haven, CT: Yale University Press, 1986.

Binenbojm, Gustavo. *A nova jurisdição constitucional*. Rio de Janeiro: Renovar, 2004.

Boeira, Nelson, trans. *Levando os direitos a sério*. São Paulo: Martins Fontes, 2010.

Brandão, Rodrigo. *Supremacia judicial versus diálogos constitucionais: A quem cabe a última palavra sobre o sentido da constituição?* Rio de Janeiro: Lumen Juris, 2012.

Brest, Paul. "The Fundamental Rights Controversy: The Essential Contradictions of Normative Constitutional Scholarship." *Yale Law Journal* 90, no. 5 (1981): 1063–1109.

Breyer, Stephen. *Active Liberty*. New York: Vintage, 2006.

Cameron, Jamie. "Dialogue and Hierarchy in Charter Interpretation: A comment on R. V. Mills." *Alberta Law Review* 38 (2001): 1051.

Campos, Carlos Alexandre de Azevedo. *Dimensões do ativismo judicial do Supremo Tribunal Federal*. Rio de Janeiro: Forense, 2014.

———. "Da Inconstitucionalidade por Omissão ao 'Estado de Coisas Inconstitucional.'" PhD diss., Faculdade de Direito - Universidade do Estado do Rio de Janeiro, 2015.

Canotilho, José Joaquim Gomes. *Direito Constitucional e Teoria da Constituição*. Coimbra: Almedina, 2003.

———. *Direito Constitucional e Teoria da Constituição*, 7th ed. Coimbra: Almedina, 2003.

———. *Estudos sobre direitos fundamentais*. São Paulo: RT/Coimbra: Coimbra Editora, 2008.

Cardoso, Rodrigo Mendes. "As teorias do constitucionalismo popular e do diálogo na perspectiva da jurisdição constitucional brasileira." *RECHTD* 6, no. 2 (2014).

Clève, Clèmerson Merlin. *Atividade Legislativa do Poder Executivo*. São Paulo: Revista dos Tribunais, 2011.

———. *O direito e os direitos: Elementos para uma crítica do direito contemporâneo*. Belo Horizonte: Fórum, 2011.

———. *A Fiscalização Abstrata de Constitucionalidade no Direito Brasileiro*. São Paulo: RT, 2000.

————. *A Fiscalização Abstrata de Constitucionalidade no Direito Brasileiro*, 2nd ed. São Paulo: RT, 2000.

———. *Jurisdição constitucional, ativismo e democracia*, Opening lecture at the IX Latin American Law Convention (*Convenção Latino-americana de Direito - Colad*), Curitiba, Paraná (October 27, 2011).

———. *Medidas provisórias*. São Paulo: Revista dos Tribunais, 2010.

———. *Para uma dogmática constitucional emancipatória*. Belo Horizonte: Fórum, 2012.

———. *Temas de Direito Constitucional*. Belo Horizonte: Fórum, 2014.

———. *Temas de Direito Constitucional*, 2nd ed. Belo Horizonte: Fórum, 2014.

———, and Alexandre Freire. *Direitos fundamentais e jurisdição constitucional*. São Paulo: Editora RT, 2014.

———, and Bruno Meneses Lorenzetto. "Constituição, Governo Democrático e Níveis de Intensidade do Controle Jurisdicional." *Revista Jurídica Luso Brasileira* 1 (2015).

Coram, Bruce T. "Second Best Theories and the Implications for Institutional Design." In *The Theory of Institutional Design*, edited by Robert E. Goodin. Cambridge, UK: Cambridge University Press, 1996.

Cover, Robert. "The Origins of Judicial Activism in the Protection of Minorities." *Yale Law Journal* 91, no. 7 (1982): 1287–1316.

Dixon, Rosalind. "Creating Dialogue about Socioeconomic Rights: Strong-Form versus Weak-Form Judicial Review Revisited." *International Journal of Constitutional Law* 5, no. 3 (2007): 391–418.

Dworkin, Ronald. *Justice for Hedgehogs*. Cambridge, MA: Harvard University Press, 2011.

———. *Justice in Robes*. Cambridge, MA: Harvard University Press, 2006.

———. *Law's Empire*. Cambridge, MA: Harvard University Press, 1986.

———. *A Matter of Principle*. Cambridge, MA: Harvard University Press, 1985.

———. "Rights as Trumps." In *Theories of Rights*, edited by Jeremy Waldron. Oxford, UK: Oxford University Press, 1984.

———. *Taking Rights Seriously*. Cambridge, MA: Harvard University Press, 1978.

Ely, John Hart. *Democracy and Distrust: A Theory of Judicial Review*. Cambridge, MA: Harvard University Press, 1980.

Enterría, Eduardo García de. *La Constitución como norma y el Tribunal Constitucional*. Madrid: Civitas, 2006.

Eskridge, William N., Jr. "Dynamic Statutory Interpretation." *University of Pennsylvania Law Review* 135, no. 6 (1987): 1479–1555.

———. "Gadamer/Statutory Interpretation." *Columbia Law Review* 90, no. 3 (1990): 609–681.

———. "The New Textualism." *UCLA Law Review* 37 (1990): 621–691.

———. "No Frills Textualism." *Harvard Law Review* 119, no. 7 (2006): 2041–2075.

Falcão, Joaquim, Ivar A. Hartmann, and Vitor P. Chaves. *III Relatório Supremo em Números: O Supremo e o tempo*. Rio de Janeiro: Escola de Direito do Rio de Janeiro da Fundação Getulio Vargas, 2014.

Fallon, Richard H., Jr. *Implementing the Constitution*. Cambridge, MA: Harvard University Press, 2001.

———. "Strict Judicial Scrutiny." *University of California Law Review* 54, no. 5 (2007): 1267–1337.

Farber, Daniel A. "Legal Formalism and the Red-Hot Knife." *University of Chicago Law Review* 66, no. 3 (1999): 597.

Ferejohn, John. "Judicializing Politics, Politicizing Law." *Law and Contemporary Problems* 65, no. 3 (2002): 41–68.

Fish, Stanley. "Mission Impossible: Settling the Just Bounds between Church and State." *Columbia Law Review* 97, no. 8 (1997): 2255–2333.

Fiss, Owen. *Libertad de Expresión y Estructura Social*. México, D.F.: Fontamara, 1997.

———. "A Life Lived Twice." *Yale Law Journal* 100, no. 5 (1991): 1117–1129.

———. "Objectivity and Interpretation." *Stanford Law Review* 34 (1982): 739–763.

———. "The Perils of Minimalism." *Theoretical Inquires in Law* 9, no. 2 (2008): 643–664.

Fonseca, Juliana Pondé. "O (des)controle do Estado no Judiciário brasileiro." PhD diss., Setor de Ciências Jurídicas - Universidade Federal do Paraná, 2015.

Forst, Rainer. "Os limites da tolerância." Translated by Mauro Victoria Soares. *Novos Estudos - CEBRAP* 84 (2009): 15–29.

Freitas, Lucas Jorge de. "Estudo da Construção do Ethos Retórico Donatista e suas Implicações no Cristianismo Africano do Século IV e V." PhD diss., Universidade de São Paulo, 2013.

Friedman, Barry. "Dialogue and Judicial Review." *Michigan Law Review* 91 (1993): 577–682.

Gadamer, Hans-Georg. *Verdade e Método*. Petrópolis: Vozes, 1997.

Garavito, César Rodríguez. "Beyond the Courtroom: The Impact of Judicial Activism on Socioeconomic Rights in Latin America." *Texas Law Review* 89 (2011): 1669–1698.

Gargarella, Roberto. *El Derecho a la Protesta: El primer derecho*. Buenos Aires: Ad-Hoc, 2005.

Ginsburg, Ruth Bader. "Speaking in a Judicial Voice." *New York University Law Review* 67 (1992): 1185–1209.

Gravito, César Rodriguez, and Diana Rodriguez Franco. *Cortes y cambio social: Como la Corte Constitucional transformo el desplazamiento forzado en Colombia.* Bogotá: Centro de Estudios de Derecho, Justicia y Sociedad, 2010.

Grinover, Ada Pellegrini, and Paulo Henrique dos Santos Lucon. "ADPF 347 e o controle judicial de políticas públicas." Folha de São Paulo, accessed October 19, 2015, http://www1.folha.uol.com.br/opiniao/2015/09/1686769-adpf-347-e-o-controle-judicial-de-politicas-publicas.shtml.

Guedes, Néviton. "Luís Roberto Barroso e a tolerância no direito." *Revista Consultor Jurídico*, accessed May 27, 2013, https://www.conjur.com.br/2013-mai-27/constituicao-poder-luis-roberto-barroso-tolerancia-direito.

Habermas, Jürgen. *Between Facts and Norms*. Cambridge, MA: MIT Press, 1998.

———. *Direito e Democracia: Entre facticidade e validade*. Translated by Flávio Beno Siebeneichler. Rio de Janeiro: Tempo brasileiro, 1997.

———. *Entre naturalismo e religião: Estudos filosóficos*. Translated by Flávio B. Siebeneichler. Rio de Janeiro: Tempo brasileiro, 2007.

———. *A inclusão do outro: Estudos de toeria política*. Translated by Denilson Luís Werle. São Paulo: Editora Unesp, 2018.

———. "Intolerance and Discrimination." *International Journal of Constitutional Law* 1, no. 1 (2003): 2–12.

———. *Theory and Practice*. Boston: Beacon Press, 1973.

Hamilton, Alexander, James Madison, and John Jay. *The Federalist Papers*. Washington, DC: Library of Congress, 1787.

Hart, Henry, Jr., and Albert M Sacks. *The Legal Process: Basic Problems in the Making and Application of Law*. New York: Foundation Press, 1994.

Hart, Herbert L. *The Concept of Law.* Oxford, UK: Oxford University Press, 1961.

———. *The Concept of Law*, 2nd ed. Oxford, UK: Clarendon, 1994.

———. *Essays in Jurisprudence and Philosophy*. Oxford, UK: Clarendon, 1983.

Hesse, Konrad. *Elementos de Direito Constitucional da República Federal da Alemanha*. Translated by Luis Afonso Heck. Porto Alegre: Sergio Antonio Fabris. 1998.

Hiebert, Janet. *Charter Conflicts: What Is Parliament's Role?* Montreal: McGill-Queen's University Press, 2002.

Hirschl, Ran. "The Judicialization of Politics." In *Oxford Handbook of Political Science*, edited by Gregory A. Caldeira, R. Daniel Kelemen, and Keith E. Whittington. Oxford, UK: Oxford University Press, 2008.

———. "The Political Origins of the New Constitutionalism." *Indiana Journal of Global Legal Studies* 11, no. 1 (2004): 71–108.

Hirst, Paul. *Representative Democracy and its Limits*. Cambridge, UK: Polity, 1990.

Hobbes, Thomas. *Leviatã*. Trasnlated by Rosina D'Angina. São Paulo: Ícone, 2000.

———. *Leviatã, ou, A matéria, forma e poder de um estado eclesiástico e civil.* São Paulo: Ícone, 2000.

Hogg, Peter W., and Allison A. Bushell Thornton. "The Charter Dialogue between Courts and Legislatures (Or Perhaps the *Charter of Rights* Isn't Such a Bad Thing After All)." *Osgoode Hall Law Journal* 35, no. 1 (1997): 75–124.

Hogg, Peter W., Allison A. Bushnell Thornton, and Wade K. Wright. "Charter Dialogue Revisited—Or 'Much Ado about Metaphors.'" *Osgoode Hall Law Journal* 45, no. 1 (2007): 1–65.

Holmes, Stephen, and Cass Sunstein. *The Cost of Rights: Why Liberty Depends on Taxes*. New York: W. W. Norton & Company, 1999.

Katznelson, Ira. "A Form of Liberty and Indulgence: Tolerance as a Layered Institution." In *Boundaries of Toleration*, edited by Alfred Stepan and Charles Taylor. New York: Columbia University Press, 2014.

Kelsen, H. *Jurisdição constitucional.* Translated by Alexandre Krug. São Paulo: Martins Fontes, 2007.

———. *Jurisdição constitucional*. Translated by Maria Ermantina de Almeida Prado Galvão. São Paulo: Martins Fontes, 2007.

Kennedy, Duncan. "Legal Formalism." In *Encyclopedia of the Social and Behavioral Sciences* 13, edited by Neil Smelser and Paul Baltes. New York: Elsevier, 2001.

King, Jeff A. "Institutional Approaches to Judicial Restraint." *Oxford Journal of Legal Studies* 28, no. 3 (2008): 409–441.

Kingwell, Mark. "Let's Ask Again: Is Law Like Literature?" *Yale Journal of Law and the Humanities* 6 (1994): 317.

Kramer, Larry D. *The People Themselves: Popular Constitutionalism and Judicial Review*. Oxford, UK: Oxford University Press, 2004.

Kymlicka, Will. "Two Models of Pluralism and Tolerance." *Analyse & Kritik*, 14, no. 1 (1992): 33–56.

Leivas, Paulo Gilberto Cogo. *Teoria dos direitos fundamentais sociais*. Porto Alegre: Livraria do Advogado, 2006.

Lima, George Marmelstein. "O Estado de Coisas Inconstitucional - ECI: Apenas um nova onda do verão constitucional?" *Direitos Fundamentais*, accessed October 5,

2015, http://direitosfundamentais.net/2015/10/02/o-estado-de-coisas-inconstitucional-eci-apenas-uma-nova-onda-do-verao-constitucional/.

Limbach, Jutta. "The Concept of the Supremacy of the Constitution." *Modern Law Review* 64, no. 1 (2001): 1–10.

Locke, John. *Os caminhos do constitucionalismo para a democracia*. Belo Horizonte: Arraes Editores, 2017.

———. *A Letter Concerning Toleration and Other Writings*. Indianapolis, IN: Liberty Fund, 2010.

Lorenzetto, Bruno Meneses. "Os Caminhos do Constitucionalismo para a Democracia." PhD diss., Universidade Federal do Paraná, Curitiba, 2014.

———. *Direito e desconstrução: As aporias do tempo, do direito e da violência*. Belo Horizonte: Arraes Editores, 2013.

———, and Tanya Kozicki de Mello. "Revisão legislativa dos atos jurisdicionais." In *Direito Constitucional Brasileiro* II, edited by Clèmerson Merlin Clève. São Paulo: Revista dos Tribunais, 2014.

Maalouf, Amin. *O mundo em desajuste: quando nossas civilizações se esgotam*. Translated by Jorge Bastos. Rio de Janeiro: DIFEL, 2011.

Macedo Junior, Ronaldo Porto. *Do Xadrez à Cortesia*: *Dworkin e a teoria do direito contemporânea*. São Paulo: Saraiva, 2013.

Manfredi, Christopher, and James B. Kelly. "Six Degrees of Dialogue: A Response to Hogg and Bushell." *Osgoode Hall Law Journal* 37, no. 3 (1999): 513–527.

Mathews, Jud, and Alec Stone Sweet. "All Things in Proportion? American Rights Doctrine and the Problem of Balancing." *Emory Law Journal* 60, no. 4 (2011): 797–875.

Mendes, Conrado Hübner. *Constitutional Courts and Deliberative Democracy*. Oxford, UK: Oxford University Press, 2013.

———. *Controle de constitucionalidade e democracia*. Rio de Janeiro: Elsevier, 2008.

———. *Direitos fundamentais, separação de poderes e deliberação*. São Paulo: Saraiva, 2011.

Mendes, Gilmar Ferreira, and Paulo Gustavo Gonet Branco. *Curso de direito constitucional*. São Paulo: Saraiva, 2012.

Michelman, Frank I. *Brennan and Democracy*. Princeton, NJ: Princeton University Press, 1999.

Miranda, Jorge. *Manual de Direito Constitucional*, Tomo III, 5th ed. Coimbra: Coimbra Editora, 2004.

Montesquieu, Charles de Secondat. *O Espírito das Leis*. Translated by Cristina Murachco. São Paulo: Martins Fontes, 2000.

Moreira, Egon Bockmann, and Heloísa Câmara. "Quem pode dar cabo deste estado de coisas?" *Gazeta do Povo*, September 29, 2015, http://www.gazetadopovo.com.br/opiniao/artigos/quem-pode-dar-cabo-deste-estado-de-coisas-2vz9g0a4fd4hj1yjq4pswibpw.

Moro, Sergio Fernando. *Legislação suspeita? Afastamento da presunção de constitucionalidade da lei*. Curitiba: Juruá Editora, 2003.

Morton, F. L., and Rainer Knopff. *The Charter Revolution and the Court Party*. Peterborough: Broadview Press, 2000.

Mouffe, Chantal. *El retorno de lo político*. Barcelona: Paidós, 1999.

Netto, Menelick de Carvalho, and Guilherme Scotti. *Os direitos fundamentais e a (in)certeza do direito: A produtividade das tensões principiológicas e a superação do sistema de regras*. Belo Horizonte: Fórum, 2011.

Neves, Marcelo. *Constitutionalism and the Paradox of Principles and Rules: Between the Hydra and Hercules*. Oxford, UK: Oxford University Press, 2021.

Nino, Carlos Santiago. *La constitución de la democracia deliberativa*. Barcelona: Gedisa, 1997.

———. *The Constitution of Deliberative Democracy*. New Haven, CT: Yale University Press, 1996.

———. *Ética y derechos humanos: Un ensayo de fundamentación*. Buenos Aires: Astrea, 1989.

Pieroth, Bodo, and Bernhard Schlink. *Direitos Fundamentais*. Translated by António Francisco de Sousa and António Franco. São Paulo: Saraiva, 2012.

Posner, Richard. "The Rise and Fall of Judicial Self-Restraint." *California Law Review* 100, no. 3 (2012): 519–556.

Post, Robert C. "Fashioning the Legal Constitution: Culture, Courts, and Law." *Harvard Law Review* 117 (2003): 4–112.

———. "Theorizing Disagreement: Reconceiving the Relationship between Law and Politics." *California Law Review* 98, no. 4 (2010): 1319–1350.

———, and Reva B. Siegel. *Constitucionalismo democrático: Por una reconciliación entre Constitución y pueblo*. Buenos Aires: Siglo Veintiuno Editores, 2013.

Rawls, John. *Political Liberalism*. New York: Columbia University Press, 1995.

Roach, Kent. "Dialogic Judicial Review and Its Critics." *Supreme Court Law Review* 23 (2004): 49–104.

Robinson, Greg, and Toni Robinson. "*Korematsu* and Beyond: Japanese Americans and the Origins of Strict Scrutiny." *Law and Contemporary Problems* 68, no. 2 (2005): 29–55.

Rodrigues, Saulo Tarso, Paulo Bonavides, Nuria Belloso Martín, and Alexandre Fernandes Silva. *Teoria da decisão judicial e teoria da justiça: Jusfilosofia e novos paradigmas constitucionais*. Curitiba: Juruá, 2015.

Rodriguez, José Rodrigo. *Como decidem as cortes? Para uma crítica do direito (brasileiro)*. Rio de Janeiro: Editora FGV, 2013.

Rorty, Richard. *The Linguistic Turn: Essays in Philosophical Method*. Chicago: University of Chicago Press, 1992.

Sadurski, Wojciech. "Constitutional Review in Europe and in the United States: Influences, Paradoxes, and Convergence." *Sydney Law School Research Paper* 11/15 (2011).

Sarlet, Ingo Wolfgang. "Os direitos sociais como direitos fundamentais: Seu conteúdo, eficácia e efetividade no atual marco jurídico-constitucional brasileiro." In *Direitos Fundamentais e estado constitucional: Estudos em homenagem a J. J. Gomes Canotilho*, edited by George Salomão Leite and Ingo Wolfgang Sarlet. São Paulo: Revista dos Tribunais/Coimbra: Coimbra Editora, 2009.

———, Luiz Guilherme Marinoni, and Daniel Mitidiero. *Curso de Direito Constitucional*. São Paulo: RT, 2012.

Sarmento, Daniel. *Direitos fundamentais e relações privadas*. Rio de Janeiro: Lumen Juris, 2003.

Scalia, Antonin. *A Matter of Interpretation: Federal Courts and the Law*. Princeton, NJ: Princeton University Press, 1998.

Schauer, Frederick. "Formalism." *Yale Law Journal* 97, no. 4 (1988): 509–548.

Shapiro, Ian. *The State of Democratic Theory*. Princeton, NJ: Princeton University Press, 2003.

Shapiro, Scott J. "The Hart–Dworkin Debate: A Short Guide for the Perplexed." *Public Law and Legal Theory Working Paper Series*, no. 77. Available at SSRN 968657, 2007.

Shklar, Judith. "The Liberalism of Fear." In *Liberalism and the Moral Life*, edited by Nancy L. Rosenblum. Cambridge, MA: Harvard University Press, 1989.

Siegel, Jonathan R. "Judicial Interpretation in the Cost-Benefit Crucible." *Minnesota Law Review* 92, no. 4 (2007): 509–548.

Silva, Virgílio Afonso da. *Direitos Fundamentais: Sonteúdo essencial, restrições e eficácia*. São Paulo: Malheiros, 2010.

———. *Direitos Fundamentais: Sonteúdo essencial, restrições e eficácia*, 2nd ed. São Paulo: Malheiros, 2010.

———. "O STF e o controle de constitucionalidade: Deliberação, diálogo e razão pública." *Revista de Direito Administrativo* 250 (2009): 197–227.

Snyder, Thimothy. *Sobre a tirania: Vinte lições do século XX para o presente*. São Paulo: Companhia das Letras, 2017.

Souza Neto, Cláudio de Pereira, and Daniel Sarmento. *Direito constitucional: Teoria, história e métodos de trabalho*. Belo Horizonte: Fórum, 2012.

Stanley, Jason. *How Fascism Works: The Politics of Us and Them*. New York: Random House, 2018.

Stegmüller, Wolfgang. *A filosofia contemporânea: Introdução crítica*. Rio de Janeiro: Forense Universitária, 2012.

Strauss, David A. "Is Carolene Products Obsolete?" *University of Illinois Law Review* 4 (2010): 1251–1270.

———. *The Living Constitution*. Oxford, UK: Oxford University Press, 2010.

Strauss, Marcy. "Reevaluating Suspect Classifications." *Seattle University Law Review* 35, no. 1 (2011): 135–174.

Streck, Lenio Luiz. "O direito como um conceito interpretativo." *Pensar* 15, no. 2 (2010): 500–513.

———. *Hermenêutica Jurídica e(m) Crise: Uma exploração hermenêutica da construção do Direito*. Porto Alegre: Livraria do Advogado, 2000.

———. *Jurisdição Constitucional e Hermenêutica: Uma nova crítica do direito*. Rio de Janeiro: Forense, 2004.

———. *Jurisdição Constitucional e Hermenêutica: Uma nova crítica do direito*, 2nd ed. Rio de Janeiro: Forense, 2004.

———. "O problema da decisão jurídica em tempos pós-positivistas." *Novos Estudos Jurídicos* 14, no. 2 (2009): 3–26.

———. *O que é isto: Decido conforme a minha consciência?* Porto Alegre: Livraria do Advogado, 2010.

———. "O que é preciso para (não) se conseguir um Habeas Corpus no Brasil." *Conjur*, accessed September 24, 2015, http://www.conjur.com.br/2015-set-24/senso-incomum-preciso-nao-obter-hc-brasil.

———. "Superando os diversos tipos de positivismo: Porque hermenêutica é *applicatio*?" *Nomos: Revista do Programa de Pós-Graduação em Direito da UFC* 34, no. 2 (2014): 3–26.

Sunstein, C. R. "If People Would Be Outraged by Their Rulings, Should Judges Care?" *Stanford Law Review* 60 (2007): 213–240.

———. "Incompletely Theorized Agreements." *Harvard Law Review* 108, no. 7, (1995): 1733–1772.

———. "Justice Breyer's Democratic Pragmatism." *Yale Law Journal* 115, no. 7 (2006): 1719–1743.

———. *One Case at a Time: Judicial Minimalism on the Supreme Court*. Cambridge, MA: Harvard University Press, 1999.

———. *The Partial Constitution*. Cambridge, MA: Harvard University Press, 1993.

———. "Second-Order Perfectionism." *University of Chicago Law and Economics*, Olin Working Paper No. 319 (2006): 2867.

———, and Adrian Vermeule. "Interpretation and Institutions." *John M. Olin Program in Law and Economics Working Paper* 101, no. 156 (2002): 885–951.

Thayer, James Bradley. *The Origin and Scope of the American Doctrine of Constitutional Law*. Boston: Little, Brown and Company, 1893.

Torres, Ricardo Lobo. *O direito ao mínimo existencial*. Rio de Janeiro: Renovar, 2009.

Tribe, Laurence. *American Constitutional Law*. New York: Foundation Press, 2000.

———. *Constitutional Choices*. Cambridge, MA: Harvard University Press, 1985.

———. *The Invisible Constitution*. New York: Oxford University Press, 2008.

———. "The Puzzling Persistence of Process-Based Constitutional Theories." *Yale Law Journal* 89, no. 6 (1980): 1063–1080.

Tushnet, Mark. *I Dissent: Great Opposing Opinions in Landmark Supreme Court Cases*. Boston: Beacon, 2008.

———. *Taking the Constitution Away from the Courts*. Princeton, NJ: Princeton University Press, 1999.

Valle, Vanice Regina Lírio do. *Políticas públicas, direitos fundamentais e controle judicial.* Belo Horizonte: Editora Fórum, 2009.

———, and Cecília de Almeida Silva. "Abertura dialógica no controle abstrato de constitucionalidade: Um olhar ainda preceitual." *A & C Revista de Direito Administrativo & Constitucional* 43 (2010).

Velasco, Marina. *O que é justiça: O justo e o injusto na pesquisa filosófica*. Rio de Janeiro: Vieira & Lent, 2009.

Vermeule, Adrian. "Collective Wisdom and Institutional Design." In *Collective Wisdom: Principles and Mechanisms*, edited by Hélène Landemore, and Jon Elster. Cambridge, MA: Cambridge University Press, 2014.

———. "Interpretive Choice." *New York University Law Review* 75 (2000): 74.

———. *Judging under Uncertainty: An Institutional Theory of Legal Interpretation.* Cambridge, MA: Harvard University Press, 2006.

Vieira, Oscar Vilhena. "A Constituição como reserva de justiça." *Lua Nova* 42 (1997): 53–97.

———. "Supremocracia." *Revista Direito GV, São Paulo* 4, no. 2 (2008).

Waldron, Jeremy. "The Core of the Case against Judicial Review." *Yale Law Journal* 115, no. 7 (2006): 1346–1406.

———. *Law and Disagreement*. Oxford, UK: Oxford University Press, 1999.

———. *Law and Disagreement*, 2nd ed. Oxford, UK: Oxford University Press, 2004.

Wedy, Gabriel, and Juarez Freitas. "O legado dos votos vencidos na Suprema Corte dos Estados Unidos." *Revista Consultor Jurídico*, March 26, 2015, http://www.conjur.com.br/2015-mar-26/legado-votos-vencidos-suprema-corte-estados-unidos.

Whittington, Keith E. "In Defense of Legislatures." *Political Theory* 28, no. 5 (2000): 690–702.

Willeman, Marianna Montebello. "Revisão parlamentar no controle de constitucionalidade, constitucionalismo popular e humildade institucional." *Revista Brasileira de Direito Público, Belo Horizonte* 11, no. 43 (2013): 29–51.

Winkler, Adam. "Fatal in Theory and Strict in Fact: An Empirical Analysis of Strict Scrutiny in the Federal Courts." *Vanderbilt Law Review* 59, no. 3 (2006): 793–872.

Wittgenstein, Ludwig. *O Livro Azul*. Lisboa: Edições 70, 1992.

———. *Philosophical Investigations*. Oxford, UK: Basil Blackwell, 1986.

Yoshino, Kenji. "The Gay Tipping Point." *UCLA Law Review* 57, no. 5 (2010): 1537–1542

Zietlow, Rebecca E. "The Judicial Restraint of the Warren Court (and Why It Matters)." *Ohio State Law Journal* 69, no. 2 (2008): 255–302.

Index

About the Authors

Clèmerson Merlin Clève is full professor of constitutional law at the Federal University of Paraná; full professor of constitutional law at the Autonomous University Center of Brazil (UniBrasil); J.S.D. in public law from Pontifical Catholic University of São Paulo; LL.M from the Federal University of Santa Catarina; and J.S.D. in public law from Université Catholique de Louvain, Belgium. He is a former state attorney in Paraná and federal prosecutor in Brazil, and currently practices as an attorney at law.

Bruno Lorenzetto is professor of law at Pontifical Catholic University of Paraná; coordinator of the Graduate Program in Law (Fundamental Rights and Democracy) and undergraduate professor at UniBrasil; J.S.D in law from the Federal University of Paraná in the area of human rights and democracy; and LL.M from the Federal University of Paraná. He conducts research in the area of public law, with an emphasis on constitutional law and legal theory.

www.ingramcontent.com/pod-product-compliance
Ingram Content Group UK Ltd.
Pitfield, Milton Keynes, MK11 3LW, UK
UKHW041839031026
15587UKWH00002B/881

9 781793 648914